The Four Pillars of Investing

The Four Pillars of Investing

Lessons for Building a Winning Portfolio

William J. Bernstein

New York   Chicago   San Francisco   Lisbon
London   Madrid   Mexico City   Milan   New Delhi
San Juan   Seoul   Singapore   Sydney   Toronto

332.6
ER
(P)

The McGraw-Hill Companies

6 7 8 9 10   DOC/DOC 1 9 8 7 6 5 4

ISBN 978-0-07-174705-9
MHID   0-07-174705-2

This publication is designed to provide accurate and authoritative information in regard to the subject matter covered. It is sold with the understanding that the publisher is not engaged in rendering legal, accounting, securities trading, or other professional services. If legal advice or other expert assistance is required, the services of a competent professional person should be sought.

> —*From a Declaration of Principles Jointly Adopted*
> *by a Committee of the American Bar Association*
> *and a Committee of Publishers and Associations*

McGraw-Hill books are available at special quantity discounts to use as premiums and sales promotions or for use in corporate training programs. To contact a representative, please e-mail us at bulksales@mcgraw-hill.com.

Contents

Preface

In the mid-1990s, I began writing a small book, *The Intelligent Asset Allocator,* which ultimately became a "successful failure": successful because it attracted positive notice and sold enough copies to please my publisher and myself, and a failure because it did not accomplish its ultimate goal. My aim had been to explain modern portfolio theory, a powerful way of understanding investing, to the general public. What I instead produced was a work comprehensible only to those with a considerable level of mathematical training and skill.

After initially failing to interest any publishers, the original electronic version of the book was placed on my Web site, www.efficientfrontier.com, at the end of 1996. Following a slow start, it gradually elicited much positive comment. The only problem was that almost all of its readers were scientists, engineers, or finance professionals.

Closer to home, my family and friends uniformly gave up on it with alarming dispatch: "Bill, you've got to be kidding. I fell asleep after five pages; this stuff is way over my head." The dividing line seemed to be slightly north of Statistics 101; if you never took it, or did but hated it, the book might as well have been written in Tamil. Eventually, in a show of unalloyed courage, McGraw-Hill did print it as a trade publication—aimed at professionals, not the general public.

The book was a methodical mathematical exercise. First, the behavior of multiple asset classes was statistically analyzed. Next, the theoretical basics of portfolio theory were examined. Ultimately, these two foundations, as well as a practical tour of the investment industry, were synthesized into a coherent investment strategy. The small minority of investors who thrive on such fare felt well rewarded. But, as with the electronic versions, most considered it more sedative than informative. Fortunately, *The Intelligent Asset Allocator's* limited success allowed me a second chance to write a book about investing for the general audience.

My watchwords in producing *The Four Pillars of Investing* were accessibility and enjoyment; I've used engaging historical vignettes wherever possible to illustrate key financial concepts and kept mathematical detail to a minimum. A well-known rule among scientists is that each successive mathematical formula cuts a book's popular readership in half; I've done my best to keep the math simple and the graphs as spare as possible. Now, almost a decade later, this title is in its seventeenth printing; so I suppose I've succeeded.

Special thanks go to those who have provided encouragement and help along the way, including Cliff Asness, John C. Bogle Sr., Scott Burns, Edward Chancellor, Mark Gochnour, Christian Oelke, John Rekenthaler, Bill Schultheis, Larry Swedroe, Robert Sidelsky, Richard Thaler, Mike Veseth, and Jason Zweig. I'll never understand what motivated Catherine Dassopoulos and Jeffrey Krames of McGraw-Hill to take an interest in an obscure electronic file by an unknown scribbler floating around in cyberspace, but their editorial and publishing support has been a constant source of delight and satisfaction. Thanks are also given to Stephen Isaacs, who shepherded this work through each step of the production process. There must be no harder job in publishing than getting an author to "kill his darlings" in the cause of producing a tighter and more muscular manuscript; Stephen accomplished this with aplomb and grace.

Author and academic Larry Cunningham and my friends Stephen Dunn and Charles Holloway spent many hours of their precious time hammering out the flaws in both finance and wordsmithing. Jonathan Clements brought not only his time but also his years of journalistic experience at Cambridge, *Forbes*, and *The Wall Street Journal* to bear in improving the book's detail and structure.

Particular thanks go to my business partner, Susan Sharin, whose unique combination of financial savvy, editorial skills, and command of the investment business landscape proved as essential in this effort as it was in my last book. Finally, to my wife, Jane Gigler, go the fondest thanks of all. Her cheerful and unending transmutation of large heaps of muddled verbiage into readable prose and amused tolerance of an obsessed author and husband are a constant source of pleasure and awe.

William Bernstein
Portland, Oregon

Introduction

I didn't start out my professional life in finance; my original training was in the sciences, and, later, in medicine. Practicing physicians, among whom I still count myself, have a richly deserved reputation as miserable investors. The conventional explanations for this are that our practices are so demanding that we don't have the time to do it properly, or that we're too egotistical to take professional advice.

In fact, neither is the case. Learning how to invest properly doesn't take an inordinate effort, and I don't find most of my colleagues overly egotistical. Medical practice is a profoundly humbling experience to anyone with a breath of intellectual honesty; the best doctors soon come to the conclusion that the more they see, the less they know. The same, not surprisingly, is true in finance.

The real reason that physicians are rotten investors is that it never occurs to them that finance is a science, just like medicine. Day-to-day medical practice is profoundly scientific, informed by a vast amount of underlying research; nowadays almost no drug or surgical treatment is adopted without rigorous trials comparing it to other accepted treatments or placebo. In short, most physicians would not commence a treatment for so much as a cold without a good deal of experimental and statistical evidence in back of it.

The most important work is reported in prestigious peer-reviewed periodicals such as *The New England Journal of Medicine* and *Lancet*. The key term here is "peer reviewed." Nothing appears in these high-level periodicals without being vetted first by the top experts in the field—requests for multiple extensive revisions are routine. Your own physician hopefully reads these top-echelon publications on a regular basis for data relevant to his practice.

Unfortunately, when doctors put on their investing hats, they completely forget their scientific training. There is, in fact, a rich and informative scientific literature about what works and what doesn't in finance; it is routinely ignored. Instead of depending on the *Journal of Finance* (the investing equivalent of *The New England Journal of Medicine*), they get their advice from *USA Today* or worse, from their stockbroker.

Of course, I'm only picking on my colleagues for fun—in this regard doctors are no different from lawyers, retail clerks, or anyone else. What's truly scandalous is that even most finance professionals are unaware of the scientific basis of investing, which consists of four broad areas, the Four Pillars of this book.

Pillar One: Theory

The most fundamental characteristic of any investment is that its return and risk go hand in hand. As all too many have learned in the past few years, a market that doubles rapidly is just as likely to halve rapidly, and a stock that appreciates 900% is just as likely to fall 90%. Or that when a broker calls suggesting that the price of a particular stock will rocket, what he's really telling you is that he is not overly impressed with your intelligence. Otherwise, you would realize that if he actually knew that the price was going to increase, he would not tell it to you or even his own mother. Instead, he would quit his job, borrow to the hilt, purchase as much of the stock as he could, and then go to the beach.

The first, and most important, part of the book will survey the awesome body of theory and data relevant to everyday investing. Don't be daunted by this; my primary mission is to present this information in terms that you will find both understandable and entertaining. We'll learn that:

- Whether you invest in stocks, bonds, or for that matter real estate or any other kind of capital asset, you are rewarded mainly for your exposure to one thing—its risk. We'll learn just how to measure that risk and explore the interplay of risk and investment return.
- Over the long haul, it is not that hard to measure the probable return of different kinds of stocks and bonds; yet even well-respected experts usually manage to do a bad job of this.
- Almost all the differences in the performances of money managers can be ascribed to luck and not to skill; you are most certainly not rewarded for trying to pick the best-performing stocks, mutual funds, stockbrokers, or hedge funds.
- The biggest risk of all is failing to diversify properly.

- It's the behavior of your portfolio as a whole, and not the assets in it, that matters most. We'll also learn that a portfolio can behave in ways radically different than its component parts, and that this can be used to your advantage. The science of mixing different asset classes into an effective blend is called "portfolio theory" and occupies center court in the grand tournament of investing.

Pillar Two: History

It is a fact that, from time to time, the markets and investing public go barking mad. Of course, the madness is obvious only in retrospect. But a study of previous manias and crashes will give you at least a fighting chance of recognizing when asset prices have become absurdly expensive and risky and when they have become too depressed and cheap to pass up. The simplest way of separating managers who would be suckered into the dot-com mania (or, more recently, home-owners who took out interest-only liar-loan mortgages) from those who would not would be to administer a brief quiz on the 1929 crash.

Finance, unfortunately, is not a "hard" science. It is instead a social science. The difference is this: a bridge, electrical circuit, or aircraft should always respond in exactly the same way to a given set of circumstances. What separates the "hard" sciences of physics, engineering, electronics, or aeronautics from the "social" sciences is that in finance (or sociology, politics, and education) apparently similar systems will behave very differently over time.

Put a different way, a physician, physicist, or chemist who is unaware of their discipline's history does not suffer greatly from the lack thereof; the investor who is unaware of financial history is irretrievably handicapped. For this reason, an understanding of financial history provides an additional dimension of expertise. In this section, we'll study the history of finance through the widest possible lens by examining:

- Just what the centuries of recorded financial history tell us about the short-term and long-term behavior of various financial assets.
- How, from time to time, the investing public becomes almost psychotically euphoric, and at other times, toxically depressed.
- How modern investment technology has exposed investors to new risks.

Pillar Three: Psychology

Most of what we fondly call "human nature" becomes a deadly quicksand of maladaptive behavior when allowed to roam free in the investment arena. A small example: people tend to be attracted to financial choices that carry low probabilities of high payoffs. In spite of the fact that the average payoff of a lottery ticket is only 50 cents on the dollar, millions "invest" in it. While this is a relatively minor foible for most, it becomes far more menacing as an investment strategy. One of the quickest ways to the poorhouse is to make finding the next Microsoft your primary investing goal.

Only recently have academics and practitioners begun the serious study of how the individual investor's state of mind affects his or her decision making; we'll survey the fascinating area of "behavioral finance." You'll learn how to avoid the most common behavioral mistakes and to confront your own dysfunctional investment behavior. You will find out, for example, that most investors:

- Tend to become grossly overconfident.
- Systematically pay too much for certain classes of stocks.
- Trade too much, at great cost.
- Regularly make irrational buy and sell decisions.

Pillar Four: Business

Investors tend to be touchingly naïve about stockbrokers and mutual fund companies: brokers are not your friends, and the interests of the fund companies are highly divergent from yours. You are in fact locked in a financial life-and-death struggle with the investment industry; losing that battle puts you at increased risk of running short of assets far sooner than you'd like. The more you know about the industry's priorities and how it operates, the more likely it is that you will be able to thwart it.

The brokerage and mutual fund businesses form a financial colossus that bestrides modern financial, and increasingly, social, and political life. (If you doubt this, just turn on your television and time the interval between advertisements for financial services.) In the book's penultimate section, then, we'll examine how the modern financial services industry is designed solely to serve itself, and how it:

- Exists almost entirely for one purpose: the extraction of fees and commissions from the investing public, and that in fact, we are all locked in a constant zero-sum battle with this behemoth.
- Operates at a level of educational, moral, and ethical imperatives that would be inconceivable in any other profession. A small example: by law, bankers, lawyers, and accountants all have a fiduciary responsibility towards their clients. Not so stockbrokers.

Only after you've mastered these four areas can you formulate an overall investment strategy. Only after you've formulated a program that focuses on asset classes and the behavior of asset-class mixtures will you have any chance for overall success. A deficiency in any of the Four Pillars will torpedo this program with brutal dispatch.

Here are a couple of examples of how a failure to master the Four Pillars can bring grief to even the most sophisticated investors:

Big time players: The principals of Long-Term Capital Management, the firm that in 1998 almost single handedly crippled the world financial system with their highly leveraged speculation, had no trouble with Pillar One—investment theory—as they were in many cases its Nobel Prize-winning inventors. Their appreciation of Pillars Three and Four—psychology and the investment business—was also top drawer. Unfortunately, despite their corporate name, none of them had a working knowledge of Pillar Two—the long-term history of the capital markets. Focusing narrowly on only several years of financial data, they forgot the fact that occasionally markets come completely off the rails, often in ways never before seen. A working knowledge of Western financial history would have warned them that their investment strategy carried with it the near certainty of self-destruction.

Small investors: On the other hand, the average investor most often comes to grief because of deficiencies in Pillars One and Three—theory and psychology. They usually fail to understand the everyday working relationship between risk and reward and routinely fail to stay the course when things get rough.

The above two examples are caricatures: the failure modes of individual investors are as varied as their personalities. In this tome, I want to provide you with these invaluable tools—the Four Pillars—to avoid the kinds of failures I've listed above. I also want to expose you to the wondrous clockwork and history of the capital markets, which are deserving of attention in their own right.

Arguably the most substantive domestic issue facing the republic is the fate of Social Security, with privatization the most frequently mentioned option. For the first time in history, a familiarity with the behavior of the financial markets has become a prerequisite for competent citizenship, apart from its obvious pecuniary value.

Using the Four Pillars

In the book's last section, we'll show how mastery of the Four Pillars can result in a coherent strategy that will enable you to accomplish investing's primary aims: achieving and maintaining financial independence and sleeping well at night. The essential mechanics of operating an efficient investment portfolio will be covered:

- Calculating how much you'll need to save and when you can retire.
- Allocating your assets among various classes of stocks and bonds.
- Choosing which mutual funds and securities to employ.
- Getting off dead center and building your portfolio.
- Maintaining and adjusting your portfolio over the long haul.

In Conclusion

Although I hope that I've conveyed my enthusiasm for financial theory, history, psychology, and strategy, I'll freely admit that I've been dealt the short straw in the subject scintillation department—this book, after all, is not a bodice-ripper or a spy thriller. There is no arguing with the fact that some areas of finance can be damnably opaque, even to cognoscenti. This book, then, should be consumed in small bites, perhaps ten or twenty pages at a time, preferably first thing in the morning.

Lastly, while I've tried to make this work as comprehensive and readable as possible, no one book can claim to be an all-encompassing source of investment instruction. At best, what is offered here is a study guide—a financial *tour d'horizon*, if you will. Personal finance, like most important aspects of life, is a never-ending quest. The competent investor never stops learning. As such, the most valuable section is the reading list of the end of Chapter 11. Remarkably, eight years after this book's original publication, it survives with only one change, which is to update the latest edition of Jack Bogle's amazing *Common Sense on Mutual Funds*. This list should guide you through the subsequent legs of the life-long journey towards financial self-sufficiency.

PILLAR ONE

The Theory of Investing

The Nature of the Beast

In 1798, a French expedition under the direct command of Napoleon invaded Egypt. His forces possessed only the most rudimentary maps and had almost no knowledge of the climate or terrain. It came as no surprise that the invasion was a disaster from start to finish when, three years later, the last French troops, dispirited, diseased, starving, and abandoned by their leader, were mopped up by Turkish and British forces.

Unfortunately, most investors muster the same degree of planning in their investing, unaware of the nature of the investment terrain. Without an understanding of the relationship between risk and reward, how to estimate returns, the interplay between other investors and themselves, and the mechanics of portfolio design, they are doomed to failure, much like Napoleon's troops. Each of these essential topics can be mastered and will be covered chapter by chapter in this book.

The first chapter, dealing with the historical returns and risks in the European and U.S. markets during the past several centuries, is the most critical. We cover a large expanse of historical territory, the premise being that the more history you know, the more prepared you will be for the future.

1

No Guts, No Glory

There are certain things that cannot be adequately explained to a virgin either by words or pictures. Nor can any description that I might offer here even approximate what it feels like to lose a real chunk of money that you used to own.
Fred Schwed, from *Where Are the Customers' Yachts?*

I'm often asked whether the markets behave rationally. My answer is that it all depends on your time horizon. Turn on CNBC at 9:31 A.M. any weekday morning and you're faced with a lunatic asylum described by the Three Stooges. But stand back a bit and you'll start to see trends and regular occurrences. When the market is viewed over decades, its behavior is as predictable as a Lakers-Clippers basketball game. The one thing that stands out above all else is the relationship between return and risk. Assets with higher returns invariably carry with them stomach-churning risk, while safe assets almost always have lower returns. The best way to illustrate the critical relationship between risk and return is by surveying stock and bond markets through the centuries.

The Fairy Tale

When I was a child back in the fifties, I treasured my monthly trips to the barbershop. I'd pay my quarter, jump into the huge chair, and for 15 minutes become an honorary member of adult male society. Conversation generally revolved around the emanations from the television set: a small household god dwarfed by its oversized mahogany frame. The fare reflected the innocence of the era: *I Love Lucy,* game shows, and, if we were especially lucky, afternoon baseball. But I do not ever recall hearing one conversation or program that included finance. The stock market, economy, machinations of the Fed, or even government expenditures did not infiltrate our barbershop world.

Today we live in a sea of financial information, with waves of stock information constantly bombarding us. On days when the markets are particularly active, our day-to-day routines are saturated with news stories and personal conversations concerning the whys and wherefores of security prices. Even on quiet days, it is impossible to escape the ubiquitous stock ticker scrolling across the bottom of the television screen or commercials featuring British royalty discoursing knowledgeably about equity ratios.

It has become a commonplace that stocks are the best long-term investment for the average citizen. At one time or another, most of us have seen a plot of capital wealth looking something like Figure 1-1, demonstrating that $1 invested in the U.S. stock market in 1790 would have grown to more than $23 million by the year 2000.

Unfortunately, for a number of reasons, no person, family, or organization ever obtained these returns. First, we invest now so that we may spend later. In fact, this is the essence of investing: the forbearance of immediate spending in exchange for future income. Because of the mathematics of compound interest, spending even a tiny fraction on a regular basis devastates final wealth over the long haul. During the last two hundred years, each 1% spent each year reduces the final amount by a factor of eight. For example, a 1% reduction in return would have reduced the final amount from $23 million to about $3 million and a 2% reduction to about $400,000. Few investors have the patience to leave the fruits of their labor untouched. And even if they did, their spendthrift heirs would likely make fast work of their fortune.

But even allowing for this, Figure 1-1 is still highly deceptive. For starters, it ignores commissions and taxes, which would have shrunk returns by another percent or two, reducing a potential $23 million fortune to the above $3 million or $400,000. Even more importantly, it ignores "survivorship bias." This term refers to the fact that only the best outcomes make it into the history books; those financial markets that failed do not. It is no accident that investors focus on the immense wealth generated by the economy and markets of the United States these past two centuries; the champion—our stock market—is the most easily visible, while less successful assets fade quickly from view.

And yet the global investor in 1790 would have been hard pressed to pick out the United States as a success story. At its birth, our nation was a financial basket case. And its history over the next century hardly inspired confidence, with an unstable banking structure, rampant speculation, and the Civil War. The nineteenth century culminated in the near bankruptcy of the U.S. Treasury, which was narrowly averted only through the organizational talents of J.P. Morgan. Worse still, for

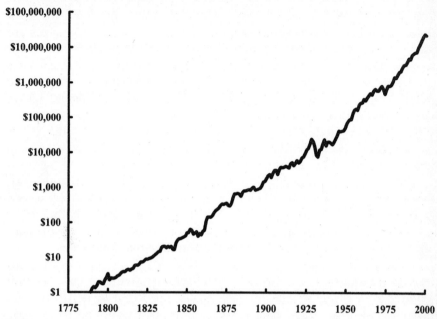

Figure 1-1. Value of $1.00 invested in U.S. stock market. (*Source:* Jeremy Siegel/ William Schwert.)

most of the past 200 years, stocks were inaccessible to the average person. Before about 1925, it was virtually impossible for even the wealthiest Americans to purchase shares in an honest and efficient manner.

Worst of all, in the year 2002, the good news about historically high stock returns is out of the bag. For historical reasons, many financial scholars undertake the serious study of U.S. stock returns with data beginning in 1871. But it's worth remembering that 1871 was only six years after the end of the Civil War, with industrial stocks selling at ridiculously low prices—just three to four times their annual earnings. Stocks today are selling at nearly ten times that valuation, making it unlikely that we will witness a repeat of the returns seen in the past 130 years.

Finally, there is the small matter of risk. Figure 1-1 is also deceptive because of the manner in which the data are displayed, with an enormous range of dollar values compressed into its vertical scale. The Great Depression, during which stocks lost more than 80% of their value, is just barely visible. Likewise, the 1973–1974 bear market, during which stocks lost more than one-half of their after-inflation value, is seen only as a slight flattening of the plot. And the October 1987 market crash is not visible at all. All three of these events drove millions of investors permanently out of the stock market. For a generation after the 1929 crash, the overwhelming majority of the investing public shunned stocks altogether.

The popular conceit of every bull market is that the public has bought into the value of long-term investing and will never sell their stocks simply because of market fluctuation. And time after time, the investing public loses heart after the inevitable punishing declines that stock markets periodically dish out, and the cycle begins anew.

With that in mind, we'll plumb the history of stock and bond returns around the globe for clues regarding how to capture some of their rewards.

Ultimately, this book is about the building of investment portfolios that are both prudent and efficient. The construction of a house is a valuable metaphor for this process. The very first thing the wise homebuilder does, before drawing up blueprints, digging a foundation, or ordering appliances, is learn about the construction materials available.

In the case of investing, these materials are stocks and bonds, and it is impossible to spend too much time studying them. We will expend a lot of energy on the several-hundred-year sweep of human investing—a topic that some may initially find tangential to our ultimate goal. Rest assured that our efforts in this area will be well rewarded. For the better we understand the nature, behavior, and history of our building materials, the stronger our house will be.

The study of financial history is an essential part of every investor's education. It is not possible to precisely predict the future, but a knowledge of the past often allows us to identify financial risk in the here and now. Returns are uncertain. But risks, at least, can be controlled. We tend to think of the stock and bond markets as relatively recent historical phenomena, but, in fact, there have been credit markets since human civilization first took root in the Fertile Crescent. And governments have been issuing bonds for several hundred years. More importantly, after they were issued, these bonds then fluctuated in price according to economic, political, and military conditions, just as they do today.

Nowhere is philosopher George Santayana's famous dictum, "Those who cannot remember the past are condemned to repeat it," more applicable than in finance. Financial history provides us with invaluable wisdom about the nature of the capital markets and of returns on securities. Intelligent investors ignore this record at their peril.

Risk and Return Throughout the Centuries

Even before money first appeared in the form of small pellets of silver 5,000 years ago, there have been credit markets. It is likely that for thousands of years of prehistory, loans of grain and cattle were made at interest; a bushel or calf lent in winter would be repaid twice over at harvest time. Such practices are still widespread in primitive societies. (When gold and silver first appeared as money, they were valued according to head of cattle, not the other way around.) But the invention of money magnified the prime question that has echoed down through investment history: How much return should be paid by the borrowers of capital to its lenders?

You may be wondering by now about why we're spending time on the early history of the credit markets. The reason for their relevance is simple. Two Nobel Prize-winning economists, Franco Modigliani and Merton Miller, realized more than four decades ago that the aggregate cost of and return on capital, adjusted for risk, are the same, regardless of whether stocks or bonds are employed. In other words, had the ancients used stock issuance instead of debt to finance their businesses, the rate of return to investors would have been the same. So we are looking at a reasonable portrait of investment return over the millennia.

The history of ancient credit markets is fairly extensive. In fact, much of the earliest historical record from the Fertile Crescent— Sumeria, Babylon, and Assyria—concerns itself with the loaning of money. Much of Hammurabi's famous Babylonian Code—the first comprehensive set of laws—dealt with commercial transactions.

A small ancient example will suffice. In Greece, a common business was that of the "bottomry loan," which was made against a maritime shipment and forfeited if the vessel sank. A fair amount of data is available on such loans, with rates of 22.5% for a round-trip voyage to the Bosphorus in peacetime and 30% in wartime. Since it is likely that fewer than 10% of ships were lost, these were highly profitable in the aggregate, though quite risky on a case-by-case basis. This is one of the first historical demonstrations of the relationship between risk and return: The 22.5% rate of interest was high, even for that period, reflecting the uncertainty of dealing with maritime navigation and trade. Further, the rate increased during wartime to compensate for the higher risk of cargo loss.

Another thing we learn from a brief tour of ancient finance is that interest rates responded to the stability of the society; in uncertain times, returns were higher because there was less sense of public trust and of societal permanence. All of the major ancient civilizations demonstrated a "U-shaped" pattern of interest rates, with high rates early in their history that slowly fell as the civilizations matured and stabilized, reaching the lowest point at the height of the civilizations' development and rising again as they decayed. For example, the apex of the Roman Empire in the first and second century A.D. saw interest rates as low as 4%.

As a general rule, the historical record suggests excellent investment returns in the ancient world. *But this record reflects only those societies that survived and prospered, since successful societies are much more likely to leave a record.* Babylonian, Greek, and Roman investors did much better than those in the nations they vanquished—the citizens of Judea or Carthage had far bigger worries than their failing financial portfolios.

This is not a trivial issue. At a very early stage in history we are encountering "survivorship bias"—the fact that only the best results tend to show up in the history books. In the twentieth century, for example, investors in the U.S., Canada, Sweden, and Switzerland did handsomely because they went largely untouched by the military and political disasters that befell most of the rest of the planet. Investors in tumultuous Germany, Japan, Argentina, and India were not so lucky; they obtained far smaller rewards.

Thus, it is highly misleading to rely on the investment performance of history's most successful nations and empires as indicative of your own future returns.

At first glance, it might appear that the above list of winners and losers contradicts the relationship between risk and return. This is an excellent example of "hindsight bias"; in 1913 it was by no means obvious that the U.S., Canada, Sweden, and Switzerland would have the highest returns, and that Germany, Japan, Argentina, and India, the lowest. Going back further, in 1650 France and Spain were the mightiest economic and military powers in Europe, and England an impoverished upstart torn by civil war.

The interest rate bottom of 4% reached in Rome is particularly relevant to the modern audience. Never before, and perhaps not since, have the citizens of any nation had the sense of cultural and political permanence experienced in Rome at its apex. So the 4% return at Rome's height may represent a kind of natural lower limit of investment returns, experienced only by the most confident (or perhaps overconfident) nations at the top of their game.

The Austrian economist Eugen von Böhm-Bawerk stated that the cultural and political level of a nation could be discerned by its interest rate: The more advanced the nation, the lower the loan rate. Economist Richard Sylla notes that a plot of interest rates can be thought of as a nation's "fever chart," with upward spikes almost always representing a military, economic, or political crisis, and long, flat stretches signifying extended periods of stability.

As we'll see, the 4% Roman rate of return is about the same as the aggregate return on capital (when stocks and bonds are considered together) in the U.S. in the twentieth century, and perhaps even a bit more than the aggregate return expected in the next century. (The 4% Roman rate was gold-based, so the return was a *real,* that is, after-inflation, return.)

The same phenomenon was observed in Europe. The primitive and unstable societies of medieval Europe initially had very high interest rates, which gradually fell as the Dark Ages gave way to the Renaissance and Enlightenment. To illustrate this point, Figure 1-2 shows European interest rates from the thirteenth through the eighteenth centuries.

One of the most important European financial inventions was the "annuity," that is, a bond that pays interest forever, without ever repaying the principal amount. This is different from the modern insurance company annuity, in which payments cease with the death of the owner. European annuities were usually issued by a government to pay for war expenses and never expired; instead, they were handed down and traded among succeeding generations of investors. Newcomers tend to recoil at a loan that yields only interest with no return of principal, but the annuity provides a very useful way of

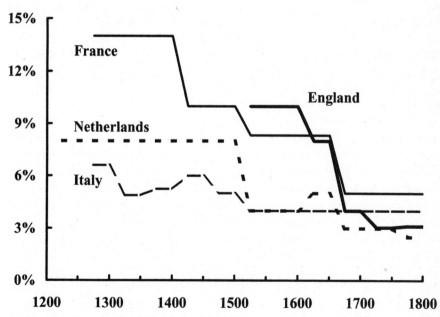

Figure 1-2. European interest rates, 1200–1800. (*Source:* Homer and Sylla, *A History of Interest Rates.*)

thinking about the *price* of a loan or bond. It's worth spending some time discussing this topic, because it forms one of the foundations of modern finance.

If you have trouble dealing with the concept of a loan which pays interest forever but never repays its principal, consider the modern U.S. 30-year Treasury bond, which yields 60 semiannual payments of interest before repaying its principal. During the past 30 years, inflation has averaged more than 5% per year; over that period the purchasing power of the original dollar fell to less than 23 cents. (In other words, the purchasing power of the dollar declined by 77%.) So almost all of the value of the bond is garnered from interest, not principal. Extend the term of the loan to 100 years, and the inflation-adjusted value of the ending principal payment is less than one cent on the dollar.

The historical European government annuity is worthy of modern consideration for one compelling reason: its value is extremely simple to calculate: divide the annual payment by the current (market) interest rate. For example, consider an annuity that pays $100 each year. At a 5% interest rate, this annuity has a value of $2,000 ($100/0.05 = $2,000). If you purchased an annuity when interest rates were 5%, and rates then increased to 10%, the value of your annuity would have fallen by half, since $100/0.1 = $1,000.

So we see that the value of a long-term bond or loan in the marketplace is inversely related to the interest rate. When rates rise, the price falls; when rates fall, the price rises. Modern long-duration bonds are priced in nearly the same way: if the bond yield rises proportionally by 1%—say from 5.00% to 5.05%—it has lost 1% of its value.

The best-known early annuity was the Venetian prestiti, used to finance the Republic's wars. These were forced loans extracted from the Republic's wealthiest citizens. The money was remitted to a central registry office, which then paid the registered owner periodic interest. They carried a rate of only 5%. Since prevailing interest rates in the nation's credit markets were much higher, the "purchase" of a prestiti at a 5% rate constituted a kind of tax levied on its owner, who was forced to buy it at face value. But the Venetian treasury did allow owners to sell their prestiti to others—that is, to change the name registered at the central office. Prestiti soon became the favored vehicle for investment and speculation among Venetian noblemen and were even widely held throughout Europe. This "secondary market" in prestiti provides economic historians with a vivid picture of a medieval bond market that was quite active over many centuries.

Consider a prestiti forced upon a wealthy citizen for 1,000 ducats, yielding 50 ducats per year, or 5%. If the prevailing interest rate in

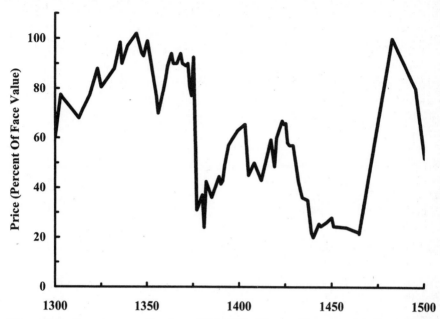

Figure 1-3. Venetian prestiti prices, 1300–1500. (*Source:* Homer and Sylla, *A History of Interest Rates.*)

the secondary market was actually 6.7%, then the owner could sell it in the market at only 75% of its face value, or 750 ducats, since 50/0.067 = 750.

I've plotted the prices of prestiti during the fourteenth and fifteenth centuries in Figure 1-3. (The "par," or face value of the bonds, is arbitrarily set at 100.) For the first time in the history of capital returns, we are now able to examine the element of *risk*. Defined in its most basic terms, risk is the possibility of losing money.

A fast look at Figure 1-3 shows that prestiti owners were certainly exposed to this unhappy prospect. For example, in the tranquil year of 1375, prices reached a high of 92 1/2. But just two years later, after a devastating war with Genoa, interest payments were temporarily suspended and vast amounts of new prestiti were levied, driving prices as low as 19; this constituted a temporary loss of principal value of about 80%. Even though Venice's fortunes soon reversed, this financial catastrophe shook investor confidence for more than a century, and prices did not recover until the debt was refinanced in 1482.

Even taking these stumbles into account, investors in medieval and Renaissance Europe earned healthy returns on their capital. But these rewards were bought by shouldering risk, red in tooth and claw. As we shall soon see, later investors in Europe and America also have experienced similar high inflation-adjusted returns. But even in the modern world, where there is return, there also lurks risk.

The point of this whole historical exercise is to establish the most important concept in finance, that *risk and return are inextricably connected*. If you desire the opportunity to achieve high returns, you have to shoulder high risks. And if you desire safety, you will of necessity have to content yourself with meager rewards. Consider the prices of prestiti in three different years:

Year	Price
1375	92 1/2
1381	24
1389	44 1/2

The Venetian investor who bought prestiti in 1375, when the Republic seemed secure, would have been badly damaged. Conversely, the investor brave enough to purchase at 1381's depressed price, when all seemed lost, would have earned high returns. High returns are obtained by buying low and selling high; low returns are obtained by buying high and selling low. If you buy a stock or bond with the intention of selling it in, say, twenty years, you cannot predict what price it will fetch at that future date. But you can state with mathematical certainty that as long as the issuing company does not go bankrupt, the lower the price you pay for it now, the higher your future returns will be; the higher the price you pay, the lower your returns will be.

This is an essential point that escapes most small investors. Even the world's most sophisticated financial economists occasionally make this mistake: in financial parlance, they "conflate expected returns with realized returns." Or, in plain English, they confuse the future with the past. This point cannot be made too forcefully or too often: high previous returns usually indicate low future returns, and low past returns usually mean high future returns.

The rub here is that buying when prices are low is always a very scary proposition. *The low prices that produce high future returns are not possible without catastrophe and risk.* The moral for modern investors is obvious: the recent very high stock returns in the U.S. would not have been possible without the chaos of the nineteenth century and the prolonged fall in prices that occurred in the wake of the Great Depression. Conversely, the placid economic, political, and social environment before the World Trade Center bombing resulted in very high stock prices; the disappearance of this apparent low-risk world produced low returns in its wake.

A Closer Look at Bond Pricing and Returns

So far, we've looked at credit and bond returns through a very wide historical lens. It's now time to focus on the precise nature of bond and debt risk and its behavior through the ages. Let's assume that you are a prosperous Venetian merchant, happily sipping bardolino in your palazzo, thinking about the value of the prestiti that your family has had registered at the loan office in the Piazza San Marco for the past few generations. From your own experience and that of your parents and grandparents, you know that the price of these annuities responds to two different factors. The first is that of absolute safety—whether or not the Republic itself will survive. When the barbarians are at the gates, interest rates rise and bond prices fall precipitously. When the danger passes, interest rates fall and bond prices rise. The risk, then, is the possibility that the bond issuer (in this case, the Republic itself) will not survive. In modern times, we worry more about simple bankruptcy than military catastrophe.

But you notice something else: Even in the most tranquil times, when credit becomes easy and interest rates fall, prices rise. When credit becomes tight and interest rates rise, prices fall. This is, of course, as it should be—the iron rules of annuity pricing mandate that if interest rates double, their value will halve.

You begin to get unnerved at the rises and falls in your family's fortune with the credit market's gyrations; you ask yourself if it is possible to reduce, or even eliminate, this risk. The answer, as we'll shortly see, is a resounding "yes!"

But before we proceed, let's recap. The first risk—that of the Turks overrunning the Republic or your neighbor's ship sinking—is called "credit risk." In other words, the possibility of losing some, or all, of your principal because of the debtor's failure. The second risk—that caused by the rise and fall of interest rates—is called "interest-rate risk." For the modern investor, interest-rate risk is virtually synonymous with inflation risk. When you buy a 30-year Treasury bond, the biggest risk you are taking is that inflation will render your future interest and principal payment nearly worthless.

The solution to interest-rate risk, then, is to lend short term. If your loan or bond is due in only one month, then you have virtually eliminated interest-rate/inflation risk, since in less than 30 days' time, you'll be able to reinvest your principal at the new, higher rate. Ever since the Babylonians began secondary trading of debt instruments, investors have sought safety from interest-rate risk in short-term loans/securities. Unfortunately, short-term loans have their own peculiar risks.

We need to get one last bit of housekeeping out of the way. For the next few chapters, we shall call short-term obligations (generally less than one year) "bills," and longer-term obligations "bonds." Direct comparisons between bill and bond rates did not become possible until the Bank of England began operations in 1694 and immediately began to dominate the English credit markets.

In 1749, the Chancellor of the Exchequer (the English equivalent of our Treasury Secretary), Henry Pelham, combined all of the government's long-term obligations. These consolidated obligations later became known as the famous "consols." They were annuities, just like the prestiti, never yielding up their principal. They still trade today, more than two-and-a-half centuries later. These consols, like the prestiti, provide historians with an unbroken record of bond pricing and rates through the centuries.

Bills, on the other hand, were simply pieces of paper of a certain face value, purchased at a discount. For example, the Bank of England might offer a bill with a face value of ten pounds. It could be purchased at a discounted price of nine pounds and ten shillings (9 1/2 pounds) and redeemed one year later at the ten pound face value. This results in a 5.26% rate of interest (10/9.5 = 1.0526).

The rates for bills (and bank deposits) and bonds (consols) in nineteenth century England are shown in Figure 1-4. The modern investor would predict that the bills would carry a lower interest than the consols, since the bills were not exposed to interest-rate (i.e., inflation) risk. But for most of the century, short-term rates were actually *higher* than long-term rates. This occurred for two reasons. First, as we'll discuss later, only in the twentieth century did sustained high inflation become a scourge; gold was money, so investors did not worry about a potential decline in its value. And second, wealthy Englishmen valued the consols' steady income stream. The return on bills was quite variable, and a nobleman desiring a constant standard of living would find the uncertainty of the bill rate highly inconvenient.

As you can see, the interest rate on short-term bills was much more uncertain than for consols. Thus, the investor in bills demanded a higher return for the more uncertain payout. Figure 1-4 also shows something far more important: the gradual decline in interest rates as England's society stabilized and came to dominate the globe. In 1897 the consol yield hit a low of 2.21%, which has not been seen since. This identifies the high-water mark of the British Empire as well as any political or military event.

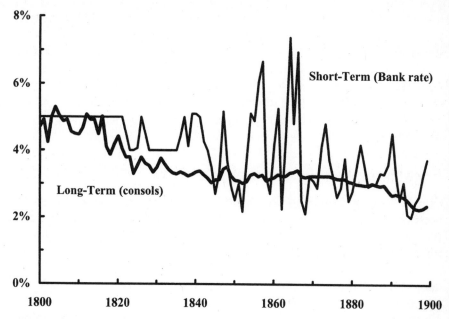

Figure 1-4. English short- and long-term rates, 1800–1900. (*Source:* Homer and Sylla, *A History of Interest Rates.*)

The tradeoff between the variability of bill payouts and the interest-rate risk of consols reverses during the twentieth century. With the abandonment of the gold standard after World War I, and the consequent inflationary explosion, the modern investor now demands a higher return from long-term bonds and annuities than from bills. This is because bonds and annuities risk serious damage from depreciating money (inflation). Thus, in recent years, long-term rates are usually higher than short-term rates, since investors need to be compensated for bearing the risk of inflation-caused damage to long-term bonds.

The history of English interest rates reinforces the notion that with high return comes risk. Anarchy and destruction lapped at Britain's very shores between 1789 and 1814, leading investors to require higher and higher returns on their funds. What they received was a 5.5% perpetual rate (remember, no inflation) with the otherwise ultrasafe consols. On the other hand, the Englishman in the late Victorian era lived in, what seemed at the time, the height of stability and permanence. With such safety came low returns. History played a cruel trick on the English investor after 1900, with low stock and bond returns being the least of his troubles.

The lesson here for the modern investor is obvious. Before the tragic events of September 11, 2001, many investors were encouraged by the apparent economic vigor and safety of the post-Cold War world. And, yet, both the logic of the markets and history show us that when the sun shines the brightest, investment returns are the lowest. This is as it should be: stability and prosperity imply high asset prices, which, because of the inverse relation between yields and prices, result in low future returns. Conversely, the highest returns are obtained by shouldering prudent risk when things look the bleakest, a theme we shall return to repeatedly.

Bond Returns in the Twentieth Century

The history of bonds in the twentieth century is unique—even the most comprehensive grasp of financial history would not have prepared the nineteenth century investor for the hurricane that buffeted the world's fixed-income markets after 1900.

In order to understand what happened, it's necessary to briefly discuss the transition from the gold standard to the paper currency system that took place in the early 1900s. We've already touched on the abandonment of the gold standard after World War I. Before then, except for very brief periods, gold *was* money. In the U.S., there is still an abundant supply of quarter ($2.50), half ($5), full ($10), and double ($20) eagles sitting in the hands of collectors and dealers; they are still legal tender. Because of that abundance, most of these coins are not worth much more than their metallic value. However, they disappeared from circulation when their gold value exceeded their face value. For example, a quarter eagle, weighing about an eighth of an ounce, contains about $35 worth of gold at present prices; you'd be foolish to exchange it for goods worth its $2.50 face value.

Over time, the value of gold relative to other goods and services remains roughly constant: an ounce of gold bought a respectable suit of men's clothes in Dante's time, and, until a just a few years ago, you could still buy a decent suit with that amount of gold. Because of the instabilities of international bullion flows resulting from post-war inflation, the gold-standard world, which had existed since the Lydian's first coinage, disappeared forever in the two decades after World War I.

Freed from the obligation of having to exchange paper money for the yellow metal, governments began to print bills, sometimes with abandon. Germany in the 1920s is a prime example. The result was the first great worldwide inflation, which accelerated in fits and starts throughout most of the century, finally climaxing around 1980, when the world's central banks and treasuries increased interest rates and finally slowed down the presses.

But the damage to investor confidence had already been done. Before the twentieth century, bond buyers had long been accustomed to dollars, pounds, and francs that did not depreciate in value over time. At the beginning of the twentieth century, investors still believed that a current dollar, pound, or franc would buy just as much in fifty years. In the decades following the conversion to paper currency, they slowly realized that their bonds, which promised only future paper currency, were worth less than they thought, producing the rise in interest rates seen in Figures 1-5 and 1-6; the result was devastating losses for bondholders.

In short, bondholders in the twentieth century were blindsided by what financial economists call a "thousand year flood": in this case, the disappearance of constant-value gold-backed money. Before the twentieth century, nations had temporarily gone off the hard-money standard, usually during wartime, but its permanent global abandonment was never contemplated until shortly before World War I. After World War I, the change was made permanent.

The shift in the investment landscape was cataclysmic, and the resulting financial damage to bonds was of the sort previously seen only with revolution and military disaster. Even in the United States, which suffered no challenge to its government or territory in the 1900s, bond losses were severe.

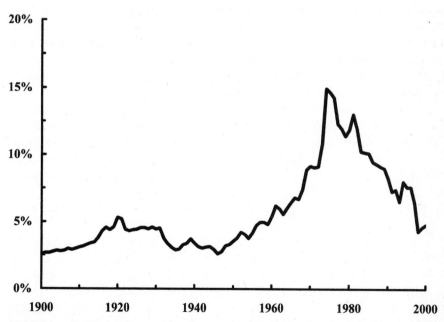

Figure 1-5. English consol/long bond rates, 1900–2000. (*Source:* Homer and Sylla, Bank of England.)

Figure 1-6. U.S. government bond rates, 1900–2000. (*Source:* Homer and Sylla, U.S. Treasury.)

Consider that in 1913, a U.S. stockholder or bondholder both received a 5% yield. The bondholder could reasonably expect that this 5% yield was a *real* one—that is, that its fixed value would not decrease over time. The stockholder, on the other hand, balanced the prospect of modest dividend growth versus the much higher risk of stocks. The abandonment of the gold standard turned all that upside down—suddenly, the future value of the bondholder's income stream was radically devalued by higher inflation, whereas that of the stockholder was enhanced by the ability of corporations to increase their earnings and dividends with inflation. It took investors more than a generation to realize this. In the process, stock prices rose dramatically and bond prices fell.

But do not lament today's paper-based currency, because the gold-based economic system, which Keynes called a "barbarous relic," was far worse. With hard currency, there is no control of the money supply—the government is committed to exchange bills for gold, or vice versa, at the will of its citizens. So it cannot expand the supply of paper money; otherwise it will risk depleting its gold supply at the hands of individuals who, detecting the increased numbers of dollar bills in circulation, appear at the Treasury's window bearing dollars. And it cannot shrink the supply of money, lest individuals, detecting the decreased number of bills, appear at the Treasury's windows bearing gold.

The problem is that national economies are subject to boom-and-bust cycles. These can be mitigated by printing more money during the busts and by taking bills out of circulation during the booms. The advantages of being able to do this under a paper-based monetary system far outweigh the inflationary tendencies of a paper money system.

Because of the abandonment of hard currency, the history of bonds in the twentieth century was not a happy one. Look again at Figure 1-5, where I've plotted British government bonds interest rates since 1900. As you can see, this is close to a mirror image of Figure 1-4, with increasing rates for most of the century. What you are looking at is a picture of the financial devastation of British bondholders. Between 1900 and 1974, the average consol yield rose from 2.54% to 14.95%, or a fall in price of 83%.

But there was even worse news. Between those two dates, inflation had decreased the value of the pound by approximately 87%, so the real principal value of the consol had fallen 98% during the period, although that loss was partially mitigated by the dividends paid out. The twentieth century history of bonds in the U.S. was almost as unhappy. Figure 1-6 plots U.S. interest rates since 1900. Once again, inflation gutted returns of U.S. bonds. Even after accounting for dividends, the real return of long-term U.S. government bonds in the twentieth century was only 2% per year.

Although it is difficult to predict the future, it is unlikely that we will soon see a repeat of the poor bond returns of the twentieth century. For starters, our survey of bond returns suggests that prior to the twentieth century, they were generous.

Second, it is now possible to eliminate inflation risk with the purchase of inflation-adjusted bonds. The U.S. Treasury version, the 30-year "Treasury Inflation Protected Security," or TIPS, currently yields 3.45%. So no matter how badly inflation rages, the interest payments of these bonds will be 3.45% of the face amount in real purchasing power, and the principal will also be repaid in inflation-adjusted dollars. (These are the equivalent of the gold-backed bonds of the last century.)

Third, inflation is a painful, searing experience for the bondholder and is not soon forgotten. During the German hyperinflation of the 1920s, bonds lost 100% of their value within a few months. German investors said, "Never again," and for the past 80 years, German central banks have carefully controlled inflation by reining in their money supply. American investors, too, were traumatized by the Great Inflation of 1965 to 1985 and began demanding an "inflation premium" when purchasing long-term bonds. For example, long-term corporate bonds currently yield more than 6%, nearly 4% above the inflation rate.

Lastly, and I'll admit this is a weak reed, it is possible that the world's central banks have finally learned how to tame the inflationary beast.

But the key point is this: bond returns in the twentieth century should not be used to predict future bond returns. The past few pages have hopefully more than adequately described bond risks. The monetary shocks of the twentieth century are among the most severe in recorded economic history, and it is more likely that inflation-adjusted bond returns going forward will be closer to the 3% to 4% rate of the previous centuries, than to the near-zero rate of the last ninety years.

The Long-Term History of Stock Returns

The history of stock returns is much more restricted. Although there has been active trading of stocks in England, France, and Holland for more than three hundred years, it is only in the past two centuries that we have information on long-term returns of stocks, beginning in the United States soon after its birth. And only in the past several decades does detailed information become available from around the globe.

At this point, it's important to clarify the difference between bonds and stocks. A bond is simply a loan. Most often, bonds have a sharply limited upside: the best that you can do is collect your interest payments and principal at maturity. A share of stock, on the other hand, represents a claim on all of the future earnings of the company. As such, its upside is potentially unlimited.

It is, of course, quite possible to suffer a 100% loss with either. If a company goes bankrupt, both its stocks and bonds may be worth nothing, although bondholders have first claim on the assets of a bankrupt company. The major difference between stocks and bonds occurs during inflation. Because a bond's payments are fixed, its value suffers during inflationary periods; it may become worthless if inflation is severe enough. Stocks are also damaged by inflation, but since a company can raise the price of the goods and services it produces, its earnings, and, thus, its value, should rise along with inflation.

This is not to say that stocks are always superior to bonds. Although stocks often have higher returns because of their unlimited upside potential and inflation protection, there are times when bonds shine.

Stocks, Bonds, and Bills in the Twentieth Century

Figure 1-7 summarizes the returns of U.S. stocks, long-term Treasury bonds, and Treasury bills since 1900. Its message should not surprise

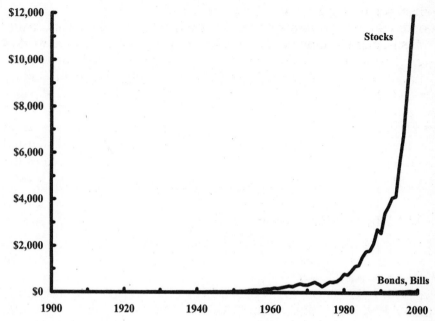

Figure 1-7. Value of $1.00 invested in stocks, bonds, and bills, 1901–2000. (*Source:* Jeremy Siegel.)

you by this point—stocks have the highest returns (9.89% annualized), followed by bonds (4.85% annualized), with "safe" bills (3.86% annualized), bringing up the rear. All of these returns are "nominal," that is, they do not take inflation into account, which, during the period, averaged 3.6%. So the "real," or inflation-adjusted, returns were about 6% for stocks, 1% for bonds, and zero for bills.

Note that the representation of wealth on the vertical scale of the graph is "arithmetic"—that is, its scale is even, with each tick mark representing the same amount of money (in this case, $1,000). This graph really doesn't convey a lot of useful information about stock returns in the first half of the century, and very little about bond or bill returns at all.

To get around this problem, finance professionals use a slightly different kind of plot to follow wealth creation over very long periods—the so-called "semilog" display shown in Figure 1-8. This means that the wealth displayed on the vertical axis is represented "logarithmically," that is, each tick represents a tenfold increase in value—from $1 to $10 to $100 to $1,000. This kind of plot is one of the most familiar teaching tools in personal finance, used by brokers and investment advisors across the nation to demonstrate the benefits of stocks to small investors. But, as we have already seen with Figure 1-1, which

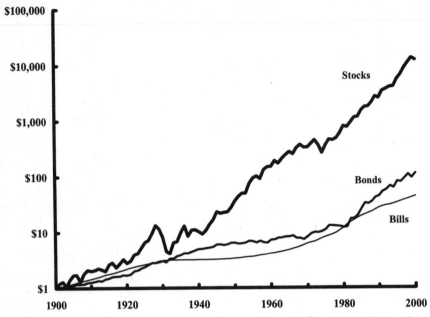

Figure 1-8. Value of $1.00 invested in stocks, bonds, and bills, 1901–2000 (semilogarithmic scale). (*Source:* Jeremy Siegel.)

is also a semilog plot, this graph can be highly deceptive, as it tends to underplay risk.

Risk—The Second Dimension

The study of investment returns is only half of the story. Distilled to its essence, investing is about earning a return in exchange for shouldering risk. Return is by far the easiest half, because it is simple to define and calculate, either as "total returns"—the end values in Figures 1-7 and 1-8, or as "annualized returns"—the hypothetical gain you'd have to earn each year to reach that value.

Risk is a much harder thing to define and measure. It comes in two flavors: short-term and long-term. Short-term risk is somewhat easier to deal with. Let's start with the annual returns of bills, bonds, and stocks, which I've plotted in Figures 1-9 through 1-11. Notice that the bills are "perfectly safe," with nary a losing year. Bonds, on the other hand, do occasionally lose money—as much as 13% in 1999, according to the long-bond data from Professor Jeremy Siegel. And finally, stocks lose money in one of every three years. Sometimes, they lose a lot.

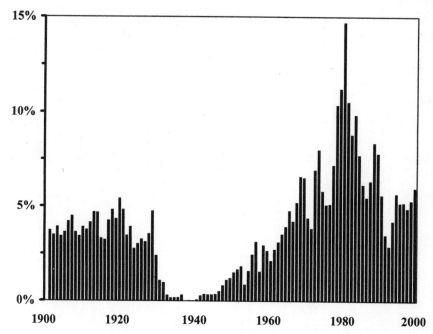

Figure 1-9. U.S. Treasury bill returns, 1901–2000. (*Source:* Jeremy Siegel.)

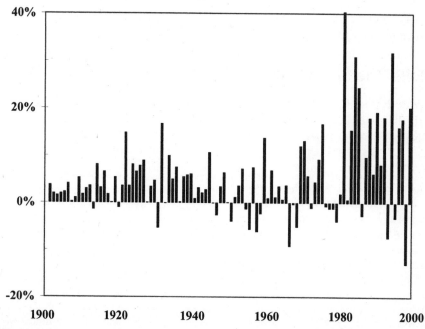

Figure 1-10. U.S. Treasury bond returns, 1901–2000. (*Source:* Jeremy Siegel.)

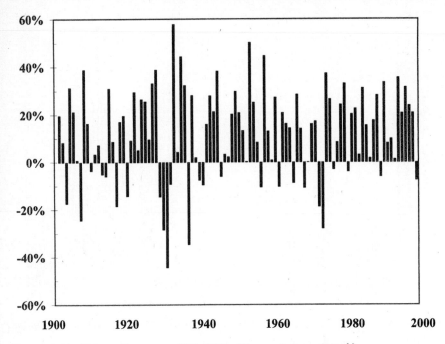

Figure 1-11. U.S. stock returns, 1901–2000. (*Source:* Jeremy Siegel.)

In fact, stocks can behave badly for years at a time. For example, from 1973 to 1974, stocks lost about 40% of their value, while inflation reduced the value of a dollar by nearly 20%, for an after-inflation cumulative loss of about one-half. And from the market peak in September 1929 to the bottom in July 1932, the market lost an astonishing 83% of its value. The loss was mitigated, however, by the approximate 20% fall in consumer prices that occurred during the period. The market recovered strongly after 1932, but in 1937, another drop of about 50% occurred.[1]

---

[1]It is relatively easy to measure short-term risk by calculating something statisticians call a "standard deviation" (SD). This can be thought about as the degree of "scatter" of a series of values about the average. For example, the average height of adult males is about 69 inches with an SD of 3 inches. This means that about one-sixth of males will be taller than 72 inches and one-sixth will be shorter than 66 inches (one SD above or below the mean); about 2% will be taller than 75 inches (two SD above the mean). For the U.S. stock market, the average annual market return is about 10%, and the SD of market returns is about 20%. So, just like the hypothetical example cited above, a return of zero is one-half SD below the mean (that is, the average return of 10% is one-half of the 20% SD). In fact, the stock market loses money about one-third of the time, as predicted by statistical theory. A "worst-case" scenario is a minus two SD result (a loss of 30%), which should occur about 2% of the time. In fact, this is

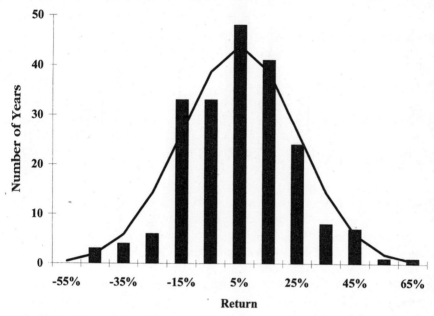

Figure 1-12. U.S. annual stock returns, 1790–2000. Actual (*bars*) versus predicted random distribution (*curve,* see footnote).

Figure 1-11 is interesting for another reason. Many investors cling to the belief that by following the right indicator or listening to the right guru, they can reduce risk by avoiding bear markets. Do you see any particular pattern to the annual returns? If you do, then you're also likely quite adept at seeing the George Washington Bridge or the face of Bruce Willis in the clouds scudding overhead. The pattern of annual stock returns is almost totally random and unpredictable. The return in the last year, or the past five years, gives you no hint of next year's return—it is a "random walk." As we'll see later, no one—not the pundits from the big brokerage firms, not the newsletter writers, not the mutual fund managers, and certainly not your broker—can predict where the market will go tomorrow or next year.

So the twentieth century has seen three severe drops in stock prices, one of them catastrophic. The message to the average investor is brutally clear: expect at least one, and perhaps two, very severe bear markets during your investing career.

---

exactly what has occurred—four times in the past 200 years (2% of years), the U.S. market lost more than 30%. In Figure 1-12, I've plotted the frequency of annual market returns (the vertical bars) versus the "theoretical" probability (the bell-shaped curve) predicted by the laws of statistics. As you can see, the agreement is quite good.

Long-term risk—the probability of running out of money over the decades—is an entirely different matter. Strangely, human beings are not as emotionally disturbed by long-term risk as they are by short-term risk. Clearly, long-term returns are much more important than the magnitude of short-term reversals.

Paradoxically, in the long run, bonds are at least as risky as stocks. This is because stock returns are "mean reverting." That is, a series of bad years is likely to be followed by a series of good ones, repairing some of the damage. Unfortunately, this is a two-edged sword, as a series of very good years is likely to be followed by bad ones, as investors have learned, to their chagrin, in the past few years. In Figure 1-13, I've plotted the annualized 30-year real (inflation-adjusted) returns of stocks. Note how placid this graph looks, with no periods of real or nominal losses. This sort of plot is often used to demonstrate that stocks become "less risky" over time.

But as we've already seen, it's easy to make graphs lie. Notice that the difference between the lowest and highest return is about 5%. Compound a 5% return difference over 30 years and you wind up with a more than fourfold difference in value. End-period wealth—the total amount of capital you have after 30 years—is a much better gauge of long-term risk than are annualized returns.

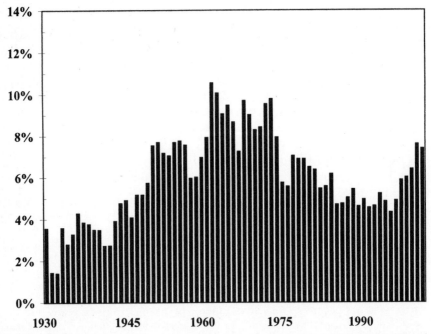

Figure 1-13. Thirty-year annualized real U.S. stock returns, 1901–2000. (*Source:* Jeremy Siegel.)

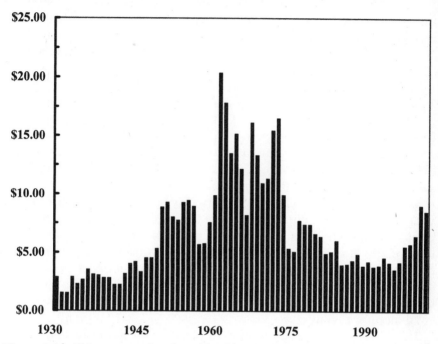

Figure 1-14. Thirty-year real end wealth of $1.00 invested in U.S. stock, 1901–2000. (*Source:* Jeremy Siegel.)

In Figure 1-14, I've plotted the real (inflation-adjusted) end wealth for $1.00 invested in each of the 30-year periods in this century. Note the enormous range of values. If these amounts represent your retirement nest egg, it can be easily seen that the gap between the best and worst 30-year periods represents the difference between a comfortable old age and the trailer park.

Retirement planning is an enormously complicated topic, which we'll explore in Chapter 12 in some detail. Obviously, your personal circumstances are critically important, but one thing is clear: an examination of historical stock returns shows that the market can perform miserably for periods as long as 15 to 20 years. For example, during the 17 years from 1966 to 1982, stock returns just barely kept up with inflation, with the brutal 1973–1974 bear market occurring in the middle of the period. Had you begun your retirement in 1966, the combination of poor inflation-adjusted returns and mandatory withdrawals would likely have devastated your assets—there would have been little or no savings left to enjoy the high returns that followed.

Bonds are even worse, since their returns do not mean revert—a series of bad years is likely to be followed by even more bad ones, as happened during the 1970s. This is the point made by Jeremy Siegel

in his superb treatise, *Stocks For The Long Run*. Professor Siegel pointed out that stocks outperformed bonds in only 61% of the years after
1802, but that they bested bonds in 80% of ten-year periods and in
99% of 30-year periods.

Looked at from another perspective, in the 30 years from 1952 to
1981, stocks returned 9.9% and bonds returned only 2.3%, while inflation annualized out at 4.3%. Thus, during this period, the bond
investor lost 2% of real value on an annualized basis, while the stock
investor made a 5.6% real annualized return. The last fifteen years of
that period were years of high inflation, so this is just another way of
saying that stocks withstand inflation better than bonds.

Short-term risk, occurring over periods of less than several years, is
what we feel in our gut as we follow the market from day to day and
month to month. It is what gives investors sleepless nights. More
importantly, it is what causes investors to bail out of stocks after a bad
run, usually at the bottom. And yet, in the long-term, it is of trivial
importance. After all, if you can obtain high long-term returns, what
does it matter if you have lost and regained 50% or 80% of your principal along the way?

This, of course, is easier said than done. Even the most disciplined
investors exited the markets in the 1930s, never to return. Obsession
with the short term is ingrained in human nature; the impulse is impossible to ignore. Your short-term investing emotions must be recognized and dealt with on their own terms. It is an easy thing to look at
the above data and convince yourself that you will be able to stay the
course through the tough times. But actually doing it is an entirely different affair.

Examining historical returns and imagining losing 50% or 80% of
your capital is like practicing an airplane crash in a simulator. Trust
me, there is a big difference between how you'll behave in the simulator and how you'll perform during the real thing. During bull
markets, everyone believes that he is committed to stocks for the
long term. Unfortunately, history also tells us that during bear markets, you can hardly give stocks away. Most investors are simply not
capable of withstanding the vicissitudes of an all-stock investment
strategy.

The data for the U.S. markets displayed in Figures 1-9 to 1-14 are
summarized in Table 1-1. It's pretty clear that there's a relationship
between return and risk—you enjoy high returns only by taking substantial risk. If you want to earn high returns, be prepared to suffer
grievous losses from time to time. And if you want perfect safety,
resign yourself to low returns. In fact, the best way to spot investment
fraud is the promise of safety and very high returns. If someone offers

Table 1-1. Historical Returns and Risks of U.S. Stocks and Bonds in the Twentieth Century

Asset	Annualized Return	Worst Real Three-Year Loss
Treasury Bills	4%	0%
Treasury Bonds	5%	−25%
Large Company Stocks	10%	−60%
Small Company Stocks	12%	−70%

(*Source:* Jeremy Siegel and Ibbotson Associates.)

you this, turn 180 degrees and do not walk—run. This is such an important point that I'm going to repeat it:

> *High investment returns cannot be earned without taking substantial risk. Safe investments produce low returns.*

We'll go into the relationship between risk and return in much more detail later, but it's worth mentioning one common example here. Almost every one of you owns a money market account from one of the large mutual fund companies. The reason you do is that money-fund yields are higher than you get from a bank passbook or checking account. This is because your money market account carries with it a slight amount of risk. Your money market owns "commercial paper" issued by large corporations, which is not insured and can default, whereas your bank accounts *are* federally insured. So you are being rewarded for taking this risk with extra return.

It's also true that the mutual fund industry does its best to soft pedal this inconvenient fact. No major fund company's money market fund has ever "broken the buck," even though commercial paper does occasionally default. In 1990, paper issued by Mortgage and Realty Trust, held by many large money market accounts, fell into default. Passing these losses onto the shareholders would have resulted in a devastating loss of confidence, and without exception, the fund companies reimbursed their money market funds. One company alone—T. Rowe Price—spent about $40 million repairing the damage. But there is no guarantee that they will always be able to do this. In addition, banks' yields are hobbled by the necessity of holding reserves—funds that cannot be loaned out.

Stock Returns Outside the U.S.

The investment stories and data presented in this chapter vividly illustrate the interplay between investment and societal risk factors and return. High-risk societies—or crisis periods in stable societies—result in high investment returns, *if those societies survive.* As we saw with Venetian prestiti, the highest returns of all were made during the transition from a high-risk to a low-risk environment. And, as we've already alluded to, the high returns of U.S. stocks were at least partly the result of the same phenomenon, drawn out over two centuries.

In fact, the U.S. stock returns of the past 200 years represent a best-case scenario. To get a more realistic view of stock returns, it's important to examine stock returns from as many nations, and over as long a period, as possible. Professors Philippe Jorion and William Goetzmann examined stock returns around the world in the twentieth century, and the picture they draw is not nearly as pretty as the American story. With their kind permission, I've reproduced their summary findings, shown in Figure 1-15. This graph is a bit confusing, but it's worth the effort to understand it.

The horizontal (bottom) axis plots the number of years each market has been in existence. Almost all of the nations on the right half of the graph—the ones with the longest market histories—are developed Western nations. Because stock markets accompany development, it is no surprise that some of the most developed countries were the first to create them. Most of these nations—especially the U.S., Canada, Sweden, Switzerland, Norway, Chile, Denmark, and Britain—have had high stock returns. (The returns shown on the vertical axis are a bit

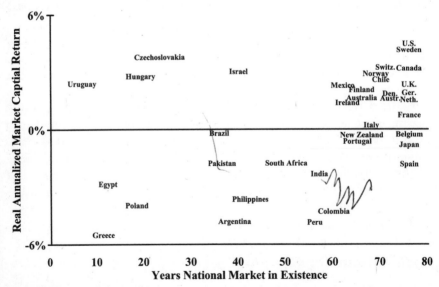

Figure 1-15. Real equity returns versus market age. (*Source:* Jorion and Goetzmann, *Journal of Finance*, 1999.)

misleading to the non-academic reader, as they subtract out the return due to inflation, and further do not include dividends.)

Now look on the left-hand portion of the graph. These are the markets with the shortest histories and are exclusively what we would today call "emerging markets." Although there is a fair amount of scatter, note how, in general, the countries clustering on the left half of the graph have lower returns than the "developed" nations on the right half of the graph.

Some consider Figure 1-15 to be an argument against investing in emerging markets. *It is no such thing.* Remember that a century ago, the U.S. was an emerging market, and that two centuries ago, England, France, and Holland were also. Rather, it is a demonstration that the markets with the best returns survive, and that those with the worst returns do not—survivorship bias, yet again.

The moral here is that because the most successful societies have the highest *past* stock returns, they become the biggest stock markets and are considered the most "typical." Looking at the winners, we tend to get a distorted view of stock returns. It helps to recall that, three centuries ago, France had the world's largest economy and just a century-and-a-half ago, that distinction belonged to England.

Yet even the detailed work cited above provides a skewed version of national security returns. You'll note that many of the names at the top of the graph are of English-speaking nations that were largely spared the destruction of the two world wars. As grievously as Britain and its Commonwealth suffered in these conflicts, they did not suffer the near total destruction of their industrial apparatus, as did Germany, the rest of continental Europe, Russia, Japan, and China. Limiting our analysis to the period following the initial phase of postwar reconstruction may provide a much less biased estimate of non-U.S. investment returns.

The Morgan Stanley Capital International Europe, Australasia, and Far East (EAFE) Index is a highly accurate measure of equity returns in the developed world outside the U.S. In Figure 1-16, I've plotted the value of a dollar invested in the S&P 500 Index and the EAFE since its inception in 1969. The returns were virtually the same: 11.89% for the EAFE versus 12.17% for the S&P 500, with end-wealths of $36.44 and $39.43, respectively.

In a world in which billions of dollars of capital can be instantaneously moved around the globe with a keystroke, this is as it should be. There is no reason why an investor from one nation should accept, as a matter of course, poor returns in his own country if he can just as easily invest abroad. If investors think that returns will be higher in Australia than in Belgium, then capital will flow from Belgium to

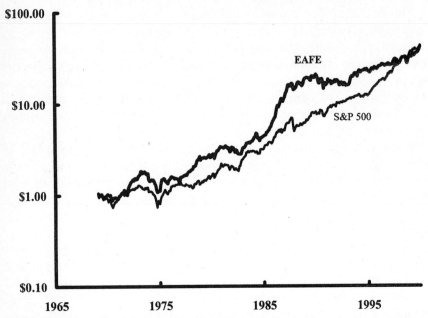

Figure 1-16. U.S. versus foreign equity, 1969 to 2000. (*Source: Principia Pro Plus* Morningstar, Inc.)

Australia. This will depress prices in Belgium, which, in turn, will increase future returns. The opposite will occur in Australia. Prices will adjust to the point where the expected returns, adjusted for risk, in both nations will be the same. Assuming that the risks are the same, there is no reason that the future return in any one nation should be higher than another. And, to the extent that one nation is perceived to be riskier than another, the nation with the highest perceived risk should have the highest future return, in order to compensate for the extra risk.

Since World War II, real long-term stock returns in the U.S. have been about 8% (after dividends and inflation are taken into account), dwarfing bond performance. But world financial history cautions us not to expect the generous rewards of U.S. stocks in the future. In fact, historical returns are of only limited use in predicting future returns. The real value of the historical record is as a gauge of risk, not return.

Size Matters

As we move forward through the twentieth century, detail about stock returns comes into increasingly sharp focus. In recent decades, financial economists have begun to study how company characteristics affect stock return.

The first company characteristic to be studied was size. The "size" of a company can be measured in many ways—the number of its employees, or the amount of sales, profits, or physical assets it owns. But the most easily measured and most important number to investors is its "market capitalization" (usually shortened to "market cap"), which is the total market value of its outstanding stock. This is an important number for many reasons, not the least of which is that most market indexes are market cap weighted, meaning that the representation of each stock in the index is proportional to its market cap. For example, as of this writing, the biggest company in the S&P 500 is General Electric, with a market cap of $460 billion. The smallest is American Greetings, with a market cap of $700 million. Thus, the S&P contains 600 times as much GE as it does American Greetings ($460 billion/$700 million = 600).

Is there a difference between the returns of small and large companies? Yes. It appears that small stocks have had higher returns than large ones. In Figure 1-17, I've plotted the returns of the stocks of the largest and smallest companies in the U.S. market from July 1926 to June 2000. This data was kindly supplied by Professor Kenneth French of MIT. He divided the markets into three groups—small, medium, and

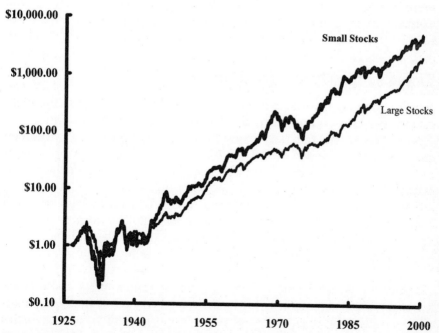

Figure 1-17. Small stocks versus large stocks, 1926–2000. (*Source:* Kenneth French.)

large. (I've omitted the medium-sized, however.) A summary of the data appears below:

Small versus Large Stocks, July 1926–June 2000

	End Wealth	Annualized Return	9/29–6/32	12/72–9/74
Small Stocks	$5,522	12.35%	−90.78%	−53.15%
Large Stocks	$2,128	10.91%	−84.44%	−43.47%

Note how small stocks have had higher returns than larger stocks, but that they also have higher risks. In both the Great Depression and the 1970s bear market, small-stocks sustained higher losses than large stocks. In addition, the small stock advantage is extremely tenuous— it's less than a percent-and-a-half per year, and there have been periods of more than 30 years when large stocks have bested small stocks. For these reasons, the small-stock advantage is controversial. But over long time periods, it is present in most foreign countries. For example, during the past 46 years, British small stocks have outperformed large stocks by 2.66% per year. During the past 31 years, the small-stock advantage in Japan has been 1.78%. Abroad, as in the U.S. small stocks were riskier. Once again, the relationship between risk and return holds up. Yes, you can have higher returns, but only by bearing more risk.

Company Quality and Stock Return

Finally, there is the issue of corporate quality. Simply put, there are "good" companies, and there are "bad" companies. And it's critical that you grasp how the market treats them and how that, in turn, affects the risk and return of your portfolio.

First, I'd like to introduce a bit of investment nomenclature. In common parlance, the shares of good companies are called "growth stocks," and those of bad companies are called "value stocks." Let's consider for a moment, Wal-Mart and Kmart. The former is financially healthy and universally admired, with legendary management, a steadily growing stream of earnings, and a huge pile of cash on hand for emergencies. The latter is a sick puppy, having recently declared bankruptcy due to marginal financial resources and a history of poor management. Even in the best of years, it had very irregular earnings. Wal-Mart is manifestly a good/growth company. Kmart is a bad/value company; without making too fine a point, it is, in fact, a real dog.

More importantly, Wal-Mart, aside from being the better company, is also the safer company. Because of its steadily growing earnings and assets, even the hardest of economic times would not put it out of business. On the other hand, Kmart's finances are marginal even in the best of times, and the recent recessionary economy very well could put it on the wrong side of the daisies with breathtaking speed.

Now we arrive at one of the most counterintuitive points in all of finance. It is so counterintuitive, in fact, that even professional investors have trouble understanding it. To wit: *Since Kmart is a much riskier company than Wal-Mart, investors expect a higher return from Kmart than they do from Wal-Mart.* Think about it. If Kmart had the same expected return as Wal-Mart, no one would buy it! So its price must fall to the point where its expected return exceeds Wal-Mart's by a wide enough margin so that investors finally are induced to buy its shares. The key word here is *expected,* as opposed to *guaranteed.* Kmart has a higher *expected* return than Wal-Mart, but this is because there is great *risk* that this may not happen. Kmart's recent Chapter 11 filing has in fact turned it into a kind of lottery ticket. There may only be a small chance that it will survive, but if it does, its price will sky-rocket. Let's assume that Kmart's chances of survival are 25%, and that if it does make it, its price will increase by a factor of eight. Thus, its "expected value" is 0.25×8, or twice its present value. The risk of owning stock in a single shaky company is very high. But in a *portfolio* of many such losers, a few might reasonably be expected to pull through, providing the investor with a reasonable return.

Thus, the logic of the market suggests that:

Good companies are generally bad stocks, and bad companies are generally good stocks.

Is this actually true? Resoundingly, yes. There have been a large number of studies of the growth-versus-value question in many nations over long periods of time. They all show the same thing: unglamorous, unsafe value stocks with poor earnings have higher returns than glamorous growth stocks with good earnings.

Probably the most exhaustive work in this area has been done by Eugene Fama at the University of Chicago and Kenneth French at MIT, in which they examined the behavior of growth and value stocks. They looked at value versus growth for both small and large companies and found that value stocks clearly had higher returns than growth stocks.

Figure 1-18 and the data below summarize their work:

	Annualized Return, 1926–2000
Large Value Stocks	12.87%
Large Growth Stocks	10.77%
Small Value Stocks	14.87%
Small Growth Stocks	9.92%

Fama and French's work on the value effect has had a profound influence on the investment community. Like all ground-breaking work, it prompted a great deal of criticism. The most consistent point of contention was that the results of their original study, which covered the period from 1963 to 1990, was a peculiarity of the U.S. market for those years and not a more general phenomenon. Their response to such criticism became their trademark. Rather than engage in lengthy debates on the topic, they extended their study period back to 1926, producing the data you see above.

Next, they looked abroad. In Table 1-2, I've summarized their international data, which cover the years from 1975 to 1996. Note that in

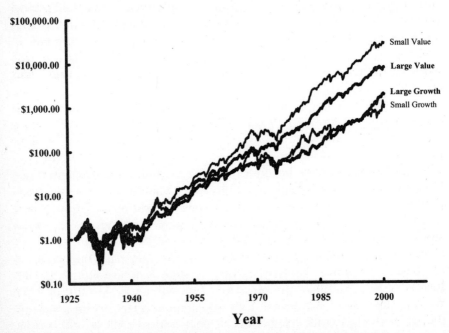

Figure 1-18. Value versus growth, 1926–2000. (*Source:* Kenneth French.)

Table 1-2. Value versus Growth Abroad, 1975–96

Country	Value Stocks	Growth Stocks	Value Advantage
Japan	14.55%	7.55%	7.00%
Britain	17.87%	13.25%	4.62%
France	17.10%	9.46%	7.64%
Germany	12.77%	10.01%	2.76%
Italy	5.45%	11.44%	−5.99%
Netherlands	15.77%	13.47%	2.30%
Belgium	14.90%	10.51%	4.39%
Switzerland	13.84%	10.34%	3.50%
Sweden	20.61%	12.59%	8.02%
Australia	17.62%	5.30%	12.32%
Hong Kong	26.51%	19.35%	7.16%
Singapore	21.63%	11.96%	9.67%
Average	**16.55%**	**11.27%**	**5.28%**

(*Source*: Fama, Eugene F., and Kenneth R. French, "Value versus Growth: The International Evidence." *Journal of Finance,* December 1998.)

all but one of the countries, value stocks did, in fact, have higher returns than growth stocks, by an average of more than 5% per year. The same was also true for the emerging-market countries studied, although the data is a bit less clear because of the shorter time period studied (1987–1995): in 12 of the 16 nations, value stocks had higher returns than growth stocks, by an average margin of 10% per year.

Campbell Harvey of Duke University has recently extended this work to the level of entire nations. Just as there are good and bad companies, so are there good and bad nations. And, as you'd expect, returns are higher in the bad nations—the ones with the shakiest financial systems—because there the risk is highest. By this point, I hope you're moving your lips to this familiar mantra: because risk is high, prices are low. And because prices are low, future returns are high.

So the shares of poorly run, unglamorous companies must, and do, have higher returns than those of the most glamorous, best-run companies. Part of this has to do with the risks associated with owning them. But there are also compelling behavioral reasons why value stocks have higher returns, which we'll cover in more detail in later chapters; investors simply cannot bring themselves to buy the shares of "bad" companies. Human beings are profoundly social creatures. Just as people want to own the most popular fashions, so too do they want to own the latest stocks. Owning a portfolio of value stocks is the equivalent of wearing a Nehru jacket over a pair of bell-bottom trousers.

The data on the performance of value and growth stocks run counter to the way most people invest. The average investor equates great companies, producing great products, with great stocks. And there is no doubt that some great companies, like Wal-Mart, Microsoft, and GE, produce high returns for long periods of time. But these are the winning lottery tickets in the growth stock sweepstakes. For every growth stock with high returns, there are a dozen that, within a very brief time, disappointed the market with lower-than-expected earnings growth and were consequently taken out and shot.

Summing Up: The Historical Record on Risk/Return

I've previously summarized the returns and risks of the major U.S. stock and bond classes over the twentieth century in Table 1-1. In Figure 1-19, I've plotted these data.

Figure 1-19 shows a clear-cut relationship between risk and return. Some may object to the magnitude of the risks I've shown for stocks. But as the recent performance in emerging markets and tech investing show, losses in excess of 50% are not unheard of. If you are not prepared to accept risk in pursuit of high returns, you are doomed to fail.

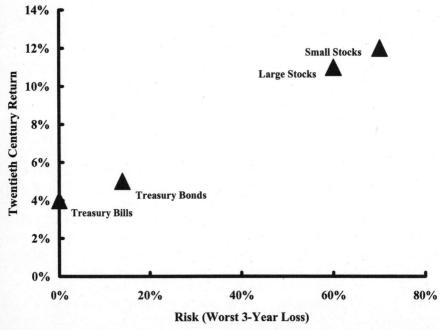

Figure 1-19. Risk and return summary. (*Source:* Kenneth French and Jeremy Siegel.)

CHAPTER 1 SUMMARY

1. The history of the stock and bond markets shows that risk and reward are inextricably intertwined. Do not expect high returns without high risk. Do not expect safety without correspondingly low returns. Further, when the political and economic outlook is the brightest, returns are the lowest. And it is when things look the darkest that returns are the highest.
2. The longer a risky asset is held, the less the chance of a loss.
3. Be especially wary of data demonstrating the superior long-term performance of U.S. stocks. For most of its history, the U.S. was a very risky place to invest, and its high investment returns reflect that. Now that the U.S. seems to be more of a "sure thing," prices have risen, and future investment returns will necessarily be lower.

The New World Order, circa 1913

The tragic events in New York, Washington, DC, and Pennsylvania in the fall of 2001 served to underscore the relationship between return and risk. Prior to the bombings, most investors felt that the world had become progressively less risky. This resulted in a dramatic rise in stock prices. When this illusion was shattered, prices reacted equally dramatically.

This is not a new story. There is no better illustration of the dangers of living and investing in an apparently stable and prosperous era than this passage from Keynes's *The Economic Consequences of the Peace*, which chronicles life in Europe just before the lights went out for almost two generations:

> The inhabitant of London could order by telephone, sipping his morning tea in bed, the various products of the whole earth, in such quantity as he might see fit, and reasonably expect their early delivery upon his doorstep; he could at the same moment and by the same means adventure his wealth in the natural resources and new enterprises of any quarter of the world, and share, without exertion or even trouble, in their prospective fruits and advantages; or he could decide, to couple the security of his fortunes with the good faith of the townspeople of any substantial municipality in any continent that fancy or information might recommend. He could secure forthwith, if he wished it, cheap and comfortable means of transit to any country or climate without passport or other formality, could dispatch his servant to the neighboring office of a bank for such supply of the precious metals as might seem convenient, and could then proceed abroad to foreign quarters, without knowledge of their religion, language, or customs, bearing coined wealth upon his person, and would consider himself greatly aggrieved and much surprised at the least interference. But, most important of all, he regarded this state of affairs as normal, certain, and permanent, except in the direction of further improvement, and any deviation from it as aberrant, scandalous, and avoidable. The projects and politics of militarism and imperialism, of racial and cultural rivalries, of monopolies, restrictions, and exclusion, which were to play the serpent to this paradise, were little more than the amusements of his daily newspaper, and appeared to exercise almost no influence at all on the ordinary course of social and economic life, the internationalization of which was nearly complete in practice.

2

Measuring the Beast

Capital value is income capitalized, and nothing else.

Irving Fisher

In the history of modern investing, one economist towers above all others in influence on the way we examine stocks and bonds. His name was Irving Fisher: distinguished professor of economics at Yale, advisor to presidents, famous popular financial commentator, and, most importantly, author of the seminal treatise on investment value, *The Theory of Interest*. And it was Fisher, who, a century ago, first attempted to scientifically answer the question, "What is a thing worth?" His career was dazzling, and his precepts are still widely studied today, more than seven decades after the book was written.

Fisher's story is a caution to all great men, because, in spite of his long list of staggering accomplishments, he will be forever remembered for one notorious gaffe. Just before the October 1929 stock market crash, he declared, "Stock prices have reached what looks like a permanently high plateau." Weeks before the start of a bear market that would eventually result in a near 90% decline, the world's most famous economist declared that stocks were a safe investment.

The historical returns we studied in the last chapter are invaluable, but these data can, at times, be misleading. The prudent investor requires a more accurate estimate of future returns for stocks and bonds than simply looking at the past. In this chapter, we're going to explore Fisher's great gift to finance—the so-called "discounted dividend model" (referred to from now on as the DDM), which allows the investor to easily estimate the expected returns of stocks and bonds with far more accuracy than the study of historical returns.[1]

---

[1]Many credit John Burr Williams, in his 1938 classic, *The Theory of Investment Value*, with the DDM, and, indeed, he fleshed out its mathematics in much greater detail than Fisher. But *The Theory of Interest*, published eight years earlier, clearly lays out the principles of the DDM with sparkling, and at times, entertaining clarity.

Bluntly stated, an understanding of the DDM is what separates the amateur investor from the professional; most often, small investors haven't the foggiest notion of how to estimate a reasonable share price for the companies they are buying.

You may find this chapter the most difficult in the book; the concepts we will explore are not intuitively obvious, and, in a few spots, you will have to put the book down and think. But if you can understand the chapter's central point—that the value of a stock or a bond is simply the *present* value of its *future* income stream—then you will have a better grasp of the investment process than most professionals.

As we've seen, the British enjoy a nearly millennial head start on us in the capital markets. This has allowed them to embed some bits of financial wisdom into their culture that we have yet to absorb. Ask an Englishman how wealthy someone is, and you're likely to hear a response like, "He's worth 20,000 per year."

This sort of answer usually confuses us less sophisticated Yanks, but it's an estimable response, because it says something profound about wealth: it does not consist of inert assets but, instead, *a stream of income.* In other words, if you own an orchard, its value is defined not by its trees and land but, rather, by the income it produces. The worth of an apartment house is not what it will fetch in the market, but the value of its future cash flow. What about your own house? Its value is the shelter and pleasure it provides you over the years.

The DDM, by the way, is the ultimate answer to the age-old question of how to separate *speculation* from *investment.* The acquisition of a rare coin or fine painting for purely financial purposes is clearly a speculation: these assets produce no income, and your return is dependent on someone else paying yet a higher price for them later. (This is known as the "greater fool" theory of investing. When you purchase a rapidly appreciating asset with little intrinsic value, you are dependent on someone more foolish than you to take it off your hands at a higher price.) There is nothing wrong with purchasing any of these things for the future pleasure they may provide, of course, but this is not the same thing as a financial investment.

Only an income-producing possession, such as a stock, bond, or working piece of real estate is a true investment. The skeptic will point out that many stocks do not have current earnings or produce dividends. True enough, but any stock price above zero reflects the fact that at least some investors consider it possible that the stock will regain its earnings and produce dividends in the future, even if only from the sale of its assets. And, as Ben Graham pointed out decades ago, a stock purchased with the hope that its price will soon rise independent of its dividend-producing ability is also a speculation, not an investment.

And lest I unnecessarily offend art lovers, it should be pointed out that even an old master, bought from the artist for $100 and sold 350 years later for $10,000,000, has returned only 3.34% per year. Ideally, a fine painting, like a house, is neither a speculation nor an investment; it is a *purchase*. Its value consists solely of the pleasure and utility it provides now and in the future. The dividend the painting provides is of the non-financial variety.

How, then, do we define a stock's stream of income? Next, how do we determine its actual worth? This is a tricky problem, which we'll tackle in steps. *In the next several pages, we'll uncover how the stock market is properly valued and how future stock market returns are estimated. These pages may prove difficult. I recommend that you slow your reading down a bit at this juncture, making sure you have carefully read each sentence before proceeding to the next.*

One of Fisher's favorite investment paradigms was a gold or lead mine that began with a maximum yield in year one, then dwindled to nothing in 10 years:

Year	Income
1	$2,000
2	$1,800
3	$1,600
4	$1,400
5	$1,200
6	$1,000
7	$800
8	$600
9	$400
10	$200
Total	**$11,000**

Now that we've defined the income stream in the above table, how do we value it? At first glance, it appears that the mine's worth is simply the sum of the income for all ten years—in this case, $11,000. But there's a hitch. Human beings prefer present consumption to future consumption. That is, a dollar of income *next year* is worth less to us than a dollar *today,* and a dollar in thirty years, a great deal less than a dollar today. Thus, the value of future income must be reduced to reflect its true present value. The amount of this reduction must take into account four things:

- The number of years you have to wait: The further in the future you receive income, the less it is worth to you now.
- The rate of inflation: The higher the rate of inflation, the less value in terms of real spending power you can expect to receive in the future.

- The "impatience" of society for future consumption: The more society prefers present to future consumption, the higher are interest rates, and the less future income is worth today. (The second and third factors can be combined into the "real rate of interest.")
- Risk itself: The greater the risk that you might not receive the income at all, the less its present value.

The simplest way to look at the problem is to imagine waiting in line to board a plane for a week in Paris. You've been working hard at your job in downtown Cleveland, and you can almost smell the crêpes on Rue Saint Germain. But wait! Just as you get to the head of the line, the ticket agent swipes your boarding pass and says, "Sorry sir, but Hillary Clinton has just arrived, and she needs your seat." (You're flying first class, of course.) "It's the last one, and the Secret Service agent demands I give it to her. Don't worry though, because I can offer you another trip in ten years."

What a raw deal! A week in Paris in ten years is not worth nearly as much to you as a trip right now. You balk. Finally, "I'm sorry, but you'll have to make it five weeks in Paris a decade from now to make it worth my while." With a sigh of defeat, the agent accepts.

What you have just done is what financial economists call "discounting to the present." That is, you have decided that a week in Paris in ten years is worth a good deal less to you than a week there right now; you have lowered the value of the future weeks in Paris to account for the fact that you will not be enjoying them for another decade. To wit, you have decided that five weeks in ten years is worth as much as just one week today. In the process of doing so, you have determined that your week-in-Paris discount interest rate is 17.5% per year; 17.5% is the rate at which one week grows to five weeks over ten years.

Here is where things start to get a bit sticky, because the discount rate (referred to from now on as the DR) and the present value are inversely related: the higher the DR, the lower the present value. This is the same as with consols and prestiti, whose values are inversely related to interest rates. For example, if you decide that a week in Paris now is worth *ten* weeks a decade from now, that implies a much higher DR of 25.9%. This is the same as saying that the present value of a week in Paris in a decade has cheapened. Again, an *increase* in the DR means that the present value of a future item has *decreased;* if the value of one week in Paris now has increased from five to ten weeks in Paris in the future, then the value of those future weeks has just fallen.

Fisher's genius was in describing the factors that affect the DR, or simply, the "interest rate," as he called it. For example, a starving man would be willing to pay much less for a delayed meal than a well-fed person. In other words, a hungry person's DR for food is very high since he has a more immediate need for it than someone who is well nourished. Fisher, in fact, uses the words "impatience" and "interest rate" interchangeably; the wastrel has a higher interest rate (DR) than the tightwad.

Another of Fisher's observations was that societies characterized by highly durable goods have lower interest rates than those that are not. Where the houses are made of bricks and stone, interest rates are low. Where the houses are made of mud and straw, rates are high.

Fisher found that, by far, the single most important factor affecting the DR is *risk*. The one week/five week Paris trip relationship discussed above assumed that the airline and travel agent were well-established and likely to still be in business in ten years when you return for your vacation. But what if you weren't so sure that they would be there for you in a decade? You would, of course, demand a longer vacation in 10 years—say 10 weeks, instead of five. In which case, you've arrived at the 25.9% DR we mentioned previously. In other words, the riskier the payoff, the higher the return you would demand.

Let's now return to our mine. We have to decide on a discount factor to apply in each successive year to its income. But before I tell you just how to estimate the DR, let's see what a given DR means. Say that we decide on an 8% DR. The table below is the same one we saw a few pages ago, but now we've added two more columns. The column labeled "Discount Factor" is the amount we must reduce the dividend by in a given future year to compute its value in the present day; the first year's income must be divided by 1.08, the second year's by 1.08 × 1.08, and so on. The last column, labeled "Discounted Income," is the resultant present value:

Year	Income	Discount Factor	Discounted Income
1	$2,000	1.0800	$1,852
2	$1,800	1.1664	$1,543
3	$1,600	1.2597	$1,270
4	$1,400	1.3605	$1,029
5	$1,200	1.4693	$817
6	$1,000	1.5869	$630
7	$800	1.7138	$467
8	$600	1.8509	$324
9	$400	1.9990	$200
10	$200	2.1589	$93
		Total	**$8,225**

For example, look at year 8. In this year, the mine earns $600 but, just like your delayed trip to Paris, this future payment of $600 is not worth $600 to you right now. To obtain the current value of this future $600, you must divide it by 1.8509 (1.08 multiplied by itself seven times), to yield a value of $324. This is the *present value* of $600 for which we must wait eight years at an 8% DR. The total present value of the mine—in effect, its "true value"—is the sum of all of the future dividends, *discounted to the present*. This is the sum at the bottom of the table: $8,225.

The next step is to apply this method to stocks. The primary job of the security analyst is to predict the dividend flow of a company so that it may be discounted to obtain the "fair value" of its stock. If the market price is below the calculated fair value, it is bought. If the market price is above the calculated fair value, it is sold. This is no easy task. (In fact, as we'll find out in Chapter 4, it is an *impossible* task.) Not infrequently, promising companies with large expected future dividend streams stumble and fall; nearly as often, companies given up for dead recover and provide shareholders with prodigious amounts of future income.

On the other hand, when you examine an entire market, consisting of hundreds or thousands of companies, these unexpected events average out. For this reason, the income stream of the market as a whole is a much more reliable calculation.

But at first, even this seems a hopeless task. Because the stock market is expected to produce dividends forever, you have to predict the future income stream for an infinite number of future years, discount the dividends for each year to the present, then add them all up. But with a few mathematical tricks, this nut is easily cracked.

A Stream of Future Dividends, Forever and Ever, Amen

To paraphrase the famous Chinese proverb, even a journey of a thousand miles must begin with a single step. Here's our first one. At the end of 2001, the Dow Jones Industrial Average was selling at around 9,000 and yielded 1.55% of that, or about $140 per year in dividends. Further, over the long haul, the Dow's dividends grow at about 5% per year. So in 2002, there should be about $147 of dividends; in 2031, $605. Now take a look at Table 2-1. In the second column, under "Nominal Dividends" ("*nominal*" refers to the actual dollar amount, *not* adjusted for inflation), I've tabulated the actual dividend for each future year; I've also plotted this rise in dividends in Figure 2-1.

We've just taken the first step in valuing the market: we've defined its future stream of dividends. Next, we must discount the actual divi-

Table 2-1. Dow Jones Industrial Average Projected and Discounted Dividends

Year	Nominal Dividends	8% Discount Factor	8% Discount Value	15% Discount Factor	15% Discount Value
2001	$140.00	1.00	**$140.00**	1.00	**$140.00**
2002	$147.00	1.08	**$136.11**	1.15	**$127.83**
2003	$154.35	1.17	**$132.33**	1.32	**$116.71**
2004	$162.07	1.26	**$128.65**	1.52	**$106.56**
2005	$170.17	1.36	**$125.08**	1.75	**$97.30**
2006	$178.68	1.47	**$121.61**	2.01	**$88.84**
2007	$187.61	1.59	**$118.23**	2.31	**$81.11**
2008	$196.99	1.71	**$114.94**	2.66	**$74.06**
2009	$206.84	1.85	**$111.75**	3.06	**$67.62**
2010	$217.19	2.00	**$108.65**	3.52	**$61.74**
2011	$228.05	2.16	**$105.63**	4.05	**$56.37**
2012	$239.45	2.33	**$102.69**	4.65	**$51.47**
2013	$251.42	2.52	**$99.84**	5.35	**$46.99**
2014	$263.99	2.72	**$97.07**	6.15	**$42.91**
2015	$277.19	2.94	**$94.37**	7.08	**$39.17**
2016	$291.05	3.17	**$91.75**	8.14	**$35.77**
2017	$305.60	3.43	**$89.20**	9.36	**$32.66**
2018	$320.88	3.70	**$86.72**	10.76	**$29.82**
2019	$336.93	4.00	**$84.32**	12.38	**$27.23**
2020	$353.77	4.32	**$81.97**	14.23	**$24.86**
2021	$371.46	4.66	**$79.70**	16.37	**$22.70**
2022	$390.03	5.03	**$77.48**	18.82	**$20.72**
2023	$409.54	5.44	**$75.33**	21.64	**$18.92**
2024	$430.01	5.87	**$73.24**	24.89	**$17.28**
2025	$451.51	6.34	**$71.20**	28.63	**$15.77**
2026	$474.09	6.85	**$69.23**	32.92	**$14.40**
2027	$497.79	7.40	**$67.30**	37.86	**$13.15**
2028	$522.68	7.99	**$65.43**	43.54	**$12.01**
2029	$548.82	8.63	**$63.62**	50.07	**$10.96**
2030	$576.26	9.32	**$61.85**	57.58	**$10.01**
2031	$605.07	10.06	**$60.13**	66.21	**$9.14**
2032	$635.33	10.87	**$58.46**	76.14	**$8.34**
2033	$667.09	11.74	**$56.84**	87.57	**$7.62**
2034	$700.45	12.68	**$55.26**	100.70	**$6.96**
2035	$735.47	13.69	**$53.72**	115.80	**$6.35**
2036	$772.24	14.79	**$52.23**	133.18	**$5.80**
2037	$810.85	15.97	**$50.78**	153.15	**$5.29**
2038	$851.40	17.25	**$49.37**	176.12	**$4.83**
2039	$893.97	18.63	**$48.00**	202.54	**$4.41**
2040	$938.67	20.12	**$46.66**	232.92	**$4.03**
2041	$985.60	21.72	**$45.37**	267.86	**$3.68**
2042	$1,034.88	23.46	**$44.11**	308.04	**$3.36**

Table 2-1. (Continued)

Year	Nominal Dividends	8% Discount Factor	8% Discount Value	15% Discount Factor	15% Discount Value
2043	$1,086.62	25.34	**$42.88**	354.25	**$3.07**
2044	$1,140.95	27.37	**$41.69**	407.39	**$2.80**
2045	$1,198.00	29.56	**$40.53**	468.50	**$2.56**
2046	$1,257.90	31.92	**$39.41**	538.77	**$2.33**
2047	$1,320.80	34.47	**$38.31**	619.58	**$2.13**
2048	$1,386.84	37.23	**$37.25**	712.52	**$1.95**
2049	$1,456.18	40.21	**$36.21**	819.40	**$1.78**
2050	$1,528.99	43.43	**$35.21**	942.31	**$1.62**
Etc.	Etc.	Etc.	Etc.	Etc.	Etc.
Sum of Discounted Dividends in All Years			**$4,667.67**		**$1,400.00**

dend in each future year to the present. To do this, we divide the dividend in each future year by the appropriate discount factor, similar to our calculation for the mine. How do we decide on a DR for the entire stock market? Similar to our hypothetically discounted future meal, *the*

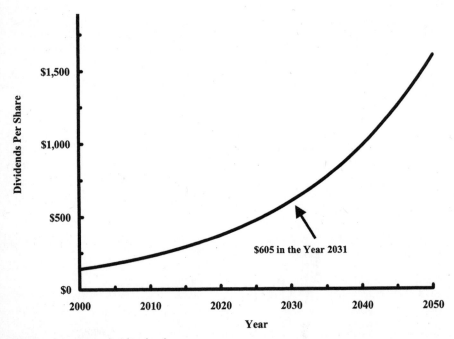

Figure 2-1. Dow dividend value.

DR of the Dow is simply the rate of return we expect from it, taking its risk into consideration.

Let's say that we expect an 8% return from stocks. So just like our mine, the market's DR, by definition, is thus 8%. As we've already determined, the Dow's dividend 30 years from now should be about $605. Similar to our mine, to get the present value of those dividends we have to divide that amount by 1.08 for each year in the future. To obtain the present value of the Dow dividend 30 years from now, in 2031, you have to divide $605 by 10.06 ($1.083^{30}$, that is, 1.08 multiplied by itself 29 times). Dividing the $605 dividend in 2031 by 10.06 yields a present value of $60. If we perceive that economic, political, or market risk has increased, we may decide that the DR should be higher; if we are really frightened about the state of the economy, the nation, or the world, we will decide that 15% is appropriate. In that case, the present value of the year 2031's $605 dividend is reduced even further, to just $9.

Take another look at Table 2-1. Again, the second column in this table displays the nominal expected dividends, which rise at a 5% annual rate in each future year. The third column is the discount factor at 8% for each year. The fourth column is the value of the dividend in that year, discounted to the present (this is calculated by dividing the actual dividend in the second column by the discount factor in the third). As with prestiti and consols, when the DR rises, prices fall; when the DR falls, prices rise.

I've also plotted these numbers in Figure 2-2. The top curve—the same curve plotted in Figure 2-1—represents the actual, or "nominal," dividends received in each future year. To reiterate, the top curve represents the actual dividend stream of the Dow received by shareholders before its value has been adjusted down to its present value. The bottom curves are the *present value* of the Dow's income stream, obtained by discounting the nominal dividends at rates of 8% and 15%.

Notice how at the higher discount rate, the discounted value of the dividends decays nearly to zero after a few decades; such is the corrosive effect of high DRs, caused by high risk or high inflation, on stock values.

Better Living Through Mathematics

Now we need only perform one more step. To obtain the "true value" of the Dow, you have to add together all of the discounted dividends for each year (excluding the first, because it has already been paid). For example at a DR of 8%, you would add up all of the numbers (except the first) in the fourth column, the one labeled "8% Discount

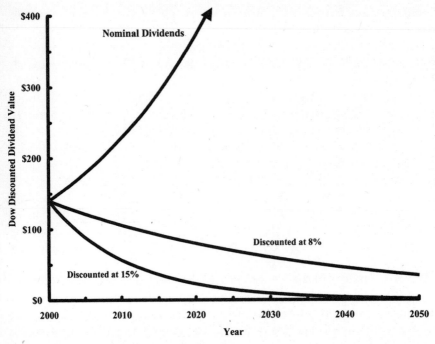

Figure 2-2. Discounted Dow dividend value.

Value." Does this seem like a hopelessly difficult task? It is, if you are doing the computation by what mathematicians call the "brute force" method, i.e., trying to add the infinite column of numbers in column four.

Fortunately, mathematicians can help us out of this pickle with a simple formula that calculates the sum of all of the desired values in column four. Here it is:

Market Value = Present Dividend/(DR − Dividend Growth Rate)

Using our assumption of a $140 present dividend, an 8% DR, and 5% earnings growth, we get:

Market Value = $140/(0.08−0.05) = $140/0.03 = $4,667

(Finance types always do their calculations with decimals; 8% becomes 0.08 in the formula.)

Oops. This formulation suggests that the Dow, currently priced at around 10,000, is about 100% overvalued compared to the 4,667 value we just computed using the rosy 8% DR − return scenario.

And if things get *really* rough, investors may decide they require a 15% DR to invest in stocks (as they did in the early 1980s, when

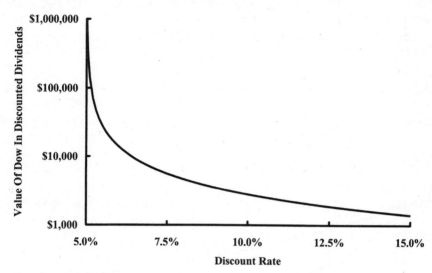

Figure 2-3. Dow fair value versus discount rate.

Treasury bonds yielded almost 16%). I've shown the relevant figures for a 15% DR in the last two columns of Table 2-1. The simplified calculation looks like this:

$$\text{Market Value} = \$140/(0.15 - 0.05) = \$140/0.10 = \$1,400$$

It is unlikely (but not impossible) that the Dow will drop as far as 1,400 at any point in the future, but recall that at least twice in this century U.S. investors indeed did demand a 15% DR.

This kind of calculation is enormously sensitive to the DR and dividend growth rate. For example, raise earnings growth to 6% and lower the DR to 7%, and you come up with a market value of 14,000. Some of you may be aware of the controversy surrounding a book by James Glassman and Kevin Hassett, provocatively titled *Dow 36,000*, in which they arrive at the title's number by fiddling with the above equation in the manner we've described.

In fact, using entirely reasonable assumptions, you can make the Dow's discounted market value almost anything you want it to be. To show how the DR affects the "fair value" of the Dow via this technique, I've plotted the Dow's "fair value" from the DDM versus the DR in Figure 2-3.

Rescued by the Gordon Equation

Why have we spent so much time and effort on the DDM when it turns out that it *cannot* be used to accurately price the stock market? For three reasons. First and foremost, because it provides an intuitive way to think about the value of a security. A stock or bond is not an abstract piece of paper that has a randomly fluctuating value; it is a claim on real future income and assets.

Second, it enables us to test the growth and return assumptions of a stock or of the entire market. At the height of the tech madness in April 2000, the entire Nasdaq market sold at approximately 100 times earnings. Applying the DDM to it revealed that this implied either a ridiculously high earnings growth rate or a low expected return. The latter seemed far more plausible to serious observers, and unfortunately, this is eventually what happened.

Third, and most important, the real beauty of the above formulas is that they can be rearranged to calculate the market's expected return, producing an equation that is at once stunningly simple and powerful:

DR (Market Return) = Dividend Yield + Dividend Growth

This formula, which is known as the "Gordon Equation," provides an accurate way to predict long-term stock market returns. For example, during the twentieth century, the average dividend yield was about 4.5%, and the compounded rate of dividend growth was also about 4.5%. Add the two together and you get 9.0%. The actual return was 9.89%—not too shabby. The approximately 1% difference was due to the fact that stocks had become considerably more expensive (that is, the dividend yield had fallen) during the period.

The Gordon Equation also has an elegant intuitive beauty. If the stock market is simply viewed as a source of dividends, then its price should rise in proportion to those dividends. So if its dividends increase at 4.5% per year, then over the very long term its price should also increase by 4.5% per year. In addition to the price increase, you also receive the actual dividend each year: the annualized total return comes from the combination of the annualized price increase (which is roughly the same as the annualized dividend growth) and the average dividend yield.

The Gordon Equation is as close to being a physical law, like gravity or planetary motion, as we will ever encounter in finance. There are those who say that dividends are quaint and outmoded; in the modern era, return comes from capital gains. Anyone who really believes that might as well be wearing a sandwich board on which is written in large red letters, "I haven't the foggiest notion what I'm talking about."

It is, of course, true that a company never has to pay out a dividend in order to provide capital gains. But even if all of the companies in the U.S. stopped paying out dividends (which they have just about done), in the long term their return would be roughly the same as their aggregate earnings growth. Thus, in a world without dividends, company earnings must grow at an average rate of 10% per year in order to provide the historical 10% long-term return of stocks. And, as we'll soon see, the long-term average rate of corporate earnings and dividend growth is only 5%. Worse, when adjusted for inflation, it has not changed in the past century.

Never forget that in the long run, it is corporate earnings growth that produces stock price increases. If, over the very long term, the annualized earnings growth is about 5%, then the annualized stock price increase must be very close to this number.

One exception to this is the case of companies that are buying back their shares. A company that has grown its earnings by 5% per year and annually buys back 5% of its outstanding shares will appreciate by 10% per year, in the long term. The opposite is true of companies that issue new stock. Averaged over the whole U.S. market, these two factors tend to cancel each other out.

The discounted dividend model is a powerful way of understanding stock and bond behavior. As we've seen, it isn't of much use in accurately predicting the fair value of the market, let alone a stock. Princeton economist Burton Malkiel famously stated that "God Almighty himself does not know the proper price-earnings multiple for a common stock." In other words, it is impossible to know the intrinsic value of a stock or the market. But the DDM is useful in more subtle, powerful ways. First, it can be used in reverse. That is, instead of entering the estimated dividend growth and DR and getting the price, we can derive these two values *from* the price of the market or for a given stock. We've already seen that in 1999, for example, applying the DDM in this manner would have told you that highly unrealistic growth expectations were embedded in the prices of tech stocks.

And, of course, the DDM gives us the Gordon Equation, which allows us to estimate stock returns. This raises an important point. Wall Street and the media are constantly obsessed with the question of whether the market is overvalued or undervalued (and by implication, whether it is headed up or down). As we've just seen, this is essentially impossible to determine. But in the process, we've just acquired a much more valuable bit of knowledge: *the long-term expected return of the market*. Think about it, which would you rather know: the market return for the next six months, or for the next 30 years? I don't know about you, but I'd much rather know the latter. And, within a reasonable margin of error, you can. But you don't sell newspapers, magazines, and airtime speculating about 30-year returns.

And what does the Gordon Equation tell us today about future stock returns? The news, I'm afraid, is not good. Dividend growth still seems to be about 5%, and the yield, as we've already mentioned, is only 1.55%. These two numbers add up to just 6.55%. Even making some wildly optimistic assumptions—say a 6% to 7% dividend growth rate—does not get us anywhere near the 10% annualized returns of the past century.

What about bonds? The expected return of a long-term bond is simply its "coupon," that is its interest payments. (For a bond, the second number in the Gordon Equation, dividend growth, is zero. In almost all cases, a bond's interest does not grow.) High-quality corporate bonds currently yield about 6%. This figure provides a reasonably accurate estimate of their future returns. If interest rates rise, their value will fall, but the rate at which the interest is reinvested will rise, and vice versa. So over a 30-year period, the total bond return cannot be very far from the 6% coupon.

What we have now is a very different picture from what transpired in the twentieth century, with its high stock returns and low bond returns. Going forward, it looks like stock and bond returns should both be in the 6% range, not the 10% historical reward. Don't shoot me, I'm only the messenger.

Viewed from an historical perspective, what has happened is that stocks have had an incredible run the past few decades. Their prices have been bid up dramatically, so their future returns will be commensurately lower. The exact opposite has happened to bonds. As we've already seen, bondholders were severely traumatized by the unprecedented monetary shift in the twentieth century. Their prices have fallen, so their expected returns have commensurately risen.

On an intellectual level, most investors have no trouble understanding the notion that high past returns result in high prices, which, in turn, result in lower future returns. But at the same time, most investors find this almost impossible to accept on an emotional level. By some strange quirk of human nature, financial assets seem to become *more* attractive after their price has risen greatly. But buying stocks and bonds is no different than buying tomatoes. Most folks are sensible enough to load up when the tomatoes are selling at 40 cents per pound and to forgo them at three dollars. But stocks are different. If prices fall drastically enough, they become the lepers of the financial world. Conversely, if prices rise rapidly, everyone wants in on the fun.

Until very recently, there was a great deal of talk about the "new investment paradigm." Briefly stated, this doctrine asserts that Fisher had gotten it all wrong: earnings, dividends, and price no longer matter. The great companies of the New Economy—Amazon, eToys, and

Cisco—were going to dominate the nation's business scene, and no price was too high to pay for the certain bonanza these firms would provide their shareholders.

Of course, we've seen this movie before. In 1934, the great investment theorist Benjamin Graham wrote of the pre-1929 stock bubble:

> Instead of judging the market price by established standards of value, the new era based its standards of value upon the market price. Hence, all upper limits disappeared, not only upon the price at which a stock *could* sell, but even upon the price at which it would *deserve* to sell. This fantastic reasoning actually led to the purchase for investment at $100 per share of common stocks earning $2.50 per share. The identical reasoning would support the purchase of these same shares at $200, at $1,000, or at any conceivable price.

Even the most casual investor will see the parallels of Graham's world with the recent tech/Internet bubble. Graham's $100 stock sold at 40 times its $2.50 earnings. At the height of the 2000 bubble, most of the big-name tech favorites, like Cisco, EMC, and Yahoo! sold at much more than 100 times earnings. And, of course, almost all of the dot-coms went bankrupt without ever having had a cent of earnings.

At the end of the day, the Fisher DDM method of discounting interest streams is the only proper way to estimate the value of stocks and bonds. Future long-term returns are quite accurately predicted by the Gordon Equation. As I've already said, these are essentially the laws of gravity and planetary motion of the financial markets. But it seems that once every 30 years or so, investors tire of valuing stocks by these old-fashioned techniques and engage in orgies of unthinking speculation. Invariably, Fisher and Graham's lesson—not to overpay for stocks—is re-learned in excruciating slow motion in the years following the inevitable market crash.

The rub is, the Gordon Equation is useful only in the long term—it tells us nothing about day-to-day, or even year-to-year, returns. And even in the very long term, it is not perfect. As we've already seen above, over the course of the twentieth century, it was off by about 1% of annualized return. This 1% difference can be attributed to the change in the dividend rate, which decreased from 4.5% to 1.4% between 1900 and 2000. In other words, stocks, which in 1900 sold for 22 times their dividends, now sell for 70 times their dividends. The ratio of price to dividends—22 in 1900, 70 in 2000—is called the "dividend multiple." (This is simply the inverse of the dividend yield: $1/.045 = 22$, and $1/.014 = 70$.) This ratio is the number of dollars you must pay to get one dollar of dividends. It is similar to the more familiar "PE multiple": price divided by earnings. The PE multiple is the most popular measure of how "expensive" the stock market is.

The Gordon Equation does not account for changes in the dividend or PE multiple. The tripling of the dividend multiple between 1900 and 2000 accounts for most of the approximately 1% difference between the 9% predicted by the Gordon Equation and the 9.89% actual return. (Compounding 0.89% over a century produces close to a tripling of the stock market's value.) Stating that there was a "tripling of the dividend multiple" is just another way of saying that an enthusiastic investing public has driven up stock prices relative to earnings and dividends by a factor of three.

Over relatively short periods of time—less than a few decades—this change in the dividend or PE multiple accounts for most of the stock market's return, and over periods of less than a few years, almost 100% of it. John Bogle, founder of the Vanguard Group of mutual funds, provides us with a very useful way of thinking about this. He calls the short-term fluctuations in stock prices due to changes in dividend and PE multiples the "speculative return" of stocks.

On the other hand, the long-term increase in stock market value is entirely the result of the sum of long-term dividend growth and dividend yield calculated from the Gordon Equation, what Bogle calls the "fundamental return" of stocks. In engineering terms, Bogle's fundamental return is the signal—a constant, reliable occurrence. Bogle's speculative return is the noise—distracting and unpredictable. For example, on October 19, 1987, the stock market fell by 23%. Certainly, on that day—Black Monday—there were no significant changes in the dividend payments or dividend growth of common stocks. The market crash of 1987, and the run up which preceded it, were purely speculative events.

The key point, which we'll return to again and again, is that the fundamental return of the stock market—the sum of dividends and dividend growth—is somewhat predictable, but only in the very long term. The short-term return of the market is purely speculative and cannot be predicted. Not by anyone. Not the panelists on *Wall Street Week*, not the "market strategists" at the biggest investment houses, not the newsletter writers, and certainly not your stockbroker.

Perhaps somewhere in a dark secret corner of Wall Street, there is one person who knows just where the market is going tomorrow. But if she exists, she would of course not tell a soul for fear of tipping off the market and damaging the enormous profits that are to be hers on the morrow. (Or, as financial economist Rex Sinquefield replies with a straight face when asked about the direction of the stock market, "I know where the market's headed, I just don't want to share that with anyone.")

A superb metaphor for the long-term/short-term dichotomy in stock returns comes from Ralph Wanger, the witty and incisive principal of the Acorn Funds. He likens the market to an excitable dog on a very long leash in New York City, darting randomly in every direction. The dog's owner is walking from Columbus Circle, through Central Park, to the Metropolitan Museum. At any one moment, there is no predicting which way the pooch will lurch. But in the long run, you know he's heading northeast at an average speed of three miles per hour. What is astonishing is that almost all of the market players, big and small, seem to have their eye on the dog, and not the owner.

As we've already mentioned, the Gordon Equation is not good news for future equity returns. Is there any way out of this gloomy scenario? Yes. There are three possible scenarios in which equity returns could be higher than the predicted 6.4%:

- Dividend growth could accelerate. Companies usually only pay part of their dividends out as earnings. At the present time, the market sells at about 25 times its annual earnings. Another way of saying this is that the "earnings yield" of the market is 4% (1/25). So, if these companies are paying out 1.4% as dividends, that leaves 2.6% to pay for growth.

    The above figures represent an average of the whole market. Many companies earn far more or far less than 4% of their market value, while many, like Microsoft, pay out zero dividends, retaining all their earnings for future growth. It is said that U.S. companies have experienced dramatic increases in productivity in the past few decades, and that this will further accelerate earnings growth beyond the 5% historical figure. This is wishful thinking.

    In the first place, before 1980, companies kept far more than 2.6% of their capital value in retained earnings. In the second place, there is voluminous evidence that excess corporate cash from "retained earnings" (that is, earnings not paid out to the shareholders, but instead reinvested in the company) tends to be wasted. And finally, it just isn't happening. In Figure 2-4, I've plotted the dividends and earnings of the stock market since 1900 (courtesy of Robert Shiller at Yale). Figure 2-4 is another one of those confusing "semilog" graphs. Their major advantage is that they allow you to estimate the percent rate of increase of earnings and dividends across a wide range of values. This is not true of standard "arithmetic" plots. With a semilog graph, a constant growth rate produces a plot that moves up at a fairly constant angle, called the slope. This is approximately what is seen in Figure 2-4.

    Those of you with an eagle eye will detect that the slope for the first 50 years seems to be ever-so-slightly less than for the last

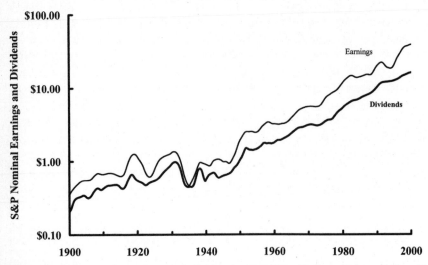

Figure 2-4. Nominal earnings and dividends, S&P 500. (*Source:* Robert Shiller, Yale University).

50. This is because of inflation. In inflation-adjusted terms, dividend growth may actually be slowing. When inflation is factored in, from 1950 to 1975, annualized earnings growth was 2.22%, and from 1975 to 2000 it was 1.90%. Clearly the rapidly accelerating trend of earnings and dividend growth frequently cited by today's New Era enthusiasts is nowhere to be seen. This analysis also demolishes another one of the supposed props of current stock valuations: stock buybacks, which should also increase per-share stock dividends. This is what is actually plotted in Figure 2-4.

• Bogle's speculative return—the growth of the dividend multiple— could continue to provide future stock price increases with further growth of the dividend multiple. Why, you might ask, can't the dividend multiple grow at 3% per year from here, yielding 3% of extra return? Unfortunately, this means that the dividend multiple would have to double every 24 years. While it is possible that this could occur for another decade or two, it is not sustainable in the long term. After all, if the dividend multiple increased at 3% per year for the next century, then stocks in 2102 would sell at 1,350 times dividends, for a yield of 0.07%! In fact, thinking about the future of the speculative return is a scary exercise. The best-case scenario has the dividend multiple remaining at its present inflated level and not affecting returns. It is quite possible, however, that we may see a reduction in this value over time. Let's say, for the sake of argument, that the dividend multiple halves from the current value, raising the dividend from its current 1.4% to 2.8%—still far lower than the 5% historical average—over the next 20 years. In that case, the speculative return will be a *negative* 3.4% per year, for a total annualized market return of 2.8%. Sound far-fetched? Not at all. If inflation stays at the 2% to 3% level of the past decade, this implies a near zero real return over 20 years. This is not an uncommon occurrence. It's happened three times in the twentieth century: from 1900 to 1920, from 1929 to 1949, and from 1964 to 1984.

- The stock market could crash. You heard me right. The most sustainable way to get high stock returns is to have a dramatic fall in stock prices. Famed money manager Charles Ellis likes to tease his friends with a clever riddle. He asks them which market scenario they would rather see as long-term investors: stocks rising dramatically and then staying permanently at that high level, or falling dramatically and staying permanently at that low level. The correct answer is the latter, since with permanently low prices you will benefit from permanently high dividends. As the old English ditty says, "Milk from the cows, eggs from the hens. A stock, by God, for its dividends!"

After several decades, the fact that you are reinvesting income at a much higher dividend rate will more than make up the damage from the original price fall. To benefit from this effect, you have to be investing for long enough—typically more than 30 to 50 years. To demonstrate this phenomenon, in Figure 2-5, I've plotted three different scenarios: (1) no change in the dividend multiple, with its current 1.4% dividend, (2) a 50% fall, resulting in a 2.8% dividend, and (3) an 80% fall, resulting in a 7% dividend.

As you can see, the more drastic 80% fall produces a quicker recovery than the 50% fall. The below table shows why:

	No Fall	50% Fall	80% Fall
Dividend Yield	1.4%	2.8%	7.0%
Dividend Growth	5.0%	5.0%	5.0%
Total Return	6.4%	7.8%	12.0%

After an 80% fall in prices, the higher long-term return eventually compensates for the initial devastation. Even better than having a long time horizon in this situation is having the wherewithal to periodically invest sums regularly at such low levels—this dramatically shortens the "break-even point."

The implications of the last scenario are profound. What this says is that a young person saving for retirement should get down on his

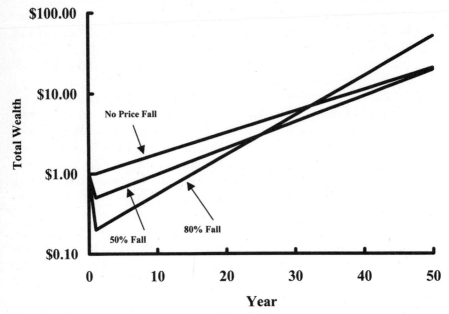

Figure 2-5. Effect of stock declines on final wealth.

knees and pray for a market crash, so that he can purchase his nest egg at fire sale prices. For the young investor, prolonged high stock prices are manifestly a great misfortune, as he will be buying high for many years to invest for retirement. Alternatively, the best-case scenario for a retiree living off of savings is a bull market early in retirement.

For the retiree, the worst-case scenario is a bear market in the first few years of retirement, which would result in a very rapid depletion of his savings from the combination of capital losses and withdrawals necessary for living expenses. To summarize:

	Market Crash	Bull Market
Young Saver	Good	Bad
Retiree	Bad	Good

How to Think about the Discount Rate and Stock Price

The relationship between the DR and stock price is the same as the inverse relationship between interest rates and the value of prestiti and consols in the last chapter: when DR goes up, the stock price goes down, and vice versa.

The most useful way of thinking about the DR is that it is the rate of return demanded by investors to compensate for the risk of owning a particular asset. The simplest case is to imagine that you are buying an annuity worth $100 per year, indefinitely, from three different borrowers:

The world's safest borrower is the U.S. Treasury. If Uncle Sam comes my way and wants a long-term loan paying me $100 per year in interest, I'll charge him just 5%. At that DR, the annuity is worth $2,000 ($100/0.05). In other words, I'd be willing to loan Uncle Sam $2,000 indefinitely in return for $100 in annual interest payments.

Next through the door is General Motors. Still pretty safe, but a bit more risky than Uncle Sam. I'll charge them 7.5%. At that DR, a perpetual $100 annual payment is worth $1,333 ($100/0.075). That is, for a $100 perpetual payment from GM, I'd be willing to loan them $1,333.

Finally, in struts Trump Casinos. Phew! For the risk of lending this group my money, I'll have to charge 12.5%, which means that The Donald's perpetual $100 payment is worth only an $800 ($100/0.125) loan.

So the DR we apply to the stock market's dividend stream, or that of an individual stock, hinges on just how risky we think the market or the stock is. The riskier the situation, the higher the DR/return we demand, and the less the asset is worth to us. Once more, with feeling:

High discount rate = high perceived risk, high returns, depressed stock price

Low discount rate = low perceived risk, low returns, elevated stock price

The Discount Rate and Individual Stocks

In the case of an individual stock, anything that decreases the reliability of its earnings and dividend streams will increase the DR. For example, consider a food company and a car manufacturer, each of which are expected to have the same average earnings and dividends over the next 20 years. The earnings and dividends of the food company, however, will be much more reliable than that of the car manufacturer—people will need to buy food no matter what the condition of the economy or their employment.

On the other hand, the earnings and dividends of auto manufacturers are notoriously sensitive to economic conditions. Because the purchase of a new car is a discretionary decision, it can easily be put off when times are tough. During recessions, it is not unusual for the earnings of the large automakers to completely disappear. So investors will apply a higher DR to an auto company than to a food company. That is why "cyclical" companies with earnings that fluctuate with business cycles, such as car manufacturers, sell more cheaply than food or drug companies.

Put another way, since the earnings stream of an auto manufacturer is less reliable than that of a food company, you will pay less for its earnings and dividends because of the high DR you apply to them. All other things being equal (which they never are!), you should earn a higher return from the auto manufacturer than from the food company in compensation for the extra risk involved. This is consistent with what we saw in the last chapter: "bad" (value) companies have higher returns than "good" (growth) companies, because the market applies a higher DR to the former than the latter. Remember, the DR is the same as expected return; a high DR produces a low stock value, which drives up future returns.

Probably the most vivid example of the good company/bad stock paradigm was provided in the popular 1982 book, *In Search of Excellence,* by management guru Tom Peters. Mr. Peters identified numerous "excellent" companies using several objective criteria. Several years later, Michelle Clayman, a finance academic from Oklahoma State University, examined the stock market performance of the companies profiled in the book and compared it with a matched group of "unexcellent" companies using the same criteria. For the five-year period following the book's publication, the unexcellent companies outperformed the excellent companies by an amazing 11% per year.

As you might expect, the unexcellent companies were considerably cheaper than the excellent companies. Most small investors naturally assume that good companies are good stocks, when the opposite is usually true. Psychologists refer to this sort of logical error as "representativeness."

The risk of a particular company, or of the whole market, is affected by many things. Risk, like pornography, is difficult to define, but we think we know it when we see it. Quite frequently, the investing public grossly overestimates it, as occurred in the 1930s and 1970s, or underestimates it, as occurred with tech and Internet stocks in the 1960s and 1990s.

The Societal Discount Rate and Stock Returns

The same risk considerations that operate at the company level are in play market-wide. Let's consider two separate dates in financial history—September 1929 and June 1932. In the fall of 1929, the mood was ebullient. Commerce and daily living were being revolutionized by the technological marvels of the day: the automobile, telephone, aircraft, and electrical power plant. Standards of living were rapidly rising. And just like today, the stock market was on everyone's lips. People had learned that stocks had much higher long-run returns than any other investment.

In *Common Stocks as Long Term Investments,* a well-researched and immensely popular book published in 1924, Edgar Lawrence Smith showed that stock returns were far superior to bank deposits and bonds. The previous decade had certainly proved his point. At the height of the enthusiasm in 1929, John J. Raskob, a senior financier at General Motors, granted an interview to *Ladies Home Journal.* The financial zeitgeist was engagingly reflected in a quote from this piece:

> Suppose a man marries at the age of twenty-three and begins a regular savings of fifteen dollars a month—and almost anyone who is employed can do that if he tries. If he invests in good common stocks and allows the dividends and rights to accumulate, he will at the end of twenty years have at least eighty thousand dollars and an income from investments of around four hundred dollars a month. He will be rich. And because anyone can do that, I am firm in my belief that anyone not only can be rich but ought to be rich.

Raskob's frugal young man was a genius indeed; compounding $15 per month into $80,000 over 20 years implies a rate of return of over 25%. Clearly, the investing public could be excused for thinking that this was the best time to invest in stocks.

Now, fast forward less than three years to mid-1932 and the depths of the Great Depression. One in three workers is jobless, the gross national product has fallen by almost half, protesting veterans have just been dispersed from Washington by Major General MacArthur and a young aide named Eisenhower, and membership in the American Communist Party has reached an all-time high. Even economists have lost faith in the capitalist system. Certainly not a good time to invest, right?

Had you bought stock at one of the brightest moments in our economic history, in September 1929, and held on until 1960, you'd have earned an annualized 7.76%, turning each dollar into $9.65. Not a bad rate of return; but for a stock investment, nothing to write home about. But had you the nerve to buy stocks in June of 1932 and hold on until 1960, you'd have earned an annualized 15.86%, turning each dollar into $58.05. Few did.

Finally, we come to the World Trade Center bombing. Before it, the world was viewed as a relatively safe place to live and invest. In an instant, this illusion was shattered, and the public's perception of risk dramatically increased; the DR rose, resulting in a sharp lowering of price. It's likely that the permanency of this feeling of increased risk will be the primary determinant of stock prices in the coming years. The key point is this: if public confidence remains depressed, prices will remain depressed, which will increase subsequent returns. And if confidence returns, prices will rise and subsequent returns will be lower.

These vignettes neatly demonstrate the relationship between societal risk and investment return. The worst possible time to invest is when the skies are the clearest. This is because perceived risks are low, causing investors to discount future stock income at a very low rate. This, in turn, produces high stock prices, which result in low future returns. The saddest part of this story is that "pie-in-the-sky investing" is both infectious and emotionally effortless—everyone else is doing it. Human beings are quintessentially social creatures. In most of our endeavors, this serves us well. But in the investment arena, our social instincts are poison.

The best possible time to invest is when the sky is black with clouds, because investors discount future stock income at a high rate. This produces low stock prices, which, in turn, beget high future returns. Here also, our psychological and social instincts are a profound handicap. The purchase of stocks in turbulent economic times invites disapproval from family and peers. Of course, only in retrospect is it possible to identify what legendary investor Sir John Templeton calls "the point of maximum pessimism"; nobody sends you an overdue notice or a bawdy postcard at the market's bottom.

So even when you are courageous and lucky enough to invest at the low point, throwing money into a market that has been falling for years is a profoundly unpleasant activity. And, of course, you are taking the risk that the system may, in fact, not survive. This brings to mind an apocryphal story centering on the Cuban Missile Crisis of 1962, which has a young options trader asking an older colleague whether to make a long (bullish) bet or a short (bearish) one. "Long!" answers the older man, without a moment's hesitation. "If the crisis resolves, you'll make a bundle. And if it doesn't, there'll be nobody on the other side of the trade to collect."

Finally, at any one moment the societal DR operates differently across the globe. Nations themselves can take on growth and value characteristics. For example, 15 years ago, the Japanese appeared unstoppable. One by one, they seemed to be taking over the manufacture of automobiles, televisions, computer chips, and even machine tools—product lines that had been dominated by American companies for decades. Signature real estate like Rockefeller Center and Pebble

Beach were being snatched up like so many towels at a blue light special. The grounds of the Imperial Palace in Tokyo were said to be worth more than the state of California.

Such illusions of societal omnipotence carry with them a very low DR. Since the Japanese income stream was discounted to the present at a very low rate, its market value ballooned, producing very low future returns. The peak of apparent Japanese invincibility occurred around 1990. A dollar of Japanese stock bought in January 1990 was worth just 67 cents 11 years later, yielding an annualized return of minus 3.59%.

In the early 1990s, the Asian Tigers—Hong Kong, Korea, Taiwan, Singapore, and Malaysia—were the most fashionable places to invest. Their industrious populations and staggering economic growth rates were awesome to behold. Once again, the investment returns from that point forward were poor. The highest return of the five markets was obtained in Hong Kong, where a dollar invested in January 1994 turned into 93 cents by year-end 2000. The worst of the five was Malaysia, where you'd have wound up with just 37 cents.

And, finally, in the new millennium, everyone's favorite market is here at home. Which gets us right back where we started this chapter, with a low discount rate, high prices, and low expected future returns.

The most depressing thing about the DR is that it seems to be quite sensitive to prior stock returns. In other words, because of human society's dysfunctional financial behavior, a rising stock market lowers the perception of risk, decreasing the DR, which drives prices up even further. What you get is a vicious (or virtuous, depending on your point of view) cycle.

The same thing happens in reverse. Because of damage done to stocks in the 1930s, the high DR for stocks outlived the Great Depression, resulting in low prices and high returns lasting for more than a quarter of a century.

Real Returns: The Outlook

It's now time to translate what we've learned into a forecast of the long-term expected returns of the major asset classes. Whenever you can, you should think about returns in "real" (inflation-adjusted) terms. This is because the use of real returns greatly simplifies thinking about the purchasing power of stocks, making financial planning easier. Most people find this a bit difficult to do at first, but after you get used to it, you'll wonder why most folks use "nominal" (before-inflation) returns.

Let's start with the historical 10% stock reward for the twentieth century. Since the inflation rate in the twentieth century was 3%, the real return was 7%. That's the easy part. The hard part is trying to use nominal returns for retirement planning. Let's say that you're going to be saving for 30 years before retiring. If you're using the 10% nominal return, you'll have to deflate that by the cumulative inflation rate over 30 years. And then, for every year after you retire, you'll have to deflate your nest egg by 3% per year to calculate your real spending power.

It is much simpler to think the problem all the way through in real terms—a 10% nominal return with 3% inflation is the same as a 7% return and no inflation[2]; no adjustments are necessary. A real dollar in 50 years will buy just as much as it will now. (And before World War I, when money really was hard gold and silver, that's how folks thought. There's an old economist's joke: An academic is questioning a stockbroker about investment returns, and asks him, "Are those real returns?" The broker responds, "Of course they are, I got them from *The Wall Street Journal* yesterday!") From now on, we're going to talk about real returns whenever possible.

For starters, the DDM tells us to expect cash to yield a zero real return, bonds to have an approximately 3% real return, and stocks in general to have about a 3.5% real return. In the current environment, is it possible to find assets with higher DRs and expected returns? Yes. As this is being written, except perhaps for Japan, foreign stocks are slightly cheaper than U.S. stocks. But even in Japan, dividend multiples are lower than in the U.S., so expected returns abroad may be slightly more than domestic expected returns. Small stocks also sell at a slight discount to large stocks around the globe, and so too have slightly higher expected returns.

Next, there's value stock investing. Value stock returns are impossible to estimate using the traditional methods, because most of the excess return arises from the slow improvement in valuations that occurs as doggy stocks become less doggy over time.

This is a difficult process to model, but a general observation or two are in order. As recently as five years ago, if you had sorted the S&P 500 by the earnings multiple ("P/E ratio": the number of dollars of stock needed to buy a dollar of current earnings), you would have found that the top 20% of stocks typically sold at about twice the multiple of the bottom 80%—at about 20 and 10 times earnings, respectively. As 2002 began, the top 20% and bottom 80% of companies sold at 64 and 20 times earnings, respectively—a more than threefold difference between top and bottom. This is not nearly as bad as the sev-

---

[2]Well, not quite. A 10% nominal return with 3% inflation actually produces a 6.80% return, since 1.10/1.03 = 1.068. But close enough for government work.

enfold difference at the market peak in the spring of 2000, but large nevertheless.

So, absent a permanent new paradigm, the historical 2% extra return from value stocks seems a good bet, yielding large-value real expected returns of about 5% and small-value real expected returns of about 7%.

Real Estate Investment Trusts (REITs) are the stocks of companies that manage diversified portfolios of commercial buildings. One example is the Washington Real Estate Investment Trust (WRE), which owns a large number of office buildings in the D.C. area. By law, WRE is required to pay out 90% of its earnings as income. Because of this enforced payment of dividends, REITs currently yield an average of about 7% per year. The downside is that because they can reinvest only a small portion of their profits, they usually carry a large amount of debt and, in the aggregate, do not grow well. Since 1972, they have increased their earnings by about 3% per year. This was about 2% *less* than the inflation rate during the period. Add a 7% dividend to a negative 2% real earnings growth and the expected real return of REITs is about 5% per year.

Stocks in many countries have been battered by the "Asian Contagion" of the late nineties, and their markets now yield 3% to 5% dividends. Most of the "Tiger" countries, as well as many South American stock markets, fall into this category. The future long-term dividend growth rate in these nations is anybody's guess, but it is quite possible that they will resume their earlier economic growth to produce healthy stock returns going forward.

The stocks of gold and silver mining companies are an intriguing asset class. They currently yield dividends of about 3%, and the most conservative assumption is that they will have zero real earnings and dividend growth, for a total real expected return of 3%—about the same as bonds and cash. In the long run, they offer excellent inflation protection. But because these stocks are very sensitive to even small changes in gold prices, they are extremely risky. We'll talk about why you might want a small amount of exposure to these companies in Chapter 4, when we discuss portfolio theory.

From time to time, it makes sense to take credit risk. This is an area we've touched on earlier. The bonds of companies with low credit ratings carry high yields—these are the modern equivalent of the Greek bottomry loans discussed in the last chapter. At present, such "high yield," or "junk," bonds, carry coupons of approximately 12%, compared to only about 5% for Treasury bonds. Are these a worthwhile investment? Many of these companies will default on their bonds and then go bankrupt. (Default does not necessarily imply bankruptcy and total loss. Many companies—about 30%—will temporarily default, then resume payment of interest and principal. Bondholders frequently recover some of their assets from bankrupt companies.)

The default rate on these companies is about 6% per year, on average, and the "loss rate"—the percent loss of capital each year from these bonds—appears to be about 3% to 4% per year. I cannot stress the word "average" enough in this context. In good times, the loss rate is near zero. And in bad times, it can be quite high—approaching 10% per year.

So, if you are earning 7% more in interest per year than with a Treasury bond, but you are losing an average of 4% per year on bankruptcies, then in the end you should still be left with 3% more return than Treasuries. Most investors would consider this to be an adequate tradeoff. But it's important to understand that during a recession, even the market value of the surviving bonds may temporarily decrease. For example, during the 1989–1990 junk bond debacle, price declines approaching 20% were common even in the healthiest issues.

If you're going to invest in junk bonds, you have to keep your eye on the yield spread between Treasuries and junk. In Figure 2-6, I've plotted this junk-Treasury spread (JTS) over the recent past. Note how the JTS is, more often than not, quite low—in fact, lower than even the historical loss rate! This irrational behavior is explained by investors "reaching for yield": unhappy with low bond and bill rates, they take on more credit risk than they had bargained for in a foolish attempt to get a few bits of extra return. When the JTS is below 5%, don't even think about buying junk. (You can find the high-yield and Treasury yields in the "Yield Comparisons" table in the back section of *The Wall Street Journal.* You'll have to subtract the Treasury yield from the junk yield yourself.)

Treasury bills are the ultimate "risk-free investment." Their expected real return is very difficult to predict, as the yield can change quite quickly and dramatically, ranging from a low of nearly zero in the late 1930s to briefly more than 20% in the early 1980s. Currently, the T-bill yield is less than 2%, or about the same as the inflation rate, for a real zero return. And, as we saw in Chapter 1, their actual long-term real return is not much greater than zero.

Lastly, there are TIPS (Treasury Inflation Protected Securities). For those investors who are risk-averse, it's tough to beat them, as they provide a 3.4% real yield. You can design the amount of inflation protection you want by balancing maturities; the maximum comes with the 3.375% TIPS of April 2032, the cost of which is 30 years of "real interest rate risk," the possibility that *real* interest rates will rise after you have bought them. This is not the same thing as (and certainly much less scary than) the inflation risk experienced by conventional bonds, where

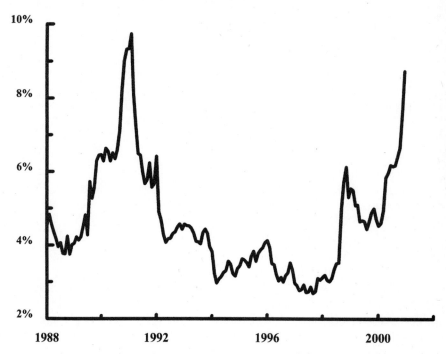

Figure 2-6. Junk-treasury spread, 1988–2000. (*Source: Grant's Interest Rate Observer.*)

the fixed interest payments can be seriously eroded by sustained inflation. After all, with TIPS, inflation is what you're protecting against.

In Table 2-2, I've summarized reasonable expected real returns,
derived from the DDM. Understand that "expected" returns are just
that. In finance, as in life, there is often a huge chasm between what
is expected and what actually transpires. The estimation of foreign
stock returns is particularly perilous. Between the breakdown of the
1944 Bretton Woods agreement, which fixed currency exchange rates
among the major developed nations, and the advent of increasingly
active foreign-currency-denominated futures and options markets, the
currencies have grown increasingly volatile. This means that the gap
between expected versus realized returns for foreign stocks is liable to
be especially large.

The "Realized-Expected Disconnect"

In the first chapter we talked about the history of past stock returns—
what economists call "realized returns." These realized returns were
quite high. In fact, in the past decade, a small industry has arisen that
thrives on the promotion and sale of this optimistic data. The message

Table 2-2. Expected Long-Term Real Returns

Asset Class	Expected Real Return
Large U.S. Stocks	3.5%
Large Foreign Stocks	4%
Large Value Stocks (foreign and domestic)	5%
Small Stocks (foreign and domestic)	5%
Small Value Stocks (foreign and domestic)	7%
Emerging Market/Pacific Rim Stocks	6%
REITs	5%
High-Yield ("Junk") Bonds	5%
Investment-Grade Corporates; TIPS	3.5%
Treasury Bills and Notes	0–2%
Precious Metals Equity	3%

of this happy band of brothers is that past is prologue: because we have had high returns in the past, we should expect them in the future.

The ability to estimate future stock and bond returns is perhaps the most critical of investment skills. In this chapter, we've reviewed a theoretical model that allows us to compute the "expected returns" of the major asset classes on an objective, mathematical basis. The message from this approach is not nearly as agreeable. Which should we believe: the optimism of historical returns, or the grim arithmetic of the Gordon Equation?

It should be obvious by now where my sympathies lie. Warren Buffett famously said that if stock returns came from history books, then the wealthiest people would be librarians. There are numerous examples of how historical returns can be highly misleading. My favorite comes from the return of long Treasury bonds before and after 1981. For the 50 years from 1932 to 1981, Treasury bonds returned just 2.95% per year, almost a full percent less than the inflation rate of 3.80%. Certainly, the historical record of this asset was not encouraging. And yet, the Gordon Equation told us that the bond yield of 15% was more predictive of its future return than the historical data. Over the next 15 years, the return of the long Treasury was in fact 13.42%—slightly lower than the predicted return because the coupons had to be reinvested at an ever-falling rate.

The fundamental investment choice faced by any individual is the overall stock/bond mix. It seems more likely that future stock returns will be closer to the 3.5% real return suggested by the Fisher DDM method than the 7% historical real gain. If, as we calculated earlier, stock and bond returns are going to be similar going forward, then even the most aggressive, risk-tolerant individual should have no more than 80% exposure to stocks.

Unfortunately, although the DDM informs us well about expected returns, it tells us nothing about future risk. We are dependent on the pattern of past returns to inform us of the potential risks of an asset. And in this regard, I believe that the historical data serve us well. Although anything is possible in finance, it is hard to imagine the stock markets of the next century throwing anything our way that would surpass the 1929–1932 bear market.

In the coming chapters, we'll explore how to use the lessons we've learned to construct portfolios that give us the best chance of reaping the most reward with the minimum necessary risk.

CHAPTER 2 SUMMARY

1. The ability to estimate the long-term future returns of the major asset classes is perhaps the most important investment skill that an individual can possess.
2. A stock or bond is worth only the future income it produces. This income stream must be reduced in value, or "discounted," to the present, to reflect the fact that it is worth less than currently received income.
3. The rate at which that income is discounted is inversely related to the asset's value; a high discount rate (DR) lowers the asset's value.
4. The DR is the same as the asset's expected return; it is determined by the asset's perceived risk. The higher the risk, the higher the DR/expected return.
5. In the long term, the asset's DR/expected return is approximately the sum of the dividend yield and the growth rate. The current high price and low dividend rate of stocks suggest that they will have much lower returns in the future than they have had in the past.
6. The above considerations pertain only to long-term returns (more than 20 years). Over shorter periods, asset returns are almost exclusively related to speculative factors and cannot be predicted.
7. The methods we discussed in this chapter suggest that the returns of stocks and bonds will be similar over the coming decades. This means that even the most aggressive investors should not have more than 80% of their savings in stocks.

3

The Market Is Smarter
Than You Are

I know what you're thinking: "Okay, you've convinced me. Future market returns will not be that high. But that doesn't matter, because I can beat the market. Or, I may not be able to beat the market myself, but I'm sure I can find a mutual fund/stock broker/financial advisor who can."

Pretend, just for a moment, you live in an obscure tropical country called "Randomovia." It's really quite a wonderful place—lush, prosperous, with universal high-speed Internet access. But it has one serious problem: a rampant chimpanzee population. In order to keep the chimps happy, the Randomovians periodically round them up, dress them in expensive suits, place them in luxurious offices, and allow them to manage the nation's investment pools. And since chimps are very jealous creatures, humans are not allowed to manage money. Further, it's a well-known fact that chimps love playing darts; they pick stocks by hurling these projectiles at the stock page.

This means three things about Randomovia:

- Over any given period of time, some of the chimpanzees will be lucky and obtain high returns.
- The past performance of a chimp at selecting stocks has no bearing on his future performance. Last year's, or last decade's, winner will just as likely be a loser as a winner next time.
- The average performance of all the chimpanzees will be the same as the market's, since chimps are the only ones who can buy and sell.

The chimps each have about a 50% chance of beating the market. There's only one problem: The investment pools they manage charge the Randomovians 2% of assets each year in expenses. In any given year, the differences in performance are great enough that the 2% expense doesn't matter that much. But because of the 2% drag, instead of 50% of the chimps beating the market each year, only about 40% of them do. With the passage of time, however, the law of averages catches up with all but the luckiest chimps. After 20 years, only about one in ten beats the market by more than their 2% annual expenses. So, the odds of your picking that winning chimpanzee are . . . one in ten.

Well, dear readers, I have very bad news. For the past several decades, financial economists have been studying the performance of all types of investment professionals, and their message is unambiguously clear: Welcome to Randomovia!

Better Living Through Statistics

Although the modern scientific revolution started with the mathematical modeling of the physical world by Copernicus, Kepler, Galileo, and Newton, it was not until the nineteenth century that social scientists—sociologists, economists, and psychologists—began the serious mathematical study of social phenomena. In Chapter 1, we saw that a dramatic improvement in the quality of financial data occurred at the beginning of the twentieth century. This was the result of a massive collaborative effort to collect and analyze stock and bond prices. As researchers began to examine the aggregate performance of stocks and bonds, it was only natural that they began by looking at the behavior of money managers.

Until relatively recently, no one questioned the notion that investing was a skill, just like medicine, law, or professional sports. Ability, training, and hard work *should* result in superior performance. The best practitioners *should* excel year after year. A skilled broker or money manager *should* be worth his weight in gold. In this chapter, we'll examine the utter demolition of that belief system and the emergence of a powerful new theory for understanding stock and bond market behavior—the efficient market hypothesis.

Alfred Cowles III Gets Burned

Most great financial innovators come from humble circumstances—nothing arouses fascination with financial assets quite like their absence. Or, as someone born to great wealth once explained to me, if you are raised in the desert, all you think about is water. But the average Western citizen, who can get it from the tap at will, hardly considers it at all. Those raised with great wealth think about money the way most of us think about water—if you want some, just turn on the faucet! Which is why Alfred Cowles III was a most unlikely financial pioneer; his family owned a large chunk of the Chicago Tribune company and was extremely wealthy. After duly graduating from Yale in 1913, he started working as a reporter, but developed tuberculosis and was sent to a sanatorium in Colorado Springs to recover. With time on his hands, he began involving himself in the family finances.

He subscribed to many financial newsletters and by the mid-1920s was regularly reading about two dozen of them. He was stunned at the abysmal quality of advice. The ferocious bear market of 1929–32 was completely unforeseen by all of them, and Cowles's family suffered as a consequence. He also found that the newsletters' recommendations during the 1920s bull market had been nothing to write home about either.

Cowles's signature characteristic was his love of collecting and analyzing data. He began recording the newsletters' recommendations and analyzing their predictive value. Eventually, he found his way to none other than Irving Fisher, who happened to be the president of a small impoverished academic organization dedicated to the study of financial data—the Econometric Society. With his family wealth, Cowles was a godsend to the struggling group, and in 1932, he endowed the Cowles Foundation, dedicated to the statistical study of financial assets.

The importance of his generosity and research cannot be overstated. He was directly responsible for the collection and analysis of most of the nation's stock and bond data from 1871 to 1930, and, more importantly, he provided the inspiration for most of the security research that followed. Without Cowles, we would still be financial cave dwellers, stumbling around blindly in the dark.

Cowles's first organized research project, predictably enough, studied financial newsletters. His report, published in the first edition of *Econometrica,* the foundation's journal, was simply titled, "Can Stock Market Forecasters Forecast?" The article had an introductory abstract consisting of just three words: "It is doubtful." He evaluated the recommendations of the most prestigious financial newsletters and financial services and analyzed the stock purchases of the largest group of institutional investors at the time—fire insurance companies.

His results were stunning. The stock-picking abilities of the financial services and insurance companies were awful—only about one-third equaled or beat the market. And the performance of the market-timing newsletters, as he had suspected for years, was even worse. In almost all cases, investors would have been better off flipping coins than following their advice. Cowles found that the very best newsletter results could easily be obtained by random choice. But what was truly stunning was that the results of the worst newsletters could *not* be explained purely by chance. In other words, although there was no evidence of skill among the best newsletter writers, the worst seemed possessed of a special ineptitude. This is a pattern that we shall encounter repeatedly: among finance professionals, the best results can easily be explained by chance, but the worst performers seem to maintain an almost uncanny incompetence.

It is no coincidence that the explosion of knowledge regarding investment management occurred when it did. The statistical computations involved in Cowles's study could not have been done by hand. He was the first financial economist to make use of the new punch card machines being produced by the Hollerith Corporation. (Another investment giant, Benjamin Graham, also had a connection with Hollerith. As a young analyst in the 1920s, he almost lost his first job by recommending that his conservative employer purchase stock in the company. A few years later, Hollerith decided that a more modern-sounding name would be appropriate: International Business Machines.)

But it was not until the commercial availability of electronic computers that things really got going. In 1964, academic Michael Jensen decided to look at the performance of mutual fund managers, testing for evidence of stock selection skill. Because most of the funds he examined held a significant portion of cash, almost all of them underperformed the market. But, of course, with their lower returns came greater safety. So he used sophisticated computer-based statistical methods to correct for the amount of cash and test the significance of his results.

Figure 3-1 is a plot of how the funds did relative to the market, adjusted for risk. It displays the performance of the funds on a gross basis, that is, before the funds' management fees are subtracted. The thick vertical black line in the middle of the graph represents the market performance. The bars on the left represent the number of funds underperforming the market, and the bars on the right represent funds outperforming it.

Only 48 funds out of 115 outperformed the market; 67 underperformed it. As predicted, the average performance was close to that of the market (actually, 0.4% less, annualized).

Figure 3-2 demonstrates fund performance on a net basis—that is, after the funds' management fees have been subtracted. This is the return that the shareholders actually see.

Essentially, this shifted fund performance about 1% to the left, so that only 39 outperformed, versus 76 underperforming. Even more

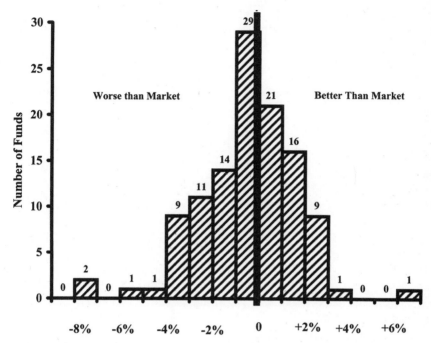

Figure 3-1. Mutual funds 1946–1964: gross returns relative to market.0 = market return, average fund = −0.4% per year. (*Source:* Michael Jensen, *Journal of Finance,* 1965.)

interesting, while only one fund outperformed the market by more than 3% per year, 21 underperformed it by more than 3%! Again, we find the pattern seen in Cowles's original work: no evidence of skill at the top of the heap, but at the bottom of the heap, the strong suggestion that some managers possess a special ineptitude.

And it goes downhill from there. All of the mutual funds studied carried sales loads (a fee, typically 8.5% of the purchase amount), which Jensen did not take into account. So the funds' investors actually obtained even lower returns than shown in Figure 3-2. Except at the bottom end, the distributions found in Figures 3-1 and 3-2 are precisely what you'd expect from a bunch of dart-throwing chimpanzees:

- The average fund produces a *gross* return equal to the market's.
- The average investor receives a *net* return equal to the market's minus expenses.
- The "best" managers produce returns that are easily explained by the laws of chance.

Are we in Randomovia yet? Almost. If we actually were in Randomovia, we would find that above-average performance does not

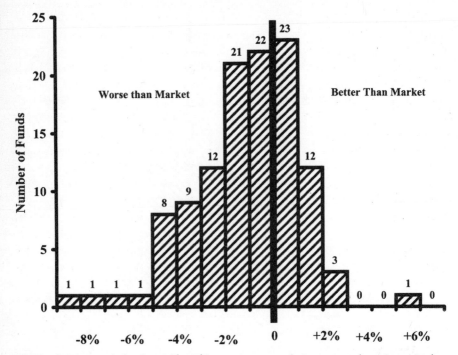

Figure 3-2. Mutual funds 1946–1964: net returns relative to market .0 = market return, average fund = −1.1% per year. (*Source:* Michael Jensen, *Journal of Finance,* 1965.)

persist, primarily due to the chimpanzees' random stock picking methodology (throwing darts). In fact, subsequent researchers soon found this to be the case in the real world as well.

Since Jensen's study, literally dozens of studies have duplicated his findings and verified the last prediction: past superior performance has almost no predictive value. Unfortunately, almost none of the subsequent studies are understandable to the lay reader. The mid-1960s, when Jensen's study was published in the *Journal of Finance,* was about the last time that the average college-educated person could get through an academic finance article without falling asleep. Vast improvements in statistical and computational sophistication in financial research meant that, in most cases, the results were impossible to translate into plain English. In Twain's words, financial research had become "chloroform in print."

Typically, these studies show that there is some brief persistence in performance; last year's top performers will beat the average fund by perhaps 0.25% to 0.5% the next year. But after that, nothing. And excellent past performance over longer periods is of no benefit at all. Since a 0.25% to 0.50% return boost is much lower than the expenses incurred in fund management, *this is not a game worth playing.*

Of the dozens of studies done on mutual fund performance persistence, the most optimistic found that if you invested in the top 10% of last year's funds, you would match, but not exceed, the performance of an index fund with low expenses. This "strategy" requires a near-total fund turnover each year. This is the best-case scenario for actively managed mutual funds—turn your portfolio over once a year, and you might—just might—match the index. And that's before taxes. In a taxable account, this strategy would eat you alive with short-term capital gains, which are penalized at your full marginal federal and state rates.

One delightful exception to the tedium of this research is an ongoing study by Dimensional Fund Advisors and S&P/Micropal, which looks at what happens to the investor who picks a mutual fund with excellent past performance. For each five-year period, they select the 30 best-performing domestic mutual funds. They then follow the performance of these best performers forward.

I've displayed their data in Figure 3-3.

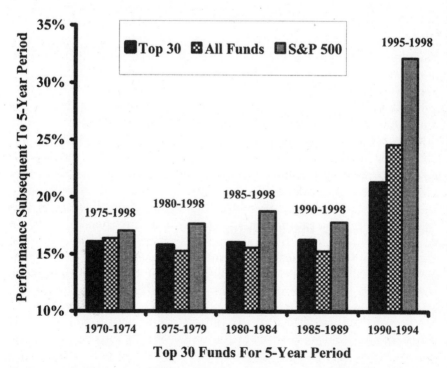

Figure 3-3. Subsequent performance of top-30 funds. (*Source:* Standard and Poor's/Mieropal/Dimensional Fund Advisors.)

In order to understand this graph, take a look at the first group of bars on the left. The first (solid) bar represents the subsequent performance of the top 30 domestic stock funds from 1970 to 1974. In other words, the funds were selected for their superior performance from 1970 to 1974; then their performance from 1975 to 1998 was followed and compared to that of the average mutual fund (checkered bar) and the S&P 500 (gray bar). Note that for some of the periods, the previous best-performing funds did slightly better than average, and for some, worse than average. *But in each instance, the previous winners underperformed the S&P 500 index going forward, sometimes by a large margin.* This is classic Randomovian behavior; we are once again looking at chimps, not skilled operators.

Actually, because of "survivorship bias," these studies understate the case against active management. We've already come across survivorship bias in Chapter 1 when we discussed the differences in stock and bond returns among nations. In this case, when you look at the prior performance of all the funds in your daily newspaper, or even a sophisticated mutual fund database like Morningstar's Principia Pro, you are not looking at the complete sample of funds; *you're looking only at those that have survived.* The funds that were recently put out of their misery because of poor performance do not make it into the record unless you go out of your way to find them. It's estimated that including these defunct funds decreases the actual average active fund performance by about 1.5% per year. So, actively managed funds are even worse than they look.

In plain English, an actively managed fund exposes you to the risk that its return may be so bad that the fund company will want to obliterate its record. In other words, you may wind up owning a fund that, like so many of Comrade Stalin's unlucky colleagues, wound up having its face airbrushed out of official photographs.

More Bad News: Market Impact

The dominance of the investment market by mutual funds is a relatively recent phenomenon. Before the 1960s, mutual funds were largely ignored by the investing public because of the high sales fees, usually 8.5%, and uninspiring performance. Further, 40 years ago, mutual funds were still associated in the public's mind with the "investment trusts" of the 1920s. These were the equivalent of today's closed-end mutual funds, except that they made extensive use of leverage (borrowed funds). Because of this leverage, many declared bankruptcy in the first stages of the 1929 crash.

All that changed in the 1960s. In 1957, Fidelity put a young manager named Gerald Tsai in charge of its Capital Fund. Tsai's specialty was growth-stock investing, and in the mid-1960s, growth companies—Xerox, IBM, LTV, Polaroid—came very much into vogue. The Go-Go Years, as they were called, were almost a carbon copy of today's tech/Internet binge. Exciting new technologies were being brought to market, and the companies at the cutting edge zoomed, eventually selling at prices approaching those seen in the more recent bubble.

Tsai was the prototypical "gunslinger," as this type of fund manager became known—aggressively buying and selling stocks at a rapid pace and ringing up attention-getting returns in the process. In the aftermath of the 1962 downturn, his Fidelity Capital Fund gained 68%, and in 1965 it gained another 50%, versus only 15% for the market. After being told by Fidelity's founder, Edward Crosby Johnson II, that he was not in line to succeed him, he left to found the high-octane Manhattan Fund.

Unfortunately for Tsai, just at that point, he was struck with a fatal case of chimpanzee syndrome. The years 1966–1967 were mediocre for Manhattan and in 1968, the patient crashed. In the first half of the year, Manhattan lost 6.6% of its value while the market gained 10%, ranking 299th among the 305 funds tracked by mutual fund expert Arthur Lipper. At that point, Tsai cashed in his chips and abandoned his shareholders, selling Manhattan to C.N.A. Financial Corporation for $30 million.

Why had things gone so horribly wrong at the Manhatttan Fund? The nation's senior financial writers spun a tale of speculation and hubris, followed by the inevitable rough justice. (At least for the shareholders. In addition to his golden parachute, Tsai eventually went on to a distinguished business career, ultimately becoming chairman of Primerica.) But the financial press missed something far more important: the Manhattan Fund was the first example of what later became an all-too-common phenomenon in the world of mutual funds—asset bloat, with its corrosive effect on returns.

In order to understand asset bloat, we'll have to step back and examine the relationship between portfolio size and investment results. Let's say that you think that the stock of XYZ company is a good buy. You call your broker and, without too much fuss, you purchase $1,000 worth. It is unlikely that anyone has noticed your order—millions of dollars worth of company stock are traded every day, and your purchase produces not a ripple in the stock's activity.

But suppose that you have $25 million to invest in the stock. Now you have a very big problem. You will not be able to complete your purchase without dramatically inflating the stock price. Another way of saying this is that at today's price, there is not nearly enough stock available for sale to meet your needs—in order to bring sufficient shares out of the woodwork, the price must be raised. The amount you pay for your shares will be considerably higher than if you had only a small order, and your overall return will be commensurately smaller. The opposite will happen if you decide to sell a large block of stock: you will seriously depress the price, again lowering your return.

This decrease in return experienced by large traders is called "impact cost," and it goes straight to the bottom line of a fund's return. Unfortunately, it is almost impossible to measure. Now it becomes clear what happened to Manhattan's unfortunate shareholders. Tsai was the first person to attain the modern label of "superstar fund manager" and, in short order, suffered its inevitable consequence, asset bloat.

In the first three months of 1968, Tsai's reputation attracted $1.6 billion into the fund—an enormous amount for the time. He was simply unable to invest that amount of cash without incurring substantial impact costs. In effect, Manhattan's shareholders paid a hefty "Tsai tax" each time he bought or sold, eventually destroying the fund's performance.

This scenario repeated itself innumerable times in the decades following Tsai's departure from the fund scene. One of the best examples of asset bloat's ramifications happened to Robert Sanborn, who, until he "retired" at a fairly young age, ran Oakmark Fund. Mr. Sanborn was an undisputed superstar manager. From its inception in 1991 to year-end 1998, Oakmark's annualized return was 24.91% versus 19.56% for the S&P 500. In 1992, it beat the benchmark by an astonishing 41.28%.

Mr. Sanborn's performance was extremely unusual in that even the most powerful statistical tests showed that this could not have been due to chance. (Unlike Tsai's record, which could easily be explained by his exposure to growth stocks and random variation.) A different story emerges when we examine the fund's performance and assets by individual year. The first row tracks the performance of Oakmark Fund relative to the S&P 500 (that is, how much better or worse it did relative to the S&P) and the second row tracks the fund's assets:

	1992	1993	1994	1995	1996	1997	1998
Return +/− S&P	41.30%	20.40%	2.00%	−3.10%	−6.70%	−0.80%	−24.90%
Assets ($millions)	328	1,214	1,626	3,301	4,194	7,301	7,667

What we see is the typical pattern of fund investors chasing performance, resulting in progressive asset bloat, with more and more investors getting lower and lower returns. It can be clearly seen that Mr. Sanborn had significant difficulties once his fund grew beyond a few billion dollars in size.

There's another depressing pattern that emerges from the above story: relatively few of a successful fund's investors actually get its high early returns. The overwhelming majority hop onto the bandwagon just before it crashes off the side of the road. If we "dollar-weight" the fund's returns, we find that the average investor in the Oakmark Fund underperformed the S&P by 7.55% annually. Jonathan Clements, of *The Wall Street Journal*, quips that when an investor says, "I own last year's best-performing fund," what he usually forgets to add is, "Unfortunately, I bought it this year."

And finally, one sad, almost comic, note. As we've already mentioned, most of the above studies show evidence of performance consistency in one corner of the professional heap—the bottom. Money managers who are in the bottom 20% of their peer group tend to stay there far more often than can be explained by chance. This phenomenon is largely explained by impact costs and high expenses. Those mangers that charge the highest management fees and trade the most frenetically, like Mr. Tsai and his gunslinger colleagues, incur the highest costs, year-in and year-out. Unfortunately, it's the shareholders who suffer most.

How the Really Big Money Invests

There is one pool of money that is even bigger and better-run than mutual funds: the nation's pension accounts. In fact, the nation's biggest investment pools are the retirement funds of the large corporations and governmental bodies, such as the California Public Employees Retirement System (CALPERS), which manages an astounding $170 billion. These plans receive a level of professional management that even the nation's wealthiest private investors can only dream of.

If you are a truly skilled and capable manager, this is the playground you want to wind up in. For example, a top-tier pension manager is typically paid 0.10% of assets under management—in other words, $10 million per year on a $10 billion pool—more than most "superstar" mutual fund managers. Surely, if there is such a thing as skill in stock picking, it will be found here. Let's see how these large retirement plans actually do.

I'm indebted to Piscataqua Research for providing me with the data in Figure 3-4, which shows the performance of the nation's largest pension plans from 1987 to 1999. The average asset allocation for almost all of these plans over the whole period was similar—about

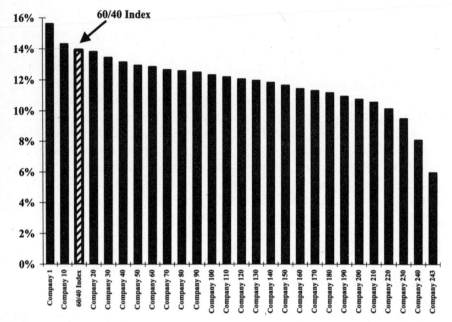

Figure 3-4. Performance of 243 large pension plans, 1987–1999. (*Source:* Dimensional Fund Advisors, Piscataqua Research.)

60% stocks and 40% bonds. So the best benchmark is a mix of 60% S&P 500 and 40% Lehman Bond Index. As you can see, more than 90% of these plans underperformed the 60/40 indexed mix. Discouraged by this failure of active management, these plans are slowly abandoning active portfolio management. Currently, about half of all pension stock holdings are passively managed, or "indexed," including over 80% of the CALPERS stock portfolio.

Small investors, though, have not "gotten it" yet; hope triumphs over experience and knowledge. If the nation's largest mutual funds and pension funds, with access to the very best information, analysts, and computational facilities, cannot successfully pick stocks and managers, what do you think *your* chances are? How likely do you think it is that your broker or financial advisor will be able to beat the market? And if there actually were money managers who could consistently beat the market, how likely do you think it would be that you would have access to them?

Comic Relief from Newsletter Writers and Other Market Timers

The straw that struggling investors most frequently grasp at is the hope that they can increase their returns and reduce risk by timing the market—holding stocks when they are going up and selling them before they go down. Sadly, this is an illusion—one that is exploited by the investment industry with bald cynicism.

It is said that there are only two kinds of investors: those who don't know where the market is going and those who don't know that they don't know. But there is a rather pathetic third kind—the market strategist. These highly visible brokerage house executives are articulate, highly paid, usually attractive, and invariably well-tailored. Their job is to convince the investing public that their firm can divine the market's moves through a careful analysis of economic, political, and investment data. But at the end of the day, they know only two things: First, like everybody else, they don't know where the market is headed tomorrow. *And second, that their livelihood depends upon appearing to know.*

We've already come across Alfred Cowles's assessment of the dismal performance of market newsletters. Some decades later, noted author, analyst, and money manager David Dreman, in *Contrarian Market Strategy: The Psychology of Stock Market Success,* painstakingly tracked opinions of expert market strategists back to 1929 and found that their consensus was mistaken 77% of the time. This is a recurring theme of almost all studies of "consensus" or "expert" opinion; it underperforms the market about three-fourths of the time.

The sorriest corner of the investment prediction industry is occupied by market-timing newsletters. John Graham and Campbell Harvey, two finance academicians, recently performed an exhaustive review of 237 market-timing newsletters. They measured the ability of this motley crew to time the market and found that less than 25% of the recommendations were correct, much worse than the chimps' score of 50%. Even worse, there were no advisors whose calls were consistently correct. Once again, the only consistency was found at the bottom of the pile; there were several newsletters that were wrong with amazing regularity. They cited one very well-known advisor whose strategy produced an astounding 5.4% loss during a 13-year period when the S&P 500 produced an annualized 15.9% gain.

More amazing, there is a newsletter that ranks the performance of other newsletters; its publisher believes that he can identify top-performing advisors. The work of Graham and Harvey suggests that, in reality, he is actually the judge at a coin flipping contest. (Although the work of Graham, Harvey, Cowles, and others does suggest one promising strategy: pick the very worst newsletter you can find. Then do the opposite of what it recommends.)

When it comes to newsletter writers, remember Malcolm Forbes's famous dictum: the only money made in that arena is through subscriptions, not from taking the advice. The late John Brooks, dean of the last generation of financial journalists, had an even more cynical interpretation: when a famous investor publishes a newsletter, it's a sure tip-off that his techniques have stopped working.

Eugene Fama Cries "Eureka!"

If Irving Fisher towered over financial economics in the first half of the twentieth century, there's no question about who did so in the second half: Eugene Fama. His story is typical of almost all of the recent great financial economists—he was not born to wealth, and his initial academic plans did not include finance. He majored in French in college and was a gifted athlete. To make ends meet, he worked for a finance professor who published—you guessed it—a stock market newsletter. His job was to analyze market trading rules. In other words, to come up with strategies that would produce market-beating returns.

Looking at historical data, he found plenty that worked—in the past. But a funny thing happened. Each time he identified a strategy that had done beautifully in the past, it fell flat on its face in the future. Although he didn't realize it at the time, he had joined a growing army of talented finance specialists, starting with Cowles, who had found that although it is easy to uncover successful *past* stock-picking and market-timing strategies, none of them worked going forward.

This is a concept that even many professionals seem unable to grasp. How many times have you read or heard a well-known market strategist say that since event X had just occurred, the market would rise or fall, because it had done so eight out of the last ten times event X had previously occurred? The classic, if somewhat hackneyed, example of this is the "Super Bowl Indicator": when a team from the old NFL wins, the market does well, and when a team from the old AFL wins, it does poorly.

In fact, if one analyzes a lot of random data, it is not too difficult to find some things that seem to correlate closely with market returns. For example, on a lark, David Leinweber of First Quadrant sifted through a United Nations database and discovered that movements in the stock market were almost perfectly correlated with butter production in Bangladesh. This is not one I'd want to test going forward with my own money.

Fama's timing, though, was perfect. He came to the University of Chicago for graduate work not long after Merrill Lynch had funded the Center for Research in Security Prices (CRSP) in Chicago. This remarkable organization, with the availability of the electronic computer, made possible the storage and analysis of a mass and quality of stock data that Cowles could only dream of. Any time you hear an investment professional mention the year 1926, he's telling you that he's gotten his data from the CRSP.

Fama had already begun to suspect that stock prices were random and unpredictable, and his statistically rigorous study of the CRSP data confirmed it. But why should stock prices behave randomly? *Because all publicly available information, and most privately available information, is already factored into their prices.*

Sure, if your company's treasurer has been recently observed to be acting peculiarly and hurriedly obtaining a Brazilian visa, you may be able to profit greatly (and illegally) from this information. But the odds that you will be able to repeat this feat with a large number of company stocks on a regular basis are zero. And with the increasing sophistication of Securities and Exchange Commission (SEC) surveillance apparatus, the chances of pulling this off even once without winding up a guest of the state grow dimmer each year.

Put another way, the simple fact that there are so many talented analysts examining stocks guarantees that none of them will have any kind of advantage, since the stock price will nearly instantaneously reflect their *collective* judgment. In fact, it may be worse than that: there is good data to suggest that the collective judgment of experts in many fields is actually more accurate than their separate individual judgments.

A vivid, if nonfinancial, example of extremely accurate collective judgment occurred in 1968 with the sinking of the submarine *Scorpion*. No one had a precise idea of where the sub was lost, and the best estimates of its position from dozens of experts were scattered over thousands of square miles of seabed. But when their estimates were averaged together, its position was pinpointed to within 220 yards. In other words, the market's estimate of the proper price of a stock, or of the entire market, is usually much more accurate than that of even the most skilled stock picker. Put yet another way, the best estimate of tomorrow's price is . . . today's price.

There's a joke among financial economists about a professor and student strolling across campus. The student stops to pick up a ten-dollar bill he has noticed on the ground but is stopped by the professor. "Don't bother," he says, "if that were really a ten-dollar bill, someone would have picked it up already." The market behaves exactly the same way.

Let's say that XYZ company is selling at a price of 40 and a clever analyst realizes that it is actually worth 50. His company or fund will quickly buy as much of the stock as it can get its hands on, and the price will quickly rise to 50 dollars per share. The whole sequence usually takes only a few days and is accomplished in great secrecy. Further, it is most often not completed by the original analyst. As other analysts notice the stock's price and volume increase, they take a closer look at the stock and also realize that it is worth 50. In the stock market, one occasionally *does* encounter ten-dollar bills lying about, but only very rarely. You certainly would not want to try and make a living looking for them.

The concept that all useful information has already been factored into a stock's price, and that analysis is futile, is known as "The Efficient Market Hypothesis" (EMH). Although far from perfect, the EMH has withstood a host of challenges from those who think that actively picking stocks has value. There is, in fact, some evidence that the best securities analysts *are* able to successfully pick stocks. Unfortunately, the profits from this kind of sophisticated stock analysis are cut short by impact costs, as well as the above-described piggybacking by other analysts.

In the aggregate, the benefits of stock research do not pay for its cost. The Value Line ranking system is a perfect example of this. Most academics who have studied the system are impressed with its theoretical results, but, because of the above factors, it is not possible to use its stock picks to earn excess profits. By the time the latest issue has hit your mailbox or the library, it's too late. In fact, not even Value Line itself can seem to make the system work; its flagship Value Line Fund has trailed the S&P 500 by 2.21% over the past 15 years. Only 0.8% of this gap is accounted for by the fund's expenses. If Value Line cannot make its system work, what makes you think that you can beat the market by reading the newsletter four days after it has left the presses?

There's yet another dimension to this problem that most small investors are completely unaware of: you only make money trading stocks when you know more than those on the other side of your trades. The problem is that you almost never know who those people are. If you could, you would find out that they have names like Fidelity, PIMCO, or Goldman Sachs. It's like a game of tennis in which the players on the other side of the net are invisible. The bad news is that most of the time, it's the Williams sisters.

It never ceases to amaze me that small investors think that by paying $225 for a newsletter, logging onto Yahoo!, or following a few simple stock selection rules, they can beat the market. Such behavior is the investment equivalent of going up against the Sixth Fleet in a rowboat, and the results are just as predictable.

Buffett and Lynch

Any discussion about the failure of professional asset management is not complete until someone from the back of the room triumphantly raises his hand and asks, "What about Warren Buffett and Peter Lynch?" Even the most diehard efficient market proponent cannot fail to be impressed with their track records and bestow on them that rarest of financial adjectives—"skilled."

First, a look at the data. Of the two, Buffett's record is clearly the most impressive. From the beginning of 1965 to year-end 2000, the book value of his operating company, Berkshire Hathaway, has compounded at 23.6% annually versus 11.8% for the S&P 500. The actual return of Berkshire stock was, in fact, slightly greater. This is truly an astonishing performance. Someone who invested $10,000 with Buffett in 1964 would have more than $2 million today. And, unlike the theoretical graphs which graced the first chapter, there are real investors who have actually received those returns. (Two of whom are named Warren Buffett and Charlie Munger, his Berkshire partner.) But it's worth noting a few things.

In the first place, Berkshire is not exactly a risk-free investment. For the one-year period ending in mid-March of 2000, the stock lost almost half its value, compared to a gain of 12% for the market. Second, with its increasing size, Buffett's pace has slowed a bit. Over the past four years, he has beaten the market by less than 4% per year. Third, and most important, Mr. Buffett is not, strictly speaking, an investment manager—he is a businessman. The companies he acquires are not passively held in a traditional portfolio; he becomes an active part of their management. And, needless to say, most modern companies would sell their metaphorical mothers to have him in a corner office for a few hours each week.

Peter Lynch's accomplishments, while impressive, do not astound as Buffett's do. Further, his personal history, while exemplary, gives pause. For starters, Lynch's public career was much shorter than Buffett's. Although he had worked at Fidelity since 1965, he was not handed the Magellan fund until 1977. Even then, the fund was not opened to the public until mid-1981—before that it was actually the private investment vehicle for Fidelity's founding Johnson family.

From mid-1981 to mid-1990, the fund returned 22.5% per year, versus 16.53% for the S&P 500. A remarkable accomplishment, to be sure, but not in the same league as Buffett's. In fact, not at all that unusual. As I'm writing this, more than a dozen domestic mutual funds have beaten the S&P 500 by more than 6%—Lynch's margin—during the past 10 years. This is about what you would expect from chance alone.

The combination of his performance and Fidelity's marketing muscle resulted in a cash inflow the likes of which had never been seen before. Beginning with assets of under $100 million, Magellan grew to more than $16 billion by the time Lynch quit just nine years later. Lynch's name and face became household items; even today, more than a decade after his retirement, his white-maned gaunt visage is among the most recognized in finance.

The combination of Magellan's rapidly increasing size and fame's klieg light took its inevitable toll. With an unlucky draw of the cards, Lynch was out of the country in the days leading up to the market crash of 1987. That year, he underperformed the market by almost 5%. Driven by mild public criticism and a stronger need to prove to himself that he still had the magic, he threw himself into his work, turning in good performances in 1988 and 1989. As the fund's assets swelled, he had to make two major accommodations.

First, he had to focus on increasingly large companies. Magellan originally invested in small- to mid-sized companies: names like La Quinta and Congoleum. But by the end of his tenure, he was buying Fannie Mae and Ford. If there is such a thing as stock selection skill, then the greatest profits should be made with smaller companies that have scant analyst coverage. By being forced to switch to large companies, which are extensively picked over by stock analysts, Lynch found the payoff of his skills greatly diminished.

Second, he had to purchase more and more companies in order to avoid excessive impact costs. By the end of his tenure, Magellan held more than 1,700 names. Both of these compromises drastically lowered his performance relative to the S&P 500 Index. Figure 3-5 vividly plots his decreasing margin of victory versus the index. During his last four years, he was only able to outperform the S&P 500 by 2%. Exhausted, he quit in 1990.

Now, having considered these two success stories, let's take a step back and draw some conclusions:

- Yes, Lynch and Buffett are skilled. But these two exceptions do not disprove the efficient market hypothesis. The salient observation is that, of the tens of thousands of money managers who have practiced their craft during the past few decades, only two showed indisputable evidence of skill—hardly a ringing endorsement of professional asset management.
- Our eyes settle on Buffett and Lynch only in retrospect. The odds of picking these two out of the pullulating crowd of fund managers ahead of time is nil. (It's important to note that just before Magellan was opened to the public, Fidelity merged two unsuc-

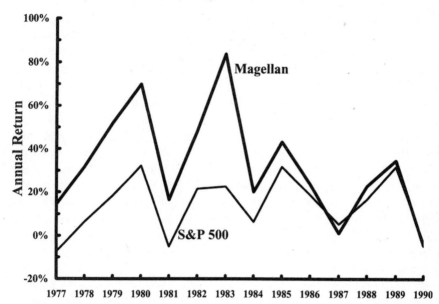

Figure 3-5. Magellan versus S&P 500: The Lynch years. (*Source:* Morningstar Principia Pro Plus.)

cessful "incubator funds"—Essex and Salem—into it.) On the other hand, there have been hundreds of stories like Tsai's and Sanborn's—managers who excelled for a while, but whose performance flamed out in a hail of assets attracted by their initial success.

- For the mutual fund investor, even Peter Lynch's performance was less than stellar. After his talent became publicly known around 1983, this intensely driven individual could continue outperforming the market for just seven more years before he saw the handwriting on the wall and quit at the top of his game. It is not commonly realized that the investing public had access to Peter Lynch for exactly nine years, the last four of which were spent exerting a superhuman effort against transactional expense to maintain a razor thin margin of victory.

The Really Bad News

It's bad enough that mutual-fund manager performance does not persist and that the return of stock picking is zero. This is as it should be, of course. These guys *are* the market, and there is no way that they can all perform above the mean. Wall Street, unfortunately, is not Lake Wobegon, where all the children are above average.

The bad news is that the process of mutual fund selection gives essentially random results. The *really* bad news is that it is expensive. Even if you stick with no-load funds, you will still incur hefty costs. Even the best-informed fund investors are usually unaware as to just how high these costs really are.

Most investors think that the fund's *expense ratio* (ER) listed in the prospectus and annual reports is the true cost of fund ownership. Wrong. There are actually three more layers of expense beyond the ER, which only comprises the fund's advisory fees (what the chimps get paid) and administrative expenses. The next layer of fees is the commissions paid on transactions. These are not included in the ER, but since 1996 the SEC has required that they be reported to share-holders. However, they are presented in the funds' annual reports in such an obscure manner that unless you have an accounting degree, it is impossible to calculate how much return is lost as a percentage of fund assets.

The second extra layer of expense is the bid/ask "spread" of stocks bought and sold. A stock is always bought at a slightly higher price than its selling price, to provide the "market maker" with a profit. (Most financial markets require a market maker—someone who brings together buyers and sellers, and who maintains a supply of securities for ready sale to ensure smooth market function. The bid/ask spread induces organizations to provide this vital service.) This spread is about 0.4% for the largest, most liquid companies, and increases with decreasing company size. For the smallest stocks it may be as large as 10%. It is in the range of 1% to 4% for foreign stocks.

The last layer of extra expense—market impact costs, which we've already discussed—is the most difficult to estimate. Impact costs are not a problem for small investors buying shares of individual compa-nies but are a real headache for mutual funds. Obviously, the magni-tude of impact costs depends on the size of the fund, the size of the company, and the total amount transacted. As a first approximation, assume that it is equal to the spread.

The four layers of mutual fund costs:

- Expense Ratio
- Commissions
- Bid/Ask Spread
- Market Impact Costs

Taken together, these four layers of expense are least for large-cap funds, intermediate for small-cap and foreign funds, and greatest for emerging market funds. They are tabulated in Table 3-1.

Table 3-1. The Expense Layers of Actively Managed Mutual Funds

	Active Fund Expenses		
	Large Cap	Small Cap/Foreign	Emerging Markets
Expense Ratio	1.30%	1.60%	2.00%
Commissions	0.30%	0.50%	1.00%
Bid/Ask Spread	0.30%	1.00%	3.00%
Impact Costs	0.30%	1.00%	3.00%
Total	**2.20%**	**4.10%**	**9.00%**

Recall that the nominal return of stocks in the twentieth century was 9.89% per year, and that, based on the DDM, the actual real returns that future investors will receive may be very much smaller. It should be painfully obvious that this is not the return that you, the mutual fund investor, will actually receive. You must subtract from that return your share of the fund's total investment expense.

Now the full magnitude of the problem becomes clear. The bottom row of Table 3-1 shows the real costs of owning an actively managed fund. In fairness, this does overstate things a bit. Money spent on research and analysis is not a total loss. As we've seen, such research does seem to increase returns, but almost always by an amount less than that spent. How much of the first expense-ratio line is spent on research? Figure about half, if you're lucky. So, even if we use the more generous historical 9.89% stock return as our guideline, active management will lose you about 1.5% in a large-cap fund, 3.3% in a foreign/small cap fund, and 8% in an emerging markets fund, leaving you with 8.4%, 6.6%, and 1.9%, respectively. Not an appetizing prospect.

The mutual fund business has benefited greatly by the high returns of recent years that have served to mask the staggering costs in most areas. One exception to this has been in the emerging markets, where the combination of low asset class returns and high expenses has resulted in a mass exodus of investors.

Bill Fouse's Bright Idea

By 1970, professional investors could no longer ignore the avalanche of data documenting the failure of supposed expert money managers. Up until that point, money management was based on the Great Man theory: find the Great Man who could pick stocks and hire him. When he loses his touch, go out looking for the next Great Man. But clearly, that idea was bankrupt: there were no Great Men, only lucky chimpanzees.

There is no greater test of character than confrontation with solid evidence that the whole of your professional life has been a lie—that the craft that you have struggled so hard to master is worthless. Most money managers fail this trial and are still in the deepest stages of denial. We'll examine their rationalizations for active management at the end of this chapter.

The cream of the crop—thoughtful and intelligent observers like Peter Bernstein (no relation), Ben Graham, James Vertin, and Charles Ellis—painfully reexamined their beliefs and adjusted their practices. Let's summarize the bleak landscape they surveyed:

- The gross returns obtained by money managers were in the aggregate the market's, since they *were* the market.
- The average net return to investors was the market return minus the expense of active stock selection. Since this averaged between 1% and 2%, the typical investor received about 1% to 2% less than the market return.
- There seemed to be few managers capable of consistently beating the market. Worst of all, there were almost no managers capable of persistently beating it by the 1% to 2% margin necessary to pay for their expenses.

One of the professionals surveying the scene in the late 1960s was a young man named William Fouse. Excited by the new techniques of portfolio evaluation, he began evaluating the performance of his colleagues at his employer, Mellon Bank. He was aghast—none of those money managers came even close to beating the market. Today, for a dollar, you can pick up *The Wall Street Journal* and compare the performance of thousands of mutual funds to the S&P 500. It's remarkable to remember that 30 years ago, investors and clients never thought to compare their performance to an index, or, in many cases, even to ask what their performance was. Sadly, the average client and his broker still do not calculate and benchmark their returns.

The solution was obvious to Mr. Fouse, however. Create a fund that would buy all the stocks in the S&P 500 Index. This could be done with a minimum of expense and was guaranteed to produce very close to the market return. His idea was met with approximately the same enthusiasm as a stink bomb at a debutante ball. Very soon he found himself looking for alternative employment. Fortunately, Fouse wound up at Wells Fargo, which provided a more receptive environment for the ideas of modern finance.

In 1971, the old-school head of the trust department, James Vertin, reluctantly gave the go-ahead and Wells Fargo founded the first index fund. It was an unmitigated disaster. Instead of using Fouse's original

S&P 500 idea, they decided to hold an equal dollar amount of all 1,500 stocks on the New York Stock Exchange. Since the stock price of its companies often moved in radically different directions, this required almost constant buying and selling to keep the values of each position equal. This, in turn, resulted in expenses equal to that of an actively managed fund. It was not until 1973 that Fouse's original idea, a fund that held all of the stocks in the S&P 500 in proportion to their market value (and thus did not need rebalancing), was adopted.

At this point, it's necessary to define what we mean by an "index fund." This usually refers to a fund that owns all, or nearly all, of the stocks in a given index, with no attempt to pick those with superior performance. Less commonly, it refers to a fund that holds all stocks meeting certain rigid criteria, usually having to do with market size or growth/value characteristics, such as price-to-book ratio. Today, almost all index funds are "cap weighted." This means that if the value of a stock doubles or falls by half, its proportional contribution in the index does as well, so it is not necessary to buy or sell any to keep things in balance. Thus, as long as the stocks remain in the index, it is not necessary to buy or sell stocks because of changes in market value.

Wells Fargo's index fund was not initially available to the general public, but that was soon to change. A few years later, in September 1976, John Bogle's young Vanguard Group offered the first publicly available S&P 500 Index fund. Vanguard's fund was not exactly a roaring success out of the starting gate. After two years, it had collected only $14 million in assets. In fact, it did not cross the billion-dollar mark—the radar threshold of the fund industry—until 1988. But as the advantages of indexing became evident to small investors, it took off. For the past few years, it has been running neck-and-neck for the number one spot in asset size with Lynch's old fund, Magellan.

Truth be told, the Vanguard 500 Index Fund has gotten a little *too* popular. Of all the major stock indexes, the S&P 500 has done the best in recent years. Much of the new assets that the fund has collected are "hot money," coming from naïve investors who are simply chasing performance.

There's another facet to this as well: Dunn's Law, a phenomenon that affects index funds. Dunn's Law states that when an index does well (that is, it does better than other asset classes), indexing that particular asset class does very well compared to actively managed funds. For example, in each of the years between 1994 and 1998, the Vanguard 500 Index Fund ranked in the top quarter in its peer group of funds—the so-called "large blend" category. But in 2000, it dropped into the lower half of the category. This was largely because the S&P

500 dramatically outperformed all other indexes from 1994 to 1998, but was the worst of the indexes in 2000.

How well has indexing worked? The proper way to judge is to compare like with like—that is, to compare a large-growth index fund with all the funds in the large growth category. Morningstar Inc. is the world's premier purveyor of mutual fund investment tools. I've used their Principia Pro software package to rank the performance of the appropriate Vanguard index fund or S&P/Barra index in its Morningstar category for the five years ending March 31, 2001. The rankings are percentile rankings, ranging from a ranking of 1 for the top percentile and 100 for the worst:

Index Fund/Index	Ranking
Vanguard Large-Cap Growth	28
Vanguard 500 Index Fund (Large-Cap Blend)	20
Vanguard Large-Cap Value Fund	34
Barra Mid-Cap Growth Index Fund	8
S&P 400 Mid-Cap Index (Mid-Cap Blend)	23
Barra Mid-Cap Value Index	24
Vanguard Small-Cap Growth Fund	73
S&P 600 Small-Cap Index (Small Cap Blend)	63
Vanguard Small-Cap Value Fund	30

So, in seven of nine categories, the index approach produces above-average results, and in four of the nine categories, top-quarter performance. A few observations are in order.

First, the Morningstar database suffers from survivorship bias—it does not include the deceased funds in each group. Were these to be included, the performance of the indexes would look even better. Second, as the time horizon lengthens, index fund relative performance improves even more. In the words of Jonathan Clements of *The Wall Street Journal,* "Performance comes and goes. Expenses are forever."

We have data for four categories—large growth, large blend, large value, and small blend—going back 15 years (ending March 31, 2001). The percentile rankings for these indexes and funds are 24, 20, 17, and 23.

Clearly, the best way to avoid the expensive chimpanzees is to simply keep your expenses to a minimum and buy the whole market with an *index* fund.

Taxes

If the case I've presented for indexing is not powerful enough for you, then consider the effect of taxes. While many of us hold funds in our retirement accounts, where taxability of distributions is not an issue, most investors also own funds in taxable, nonsheltered accounts.

While it is probably a poor idea to own actively managed funds in general, it is truly a terrible idea to own them in taxable accounts, for two reasons. First, because of their higher turnover, actively managed funds have higher distributions of capital gains, which are taxed at both the federal and state level. The typical actively managed fund distributes several percent of its assets each year in capital gains. If turnover is high enough, a substantial portion of these will be short-term, which are taxed at the higher ordinary rate: this will amount to a 1% to 4% drag on performance each year. Many index funds allow your capital gains to grow largely undisturbed until you sell.

There is another factor to consider as well. Most actively managed funds are bought because of their superior performance. But, as we've demonstrated above, outperformance does not persist. As a result, most small investors using active-fund managers tend to turn over their mutual funds once every several years in the hopes of achieving better returns elsewhere. What actually happens is that they generate more unnecessary capital gains and resultant taxes. *For the taxable investor, indexing means never having to pay the tax and investment consequences of a bad manager.*

Why Can't I Just Buy and Hold Stocks on My Own?

Some of you may ask, "If the markets are efficient, why can't I simply buy and hold my own stocks? That way, I'll never sell them and incur capital gains as I would when an index occasionally changes its composition, forcing capital gains in the index funds that track it. And since I'll never trade, my expenses will be even lower than an index fund's."

In fact, until recently, periodic turnover in the stock composition of some indexes *has* been a problem at tax time. An excellent example is Vanguard's Small-Cap Index Fund, which in recent years has penalized its taxable shareholders by distributing about 10% of its value each year as capital gains. Fortunately, there are now "tax-efficient" index funds designed for taxable accounts, which are generally able to avoid capital gains. In 1999, Vanguard created its Tax-Managed Small-Cap Index Fund, which minimizes both capital gains and dividend distributions.

But there is a much more important reason why you should not attempt to build your own portfolio of stocks, and that is the risk of buying the wrong ones. You may have heard that you can obtain adequate diversification by holding as few as 15 stocks. This is true only in terms of lowering short-term volatility. But the biggest danger facing your portfolio is not short-term volatility—it's the danger that your portfolio will have low long-term returns.

In other words, you can buy a 15-stock portfolio that has low volatility, but it may put you in the poorhouse just the same. In order to demonstrate the risks of not owning enough stocks, Ronald Surz of PPCA Inc., a provider of investment software, kindly supplied me with some data he generated on the returns of random stock portfolios, which I plotted in Figure 3-6. Mr. Surz examined 1,000 random portfolios of 15, 30, and 60 stocks. What you are looking at is the final wealth of these portfolios relative to the market. For example, look at the cluster of bars on the left—the 15-stock portfolios.

First, note the middle black bar and the thick horizontal line through it, which represents the market return at the 50th percentile (the median performance). By definition, this returned $1.00 of wealth after 30 years relative to the market—that is, it got the market return. The bar at the extreme left, representing 5th percentile performance, beating 95% of all of the random portfolios, returned two-and-one-half times the wealth of the market portfolio. At the 25th percentile—the top quarter of performance—you got almost 50% more than the market's final wealth.

Figure 3-6 shows us just how much luck can contribute to portfolio performance. The 60-stock portfolios are about the size of a small mutual fund. Notice that, purely by chance, one out of 20 of the portfolios had a 30-year wealth of $1.77 or more, relative to the market's $1.00. This means that, by accident, these portfolios beat the market by more than 2% per year over 30 years—enough to put any manager in the Mutual Fund Hall of Fame. (The 95th-percentile-by-accident portfolios would similarly be expected to beat the market by more than 10% in any one-year period.)

Now, go back to the 15-stock portfolios on the left. If you were unlucky and got bottom quarter performance (the fourth bar), after 30 years you only received 70 cents on the dollar. And if you were really unlucky and got bottom 5% performance (95th percentile), then you received only 40 cents on the dollar.

Note how adding more stocks (the 30-stock and 60-stock portfolios) moderates the differences in returns—the lucky picks don't do quite as well, and the bad draws don't do quite as badly. Finally, if you own all the stocks in the market, you will always get the market return, with no risk of failing to obtain it.

Figure 3-6 demonstrates the central paradox of portfolio diversification. Obviously, a concentrated portfolio maximizes your chance of a superb result. Unfortunately, at the same time, it also maximizes your

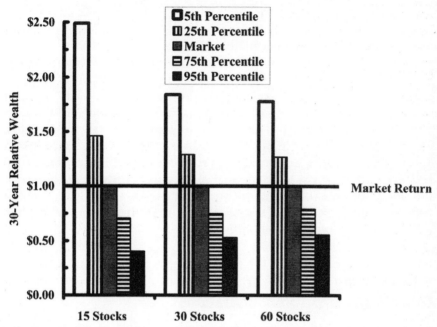

Figure 3-6. 30-year wealth of nondiversified portfolios relative to the S&P 500. (*Source:* Ronald Surz.)

chance of a poor result. This issue gets to the heart of why we invest. You can have two possible goals: One is to maximize your chances of getting rich. The other is to minimize your odds of failing to meet your goals or, more bluntly, to make the likelihood of dying poor as low as possible.

It's important for all investors to realize that these two goals are mutually exclusive. For example, let's say that you have $1,000 and want to turn it into $1,000,000 within a year. The only legal way that you have a prayer of doing so is to go out and buy 1,000 lottery tickets. Of course, you will almost certainly lose most of your money. On a more mundane level, let's say that in order to retire in ten years, you need to obtain a 30% annualized return during that period. It is quite possible to do this: 113 of the 2,615 stocks with ten-year histories listed in the Morningstar database have had ten-year annualized returns in excess of 30%. Of course, 496 of those 2,615 stocks had *negative* returns and that doesn't count the bankrupted stocks missing from the database. In fact, only 885 of the stocks had returns higher than the S&P 500.

In other words, concentrating your portfolio in a few stocks maximizes your chances of getting rich. Unfortunately, it also maximizes your chance of becoming poor. Owning the whole market—indexing—minimizes your chances of both outcomes by guaranteeing you the market return.

A recent innovation—stock "folios"—have been touted as an inexpensive and tax-efficient way for small investors to own portfolios of 30 to 150 stocks. As you can see, these new vehicles fail to provide investors with an adequate degree of diversification.

Take a long, hard look at Figure 3-6. Realize that the market return is by no means certain: neither I nor anyone else really knows precisely what it will be. Failing to diversify properly is the equivalent of taking that uncertain return and then going to Las Vegas with it. It's bad enough that you have to take market risk. Only a fool takes on the additional risk of doing yet more damage by failing to diversify properly with his or her nest egg. Avoid the problem—buy a well-run index fund and own the whole market.

Why Indexing "Doesn't Work," and Other Transparent Rationalizations

It should be painfully apparent by now that most of the investment industry is engaged in nonproductive work. When faced with ironclad data, it takes intellectual honesty in tank-car quantity to admit that you are harming your clients, or that your entire professional life has been for naught. Unfortunately, the investment industry is not known for an abundance of critical self-examination.

It is much easier to offer excuses and rationalizations about why you should avoid indexing and continue to use active management. Here are the most common ones you'll hear:

- "Indexing did terribly last year." It's true. In some years, "indexing" (by which is usually meant the S&P 500) does sometimes underperform most actively managed funds. For example, in 1977, 1978, and 1979, Vanguard's S&P 500 index fund ranked in the 85th, 75th, and 72nd percentiles of all stock funds. The reason was Dunn's Law: in those three years, small stocks did much better than large stocks. Since the S&P 500 consists only of the largest stocks, it could not benefit from holding better-performing small stocks, whereas the active managers were free to own them. In fact, in any given year, you can predict roughly how well an S&P 500 index fund will rank by comparing the returns of small versus large stocks—it will do well when large stocks do better, and worse when small stocks do better. There's an even more important point to be made here, which is that the "index advantage," typically 1% to 2% per year, is small enough that, in any given year, a large number of actively managed funds will beat the market. Remember Mr. Clements' dictum: "Performance comes and goes. Expenses are forever." As the time horizon lengthens, the odds that an active manager will beat the index by enough to pay for her expenses slowly vanish.

- "Indexing works fine for large stocks, but in the less efficient small-cap market, active analysis pays off." This is really the flip side of Dunn's Law. It's true: indexing small stocks has not worked terribly well over the past decade. But it is because small-cap stocks have not done well.

  Dimensional Fund Advisors runs the oldest small-cap index fund: It ranks in the 23rd percentile of all *surviving* small cap funds for the past 15 years. In those years when small caps have done well, indexing them has also done well. For example, for the years 1992–1994, this Fund ranked in the 13th percentile of the Morningstar small-cap category, and, for the three years ending August 2001, in the 29th percentile. If survivorship bias were taken into account, it would almost certainly have had even higher rankings. Even if it is possible for active managers to successfully pick small stocks, transactional costs in this arena are much higher than with large stocks, so any gains from stock picking will be more than offset by the costs of trading small stocks.

- "Active managers do better than index funds in down markets." This is flat-out wrong—they certainly do not. For example, from January 1973 to September 1974, according to Lipper Inc., the average domestic stock fund lost 47.9%, versus a loss of 42.6% for the S&P 500. And from September to November 1987, the average stock fund lost 28.7%, only slightly better than the S&P 500's 29.5% loss. This is particularly amazing in view of the fact that most actively managed funds generally carry about 5% to 10% in cash, whereas, by definition, index funds hold hardly any.

- "Index funds expose you to forced capital gains in the event of a market panic." The argument here is a subtle one: During a market panic, investors will pull their money out of index funds, forcing the funds to sell appreciated shares, saddling the remaining shareholders with unwanted capital gains. Even at first glance, this is a nonstarter. Most index fund investors, like active fund investors, are simply chasing performance and, as such, tend to buy at high prices. As prices fall, the fund can sell those shares at a loss. The fund most vulnerable to this concern is the Vanguard 500 Index Fund, which, because of its age and size, contains some shares bought 25 years ago at a small fraction of their current value. After the events of September 11, its share-holders did not panic and the fund experienced only minuscule net sales. By month's end, the fund contained less than 10% embedded capital gains. Any further fall in prices, even if it pre-cipitated panic selling of the fund, would thus also have com-pletely wiped out the embedded capital gains problem. At the present time, no other Vanguard stock-index fund has any signif-icant remaining embedded capital gains exposure. Vanguard's popular Total Stock Market Fund, which tracks the Wilshire 5000, has a significant *negative* capital gains exposure.

- "An index fund dooms you to mediocrity." Absolutely not: it vir-tually guarantees you superior performance. Over the typical ten-year period, most money managers would kill for index-match-ing returns. Money manager and author Bill Schultheis likens the active-versus-indexed fund choice to a shell game in which there are ten boxes, with the following amounts under each box:

$1,000	$2,000	$3,000	$4,000	$5,000
$6,000	$7,000	$8,000	$9,000	$10,000

You can pick a random box, or you can take a guaranteed pay-ment of $8,000. Yes, it's possible to beat the index, but since we've shown that because of expenses, active managers do worse than chimpanzees, the more likely probability is that you'll also do much worse.

Finally, there is one legitimate criticism that can be leveled at an indexing strategy: You will never have exceptional returns; you will never get fabulously rich. As we've already discussed, poorly diversified strategies do indeed maximize your chances of winding up with bags of money. Unfortunately, they also maxi-mize your chances of ending your days in a trailer park. Giving up a shot at the brass ring does bother a lot of investors. But that's your own choice; no one else can make it for you.

The market possesses an awesome power that cannot be easi-ly overcome. Were Obi-Wan Kenobi an investment advisor, it's clear what he'd tell his clients: "Use the force. Index your invest-ments."

CHAPTER 3 SUMMARY

1. There is almost no evidence of stock-picking skill among profes-sional money managers; from year to year, manager relative per-formance is nearly random.

2. There is absolutely no evidence that anyone can time the market.
3. The gross (before expenses) return of the average money manager is the market return.
4. The expected net (after expenses) return of a money manager is the market return minus expenses.
5. The most reliable way of obtaining a satisfying return is to index (own the whole market).

4

The Perfect Portfolio

Let's summarize the practical lessons from the first three chapters:

- Risk and reward are inextricably intertwined. If you desire high returns, you will have to purchase risky assets—namely, stocks.
- You are not capable of beating the market. But do not feel bad, because no one else can, either.
- Similarly, no one—not you, not anyone else—can time the market. As Keynes said, it is the duty of shareholders to periodically suffer loss without complaint.
- Owning a small number of stocks is dangerous. This is a particularly foolish risk to take, since, on average, you are not compensated for it.

We have already come to some conclusions about what this means: the intelligent investor's stock exposure should be to the entire market. What we haven't yet discussed is exactly how much of your assets you should expose to the market, or even what we mean by "the market."

These two issues—how much of your overall assets you should place in stocks and how you should allocate your assets between different classes of stocks—form the core of "asset allocation." In the 1980s, famed investor Gary Brinson and his colleagues published a pair of papers purporting to demonstrate that more than 90% of the variation in investment returns is due to asset allocation and less than 10% to timing and stock selection.

These articles have been hotly contested by practitioners and academicians ever since. However, this controversy completely misses the point: it does not matter how much of your return is determined by timing or stock selection—no sane investor denies that these are important determinants of return. It's just that you can't control the results of timing and selection—asset allocation is the only factor you can positively impact. *In other words, since you cannot successfully time the market or select individual stocks, asset allocation should be the major focus of your investment strategy, because it is the only factor affecting your investment risk and return that you can control.*

It's important to make perfectly clear what we can and cannot do. In examining the behavior of different kinds of portfolios, all we have to rely on is the historical record. It is easy to obtain the monthly or annual returns of various classes of stock assets, feed them into a spreadsheet or a device called a "mean variance optimizer" (MVO) and determine precisely which combinations of these assets worked the best. But we can only do this in the past tense; it tells us nearly nothing about future portfolio strategy. If anyone tells you that he knows the future's best allocation, nod slowly, slide back several steps, turn, and run like hell.

Let me give you a simple example. For the 20 years from 1970 to 1989, the best performing stock assets were Japanese stocks, U.S. small stocks, and precious metals (gold) stocks. At the end of that period, MVOs began making their way to the desktops of financial planners. In went the historical data and out came portfolios consisting almost exclusively of, you guessed it, Japanese, U.S. small company, and gold stocks. These turned out to be the worst performing assets over the next decade. In fact, designing stock portfolios based on past performance is usually a prescription for disaster.

Is it possible to predict which portfolios will perform best in the future? Of course not. In order to do so, you need to be able to predict future asset class behavior with a high degree of accuracy. This is the same thing as timing the market which, you already know, cannot be done. And if it could, you would not need an MVO or any of its fancier relatives. You would simply go out and buy the best performing assets. (Or, to paraphrase Will Rogers, buy only those stocks that are going to go up.)

The Portfolio's the Thing

First and foremost, it's important that you manage all of your financial assets—retirement accounts, taxable accounts, kids' college money, emergency money, etc.—as a *single portfolio*. For example, assume you own an S&P 500 index fund. If it returns, say, 10% in a given year, does it bother you that some of the stocks in it may have lost more than 80% of their value, as will happen to a few each year? Of course not. A globally diversified portfolio behaves the same way, except that the performance of each component is now more visible to you in the form of returns data in the daily paper and your quarterly statements. As an example, I've listed the returns for 1998, 1999, and 2000 for some of the most commonly used stock asset classes:

Asset Class	1998	1999	2000
U.S. Large Stocks (S&P 500)	28.58%	21.04%	−9.10%
U.S. Small Stocks (CRSP 9–10)	−7.30%	27.97%	−3.60%
Foreign Stocks (EAFE)	20.00%	29.96%	−14.17%
REITs (Wilshire REIT)	−17.00%	−2.57%	31.04%

This three-year sequence is a pretty typical one. Let's start with 1998. In the first place, a diversified portfolio did reasonably well in that year. U.S. large stocks did the best, but REITs lost a lot of money. Many investors got discouraged that year and sold their REITs. They were soon sorry because by 2000, stock returns were generally poor and REITs were the only stock asset with superlative returns. Foreign and U.S. large stocks, which delivered excellent returns in the first two years, took a nosedive in 2000.

The key is to ignore the year-to-year relative performance of the individual asset classes—their behavior usually averages out over the years—it is the *long-term* behavior of your whole portfolio that matters, not its day-to-day variation. If you cannot help focusing on the performance of the individual asset classes in your portfolio, at least do so only over as long a period as possible.

With training and experience, most investors take these normal asset class ups and downs in stride. (There is even a way to take advantage of them, which we'll discuss later in the chapter.) But some investors cannot. If you are such an individual and become upset when one of your asset classes does poorly, even when the rest of your portfolio is doing well, then you should not be managing your own money. I can guarantee you that each and every year you will have at least one or two poorly performing assets. And in some years, like 2000, most will behave miserably.

If you cannot handle the routine asset class volatility inherent in the capital markets, then you should have a reputable financial advisor making your investment decisions. Your decisions will forever be clouded by your emotional responses to normal market activity.

Our exploration of the asset allocation process will proceed in several steps. We'll start with the most important allocation question of all: the decision of how much of your capital to put at risk.

Step One: Risky Assets, Riskless Assets

Distilled to its essence, there are only two kinds of financial assets: those with high returns and high risks, and those with low returns and low risks. The behavior of your portfolio is determined mainly by your mix of the two. As we learned in Chapter 1, all stocks are risky assets, as are long-term bonds. The only truly riskless assets are short-term, high-quality debt instruments: Treasury bills and notes, high-grade short-term corporate bonds, certificates of deposit (CDs), and short-term municipal paper. To be considered riskless, their maturity should be less than five years, so that their value is not unduly affected by inflation and interest rates. Some have recently argued that Treasury Inflation Protected Securities (TIPS) should also be considered riskless, in spite of their long maturities, because they are not negatively affected by inflation.

What we'll be doing for the rest of this chapter is setting up a "laboratory" in which we create portfolios composed of various kinds of assets in order to see what happens to them as the market fluctuates. How we compute the behavior of these portfolios is beyond the scope of this book; for those few of you who are interested, I suggest that you read the first five chapters of my earlier book, *The Intelligent Asset Allocator*. Suffice it to say that it is possible to simulate with great accuracy the *historical* behavior of portfolios consisting of many assets. Keep in mind that this is not the same as predicting the *future* behavior of any asset mix. As we discussed in the first chapter, historical returns are a good predictor of future risk, but not necessarily of future return.

Let's start with the simplest portfolios: mixtures of stocks and T-bills. I've plotted the returns of Treasury bills, U.S. stocks, as well as 25/75, 50/50, and 75/25 mixes of the two, in Figures 4-1 through 4-5. In order to give an accurate idea of the risks of each portfolio, I've shown them on the same scale.

As you can see, when we increase the ratio of stocks, the amount lost in the worst years increases. This is the face of risk. In Table 4-1, I've tabulated the return, as well as the damage, in the 1973–74 bear markets for a wide range of bill/stock combinations. Finally, in Figure 4-6, I've plotted the long-term returns of each of these portfolios versus their performance in 1973–1974.

Figure 4-6 provides the conceptual heart of this chapter, and it's worth dwelling on for a few minutes. What you are looking at is a map of portfolio return versus risk. The numbers along the left-hand edge of the vertical axis represent the annualized portfolio returns. The higher up on the page a portfolio lies, the higher its return. The num-

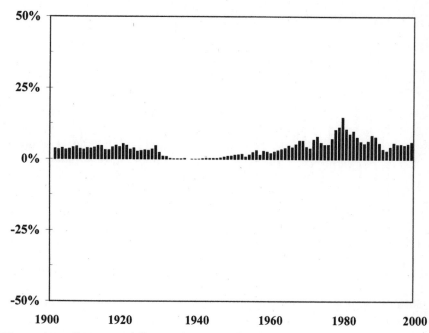

Figure 4-1. All Treasury bill annual return, 1901–2000. (*Source:* Jeremy Siegel.)

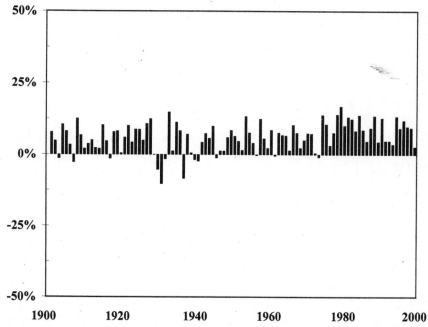

Figure 4-2. Mix of 25% stock/75% Treasury bill annual returns, 1901–2000. (*Source:* Jeremy Siegel.)

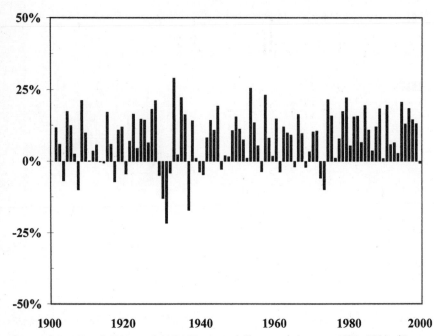

Figure 4-3. Mix of 50% stock/50% Treasury bill annual returns, 1901–2000. (*Source:* Jeremy Siegel.)

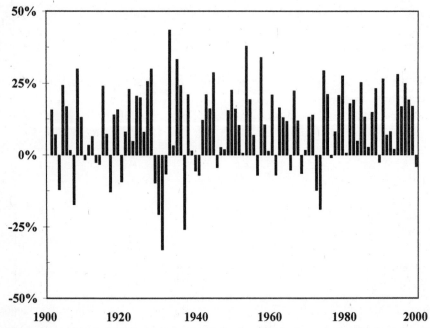

Figure 4-4. Mix of 75% Stock/25% Treasury bill annual returns, 1901–2000. (*Source:* Jeremy Siegel.)

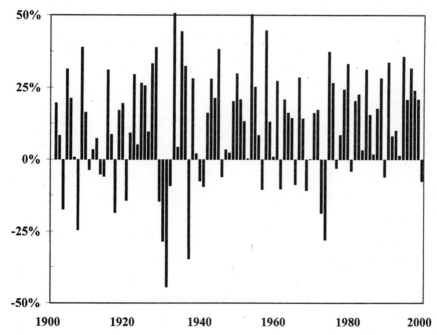

Figure 4-5. All-stock annual returns, 1901–2000. (*Source:* Jeremy Siegel.)

bers on the horizontal axis, at the bottom of the graph, represent risk. The further off to the left a portfolio lies, the more money it lost in 1973–74, and the riskier it is likely to be in the future.

It's important to clear up a bit of confusing terminology first. Until this point in the book, we've used two designations for fixed-income securities: bonds and bills, referring to long- and short-duration obligations, respectively. Bonds and bills are also different in one other respect: bonds most often yield regular interest, whereas bills do not— they are simply bought at a discount and redeemed at face value. The most common kinds of bills in everyday use are Treasury bills and commercial paper, the latter issued by corporations.

Long-duration bonds are generally a sucker's bet—they are quite volatile, extremely vulnerable to the ravages of inflation, and have low long-term returns. For this reason, they tend to be bad actors in a portfolio. Most experts recommend keeping your bond maturities short— certainly less than ten years, and preferably less than five. From now on, when we talk about "stocks and bonds," what we mean by the latter is any debt security with a maturity of less than five to ten years— T-bills and notes, money market funds, CDs, and short-term corporate, government agency, and municipal bonds. *For the purposes of this book, when we use the term "bonds" we are intentionally excluding*

Table 4-1. 1901–2000, 100-Year Annualized Return versus 1973–1974 Bear Market Return

Stock/Bill Composition	Annualized Return 1901–2000	Total Return 1973–1974
100%/0%	9.89%	−41.38%
95%/5%	9.68%	−38.98%
90%/10%	9.46%	−36.52%
85%/15%	9.23%	−34.03%
80%/20%	8.99%	−31.48%
75%/25%	8.74%	−28.89%
70%/30%	8.48%	−26.25%
65%/35%	8.21%	−23.57%
60%/40%	7.93%	−20.84%
55%/45%	7.64%	−18.07%
50%/50%	7.35%	−15.25%
45%/55%	7.04%	−12.38%
40%/60%	6.72%	−9.47%
35%/65%	6.40%	−6.51%
30%/70%	6.06%	−3.51%
25%/75%	5.72%	−0.46%
20%/80%	5.36%	2.64%
15%/85%	5.00%	5.78%
10%/90%	4.63%	8.97%
5%/95%	4.25%	12.21%
0%/100%	3.86%	15.49%

long-term treasuries and corporate bonds, as these do not have an acceptable return/risk profile. I'll admit that this is a bit confusing. A more accurate designation would be "stocks and relatively short-term fixed-income instruments," but this wording is unwieldy.

The data in Table 4-1 and the plot in Figure 4-6 vividly portray the tradeoff between risk and return. The key point is this: the choice between stocks and bonds is not an either/or problem. Instead, the vital first step in portfolio strategy is to assess your risk tolerance. This will, in turn, determine your overall balance between risky and riskless assets—that is, between stocks and short-term bonds and bills.

Many investors start at the opposite end of the problem—by deciding upon the amount of return they require to meet their retirement, educational, life style, or housing goals. This is a mistake. If your portfolio risk exceeds your tolerance for loss, there is a high likelihood that you will abandon your plan when the going gets rough. That is not to say that your return requirements are immaterial. For example, if you have saved a large amount for retirement and do not plan to leave a large estate for

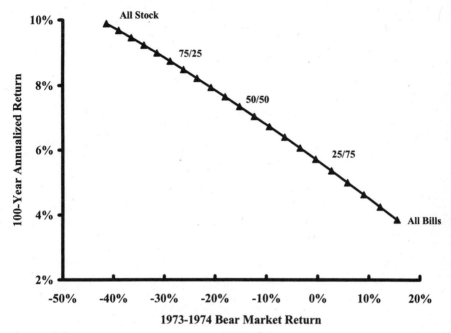

Figure 4-6. Portfolio risk versus return of bill/stock mixes, 1901–2000.

your heirs or to charity, you may require a very low return to meet your ongoing financial needs. In that case, there would be little sense in choosing a high risk/return mix, no matter how great your risk tolerance.

There's another factor to consider here as well, and that's the probability that stock returns may be lower in the future than they have been in the past. The slope of the portfolio curve in Figure 4-6 is steep—in other words, in the twentieth century, there was a generous reward for bearing additional portfolio risk. It is possible, for example, that the future risk/reward plot may look something like Figure 4-7, with a much lower difference in returns between risky and risk-free investments. In this illustration, I've assumed a 7% return for stocks and a 5.5% return for bonds. In such a world, it makes little sense to take the high risk of an all-stock portfolio.

Finally, it cannot be stressed enough that between planning and execution lies a yawning chasm. It is one thing to coolly design a portfolio strategy on a sheet of paper or computer monitor, and quite another to actually deploy it. Thinking about the possibility of losing 30% of your capital is like training for an aircraft crash-landing in a simulator; the real thing is a good deal more unpleasant. If you are just starting out on your investment journey, err on the side of conservatism. It is much better to underestimate your risk tolerance at an

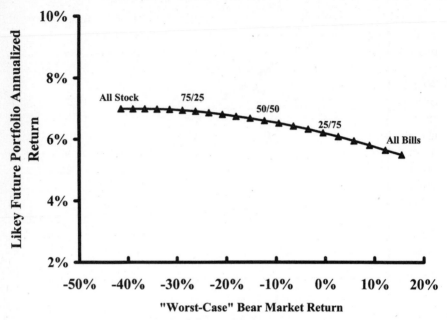

Figure 4-7. Likely future portfolio risks/returns.

early age and adjust your risk exposure upwards later than to bite off more than you can chew up front.

Millions of investors in the 1920s and 1960s thought that they could tolerate a high exposure to stocks. In both cases, the crashes that followed drove most of them from the equity markets for almost a generation. Since the risk of your portfolio is directly related to the percentage of stocks held, it is better that you begin your investment career with a relatively small percentage of stocks. This flies directly in the face of one of the prime tenets of financial planning conventional wisdom: that young investors should invest aggressively, since they have decades to make up their losses. The problem with an early aggressive strategy is that you cannot make up your losses if you permanently flee the stock market because of them.

This all adds up to one of the central points of asset allocation: Unless you are absolutely certain of your risk tolerance, you should probably err on the low side in your exposure to stocks.

Step Two: Defining the Global Stock Mix

Why diversify abroad? Because foreign stocks often zig when domestic markets zag, or at least may not zig as much. Let's look at the most recent data.

In the early part of this century, the international capital markets were a good deal more integrated than they are now. It was commonplace for an Englishman to buy American bonds or French stocks, and there were few barriers to cross-border capital flow. The two World Wars changed that; the international flow of capital recovered only slowly afterwards. The modern history of international diversification properly begins in 1969, with the inception of Morgan Stanley's EAFE (Europe, Australasia, and Far East) Index. As of year-end 2000, there is a 32-year track record of accurate foreign returns. For the period, this index shows an 11.89% annualized return for foreign investing, versus 12.17% for the S&P 500.

Why invest in foreign stocks if their returns are the same, or perhaps even less than U.S. stocks? There are two reasons: risk and return. In Figure 4-8, I've plotted the annual returns of the two indexes. Note how there can be a considerable difference in return between the two in any given year. Particularly note that during 1973 and 1974, the EAFE lost less than the S&P: a total 33.16% loss for the EAFE versus a

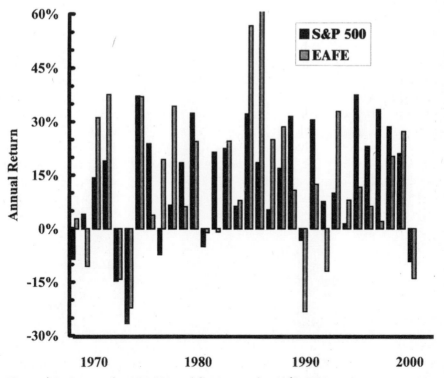

Figure 4-8. Returns for S&P 500 and foreign stocks, 1962–2000.

37.24% loss for the S&P 500. What this means is that foreign investing provided a bit of cushion to the global investor.

An even more vivid case for diversifying into foreign stocks is made by looking at returns decade by decade, as shown in Figure 4-9. Notice how during the 1970s, the return of the S&P 500 was less than inflation—that is, it had a negative real return—whereas the EAFE beat inflation handily. You'll also see that the EAFE beat the S&P 500 by a similar margin in the 1980s.

Thus, for a full two decades you would have been very happy with global diversification. This would have been particularly true if these two decades had been your retirement years, since a U.S.-only portfolio would have very likely run out of money due to its relatively low returns. In the 1990s, the law of averages finally caught up with foreign stocks, souring many on global diversification.

Despite the slightly lower rewards of foreign stocks, the most powerful argument, paradoxically enough, can actually be made on the basis of return. Most investors do not simply select an initial allocation and let it run for decades without adjustment. Because of the varying returns of different assets over the years, portfolios must be "rebal-

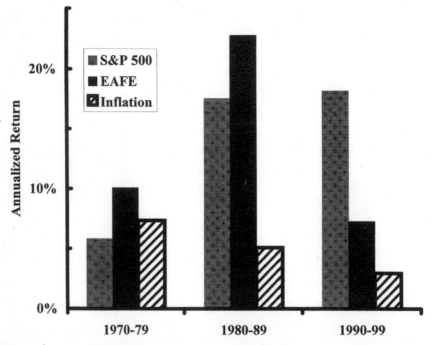

Figure 4-9. S&P 500, EAFE, and inflation, by decade. (*Source:* Morningstar Inc.)

anced." To see what rebalancing means, let's look at the two-year period from 1985 to 1986.

The overall return of the S&P 500 for those years was quite high—57%—but the return of the EAFE was off the charts—166%! Had you started with a 50/50 portfolio at the beginning of the period, at the end, it would have been 63% foreign and 37% domestic. Rebalancing the portfolio means selling enough of the better performing asset (in this case, the EAFE) and with the proceeds buying the worse performing asset (the S&P 500) to bring the allocation back to the 50/50 policy.

Had you rebalanced a 50/50 S&P 500/EAFE portfolio every two years between 1969 and 2000, it would have returned 12.62%. This was almost one-half percent better than the best-performing asset, the S&P 500. Why? Because when you rebalance back to your policy allocation (your original 50/50 plan), you are generally selling high (the best performer) and buying low (the worst performer). So, over the long haul, international diversification not only reduces risk, but it may also increase return. But be warned: as the past decade has clearly taught us, foreign diversification is not a free lunch, especially if your time horizon is less than 15 or 20 years.

Until recently, the average U.S. investor did not have to worry about diversifying abroad—it simply wasn't an option. Although domestic investors have been able to purchase foreign stocks for more than a century, in practice this was expensive, cumbersome, and awkward; it could only be done one stock at a time. Although the first U.S.-based international fund opened its doors almost five decades ago, it wasn't until the early 1980s that these vehicles became widely available. In 1990, the Vanguard Group made available the first easily accessible, low-cost indexed foreign funds.

What is the proper allocation to foreign stocks? Here we run into an enormous problem—one that makes even the most devout believer in efficient markets a bit queasy. The rub is that the total market cap of non-U.S. stocks is about $20 trillion versus only $13 trillion for the U.S. market. If you believe that the global market is efficient, then you should own every stock in the world in cap-weighted fashion, meaning that foreign companies would comprise 60% of your stock exposure. This is more than even the most enthusiastic proponents of international diversification can swallow.

So what's a reasonable foreign allocation? Certainly less than 50% of your stock pool. For starters, foreign stocks are more volatile, in general, than domestic stocks on a year-by-year basis. Second, they are more expensive to own and trade. For example, the Vanguard Group's foreign index funds, on average, incur about 0.20% more in annual expenses than their domestic index funds. Finally, a small portion of the dividends of foreign stocks are taxed by their national governments. Although these taxes are deductible on your tax returns, this deduction does not apply to retirement accounts. Here, it is lost money.

Experts differ on the "optimal" foreign stock exposure, but most agree it should be greater than 15% of your stock holdings and less than 40%. Exactly how much foreign exposure you can tolerate hinges on how much "tracking error" (the difference between the performance of your portfolio and the S&P 500) you can bear. Take a look again at Figure 4-9. An investor with a high foreign exposure would have suffered accordingly in the nineties. Although their returns would have been satisfying, they would have been much less than those obtained by their neighbors who had not diversified. So although the long-term return of a globally diversified stock portfolio should be slightly higher than a purely domestic one, there will be periods lasting as long as 10 or 15 years when the global portfolio will do worse.

If this temporary shortfall relative to the S&P 500—tracking error—bothers you greatly, then perhaps you should keep your foreign exposure relatively low. If it does not bother you at all, then you may be able to stomach as much as 40% in foreign stocks. But whatever allocation you settle on, the key is to *stick with it* through thick and thin, including rebalancing back to your target percentage on a regular basis.

Step Three: Size and Value

Steps one and two—the stock/bond and domestic/foreign decisions—constitute asset allocation's heavy lifting. Once you've answered them, you're 80% of the way home. If you're lazy or just plain not interested, you can actually get by with only three asset classes, and thus, three mutual funds: the total U.S. stock market, foreign stocks, and short-term bonds. That's it—done.

However, there are a few relatively simple extra portfolio wrinkles that are worth incorporating into your asset allocation repertoire. We've already talked about the extra return offered by value stocks and small stocks. The diversification benefits of small stocks and value stocks are less certain. For example, during the 1973–74 bear market, value stocks did much better than growth stocks; the former lost only 23% versus 37% for the latter. But during the 1929–32 bear market, value stocks lost 78% of their worth, versus "only" 64% for growth stocks. The academicians who have most closely examined the value effect—Fama and French—insist that the higher return of value stocks reflects the fact that these companies are riskier than growth stocks because they are weaker and thus more vulnerable in hard times. Fama and French's theory is consistent with stock performance during the 1929–32 bear market.

But there are also times when growth stocks demonstrate their own peculiar risks. As we'll see in the next chapter, from time to time, the public becomes overly enthusiastic about the prospects for companies at the leading edge of the era's technology. These growth stocks can appreciate beyond reason—as happened in the late 1990s in the technology and Internet areas. When the bubble deflates, however, large sums can be lost. On the other hand, we usually don't have to worry about a bubble in bank, auto, or steel stocks.

There can be no question that small stocks are riskier than large stocks. Small companies tend to be insubstantial and fragile. More importantly, they are thinly traded—relatively few shares change hands during an average day, and in a general downturn, a few motivated sellers can dramatically lower prices. From 1929 to 1932, small stocks lost 85% of their value, and from 1973 to 1974, a 58% loss was incurred. Why invest in small stocks at all? Because over the very long haul, they do offer higher returns; this is particularly true for small value stocks, as we saw in Figure 1-18.

How much of your portfolio should be held in small and value stocks? Again, it depends on the amount of tracking error you can tolerate. Small stocks and value stocks can underperform the broad market indexes for very long periods of time—in excess of a decade, as occurred in the 1990s. To demonstrate this, I've plotted the returns of the market, small stocks, large-value stocks, and small-value stocks for the past three decades in Figure 4-10. From 1970 to 1999, small-value stocks had the highest return (16.74% annualized), followed by large-value stocks (15.55%), the S&P 500 (13.73%), and small stocks (11.80%).

But Figure 4-10 also shows that during the last ten years of the period, this pattern was virtually reversed, with the S&P 500 being the best-performing asset, and small value stocks, the worst. So, again, it comes down to tracking error: how long are you willing to watch your portfolio underperform the market before it (hopefully) turns around and pays off? If you cannot tolerate playing second fiddle to your more conventionally invested neighbors at cocktail parties, then small stocks and value stocks are not for you.

What is the maximum you should allot to small stocks and value stocks? This is a tremendously complex subject that we'll tackle in some detail in Chapter 12. In general, you should own more large-cap stocks than small-cap stocks. In the large-cap arena, you should have

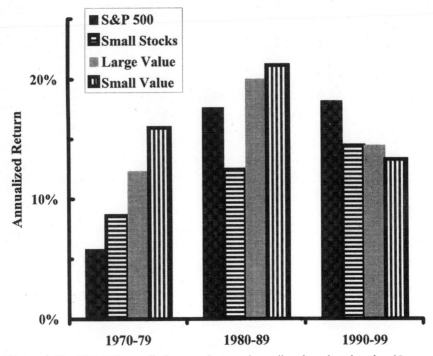

Figure 4-10. S&P 500, small, large value, and small value, by decade. (*Source:* Dimensional Fund Advisors, Morningstar Inc.)

a reasonable balance of value and growth stocks. Small-growth stocks have relatively low returns and high risks, so your allocation to small value should be much larger than to small growth. But realize that the more you stray from the S&P 500, the more often your portfolio will dance to its own drummer. This will distress investors who do not like to temporarily underperform the market.

Step Four: Sectors

What about industry sectors: tech, autos, banks, airlines, and the like? They are hardly worth the trouble; once you're exposed to the whole market via an index fund, you already own them. The only way you can improve on the market return by using sectors is by picking the areas with the future highest returns. And, as we've already seen in the preceding chapter, lots of luck.

There's another reason why it's generally a bad idea to focus on sectors: they can virtually disappear. For example, at the turn of the last century, railroad companies constituted most of the U.S. market's total value. But by 1950, they had been devastated by the automobile and the aircraft. In 1980, the market was dominated by oil stocks, but within a decade, they had shrunk to one-quarter of their former share of market capitalization. The real risk in the sector game is that you may wind up owning the next generation's buggy whip and leather industries.

But with some trepidation, I think that there are two sectors worth considering: REITs (real estate investment trusts) and precious metals stocks. Of the two, a much stronger case can be made for REITs. Their historical returns, as well as their expected future returns, are probably comparable to the market's. And, as we saw a few pages ago, they can do quite well when everything else has gone down the tubes. Unfortunately, the same table showed that the opposite is also true: they can do poorly when the rest of the market is going great guns. (Or, as Dan Wheeler of Dimensional Fund Advisors puts it, the problem with diversification is that it works, whether or not we want it to.) Again, it all comes down to tracking error: how much does it bother you when an asset grossly underperforms the rest of the market? Because of the high volatility and tracking error of REITs, the maximum exposure you should allow for this asset class is 15% of your stock component.

Precious metals stocks—companies that mine gold, silver, and platinum—historically have had extremely low returns, perhaps a few percent above inflation. Not only that, they tend to have very poor returns for very long periods of time and are extremely volatile. Why expose yourself to this asset class? For three reasons.

First, precious metals stock returns are almost perfectly uncorrelated with most of the world's other financial markets. During a global market meltdown, they are liable to do quite well. For example, from 1973 to 1974, gold stocks gained 28%. We don't have exact returns for gold stocks from 1929 to 1932, but anecdotally, they seemed to have done quite well at that time as well, when everything else was getting hammered.

Second, precious metals stocks will be profitable if inflation ever again rears its ugly head. During such periods, "hard assets" such as precious metals, real estate, and "collectibles" (e.g., art, rare coins, etc.) tend to do very well.

And third, this asset's random volatility will work in your favor via the rebalancing mechanism. If you can hold precious metals stocks in a retirement account and trade them without tax consequences, the natural buy-low/sell-high discipline of the rebalancing process should earn 3% to 5% per year in excess of the low baseline return for this asset. Be forewarned that this process takes discipline, because you will be continually moving against the crowd's sentiment. While you are selling, you will be reading and hearing some very compelling reasons to buy, and when you are buying, you will find that others consider it an act of lunacy.

This brings up a very interesting point about asset classes in general. Some bring a bit more to the portfolio than their historical rates of return would suggest. The benefit occurs when an asset is extremely volatile and does not move in synch with the rest of the market. Gold stocks are the epitome of this behavior. REITs, emerging markets stocks, and small international stocks also do this. In general, this kind of behavior can only be taken advantage of in sheltered accounts or in accounts that have high inflows of funds, as it is dependent on the rebalancing technique discussed above.

That said, precious metals are strictly optional. If gold stocks make you queasy, don't buy them. But if you do buy this asset class, it should be no more than a few percent of your portfolio.

Some Working Illustrations

It's time to show you what the overall process looks like with a few examples. First of all, to reiterate: there will be an optimal allocation among different kinds of stocks over the next 10, 20, or 30 years. Unfortunately, *there is no way of knowing in advance what it will be.* (Over the shorter periods, it will likely consist of a 100% allocation to the best-performing asset, and over longer periods, to a mixture of two or three of them.) The important thing, then, is that your asset allocation be properly diversified and behave tolerably well under most circumstances.

Let's start with a theoretical fellow named Charlie Cringe. Charlie hates investing and wants to keep it as simple as possible. Further, it drives him nuts when his neighbor, Harry Hubris, brags about how well his blue chips are doing. Charlie's no spring chicken: he'll be retiring in a few years and has lived through a few bear markets. He knows that he can't sleep at night owning more than 50% stocks. Here's a reasonable allocation for Charlie:

- 35% U.S. stock market (the "total market," not just the S&P 500)
- 10% Foreign stocks
- 5% REITs
- 50% Short-term bonds

The performance of the equity portion of Charlie's portfolio will never stray too far from that of the overall market, making cocktail hour with Harry much less stressful. Best of all, he should only have to spend a few hours per year following and rebalancing his portfolio.

On the other hand, consider Wendy Wonk, who runs the computer network in the accounting department of a large company. She's 28 years old, and numbers don't scare her one bit. Not only that, but she inherited her father's love of investing and is something of a risk taker. Here's what Wendy might do:

- 10% S&P 500
- 10% U.S. large-value stocks
- 5% U.S. small stocks
- 7.5% U.S. small-value stocks
- 7.5% REITs
- 2.5% Precious metals stocks
- 10% European stocks
- 7.5% Japanese and Pacific Rim stocks
- 7.5% Emerging markets stocks
- 7.5% International value stocks
- 25% Short-term bonds

First, note that she's at 75/25 stocks/bonds. This is about as much equity exposure as anyone should have, given the expected returns of stocks and bonds. Next, notice that nearly half of her stock exposure is foreign, and that only a small corner of it owns the S&P 500.

The next cubicle happens to be occupied by an unpleasant creature named Bonnie Bore, who's forever going on about her Microsoft options. But Wendy knows that Bonnie couldn't invest her way out of the lady's room, and on days when the big blue chips soar above all other asset classes (and Wendy's portfolio), she couldn't care less.

Finally, this is not a simple portfolio: Wendy owns no less than ten different stock asset classes; she tells me that she's thinking of adding in some junk and international bonds, and I can't come up with good reasons not to.

Wendy will probably do better than Charlie. Not only does she have a higher stock exposure, but she's also much more exposed to value and small stocks, which should earn higher returns. Of course, we can't be sure—in finance, nothing's for certain. But even if we knew positively that she would have better returns than Charlie, he's still better off sticking with his less efficient portfolio. He'll be able to manage it without exhausting his limited patience for finance and stay the course when the chips are down.

Charlie and Wendy are only two extreme illustrations. For example, a case mid-way between the two might look like this:

- 25% U.S. total stock market
- 10% U.S. large-value stocks

- 10% U.S. small-value stocks
- 5% REITS
- 10% Foreign stocks
- 40% Short-term bonds

Your asset allocation may need to be radically different from the above examples based on your own circumstances, the most critical being your tax structure. (That is, how much of your assets are held in ordinary taxable accounts, and how much in sheltered retirement and annuity accounts.) We'll explore this in much greater detail in Chapter 12.

The comparison between Charlie and Wendy highlights the tradeoff between the benefits of diversification and the pain of tracking error. The superior expected return and risk of a highly diversified portfolio come at the price of tracking error—the risk that your portfolio will significantly lag the S&P 500, and thus the portfolios of your friends and neighbors—for years at a time, as happened during the late 1990s.

CHAPTER 4 SUMMARY

1. Past portfolio performance is only weakly predictive of future portfolio behavior. It is a mistake to design your portfolio on the basis of the past decade or two.
2. Your exact asset allocation is a function of your tolerance for risk, complexity, and tracking error.
3. The most important asset allocation decision revolves around the overall split between risky assets (stocks) and riskless assets (short-term bonds, bills, CDs, and money market funds).
4. The primary diversifying stock assets are foreign equity and REITs. The former should be less than 40% of your stock holdings, the latter less than 15%.
5. Exposure to small stocks, value stocks, and precious metals stocks is worthwhile, but not essential.

PILLAR TWO

The History of Investing

When Markets Go Berserk

About once every generation, the markets go barking mad. When this happens, most investors sustain serious damage, many are totally ruined. Unless you have been living at the bottom of a well these past several years, you are keenly aware that we are in the midst of such a period.

Markets can crash, but it is less well known that markets can also become depressed for decades at a time. The following two chapters will deal with the periods of euphoria and depression that occur on a fairly regular basis. The average investor lives through at least a few markets of both types.

Even with an appreciation of their behavior, dealing with both buoyant and morose markets is difficult. Sometimes even the best-prepared can fail. But if you are unprepared, you are *sure* to fail.

5

Tops: A History of Manias

Progress, far from consisting in change, depends on retentiveness. Those who cannot remember the past are condemned to repeat it.

George Santayana

There is nothing new—only the history you haven't read.

Larry Swedroe

Men of business have keen sensations but short memories.

Walter Bagehot

To many readers, this section on booms and busts will seem out of place. After all, this book is a humble how-to tome; it has no pretension of being a documentary work. But of the four key areas of investment knowledge—theory, history, psychology, and investment industry practices—the lack of historical knowledge is the one that causes the most damage. Consider, for example, the principals of Long Term Capital Management, whose ignorance of the vagaries of financial history almost single-handedly brought the Western financial system to its knees in 1998.

A knowledge of history is not essential in many fields. You can be a superb physician, accountant, or engineer and not know a thing about the origins and development of your craft. There are also professions where it is essential, like diplomacy, law, and military service. But in no field is a grasp of the past as fundamental to success as in finance.

Academics love to argue whether the primary historical driving forces over the ages are repetitive and cyclical or non-repetitive and progressive. But in finance, there is no controversy: the same speculative follies play out with almost clock-like regularity about once a generation. The aftermaths of these binges are a bit less uniform, but just as worthy of study.

I'm writing this chapter with great trepidation, because as my keyboard clacks, we are likely just past the cusp of one of the greatest speculative bubbles of all time. For this generation, the horses are already out of the barn, and it may be another 30 years—the typical interval between such episodes—until the warning implicit in this story is again fully useful.

I do not know if this time we will see the usual sequel that issues from periods of speculation, in which prices plummet as investors flee all except the safest securities, having previously embraced the riskiest. Although this chapter has just lost much of its timeliness, it is still the most important one in the book. For even if you can master the theory, psychology, and business of investing, your efforts will still come to naught if you cannot keep your head when everyone around you has lost his.

General Considerations

Manifestly, technological progress drives economic progress, which in turn drives stock prices. Should some malign force suddenly stop all scientific and technological innovation, then our standard of living would remain frozen at the present level; corporate profits would remain stationary, and stock prices, although fluctuating as they always have, would not experience any long-term rise. This point cannot be made forcefully enough: the great engine of stock returns is the *rate* of technological progress, not its absolute level.

I recently spoke at an investment conference at which a member of the audience, knowing that I was a physician, asked how the great strides in biotechnology were revolutionizing my medical practice. My reply was that these advances—gene therapy, DNA-based diagnostic testing, the flow of new surgical and angiography tools—had brought only marginal improvements on a day-to-day basis.

In fact, the greatest single advance in medicine occurred more than six decades ago, with the invention of sulfa drugs and penicillin. At a stroke, literally millions of lives, which had been previously lost to diseases such as bacterial pneumonia and meningitis, could now be saved. Not only that, those saved were predominantly the young. In contrast, today's advances disproportionately benefit the elderly. I do not think it likely that we shall again see the kind of medical progress experienced at the dawn of the antibiotic era.

We tend to think of technological progress as an ever-accelerating affair, but it just isn't so. Technological innovation comes in intense spurts. And the most impressive blooms were not at all recent. If you want to see the full force of scientific progress on human affairs, you have to go back almost two centuries. The technological explosion that occurred from 1820 to 1850 was undoubtedly the most deep and far reaching in human history, profoundly affecting the lives of those from the top to the bottom of the social fabric, in ways that can hardly be imagined today. Within a brief period, the speed of transportation increased tenfold, and communications became almost instantaneous.

For example, as late as the early 1800s, it took Jefferson ten days to travel from Monticello to Philadelphia, with considerable attendant expense, physical pain, and peril. By 1850, the steam engine made the same journey possible in one day, and at a tiny fraction of its former price, discomfort, and risk. Consider this passage from Stephen Ambrose's *Undaunted Courage:*

> A critical fact in the world of 1801 was that nothing moved faster than the speed of a horse. No human being, no manufactured item, no bushel of wheat, no side of beef, no letter, no information, no idea, order or instruction of any kind moved faster. Nothing had moved any faster, and, as far as Jefferson's contemporaries were able to tell, nothing ever would.

The revolution in communication was even more dramatic. For most of recorded history, information traveled as slowly as physical goods. With the invention of the telegraph by Cooke and Wheatstone in 1837, instantaneous telegraphy abruptly changed the face of economic, military, and political affairs in ways that can scarcely be comprehended by even our modern technologically jaded sensibilities. It is humbling to realize that the news of Grover Cleveland's election in 1884 traveled from New York to San Francisco and London almost as quickly as it would today. In other words, for the past century and a half, the transmission of essential news has been instantaneous. The advent of modern communication technology has simply facilitated the rapid dissemination of increasingly trivial information.

But that does not mean that the economic and financial effects of technological revolutions occur immediately. Not at all. The steam and internal combustion engines did not completely displace horses in the transport of bulk goods for nearly a century, and it took several decades for computers to travel from the laboratory into the office, and, finally, into the home. Immediately after their invention, the telegraph and telephone were the toys and tools of the wealthy. Ordinary people did not begin to routinely make long-distance calls until relatively recently.

I find the following analogy useful for understanding the diffusion of technology. Imagine a well hand pumped by a ponderous handle. Once every several seconds, a gush of water issues from the spout. The water is then funneled into a long pipe. From the perspective of the person at the pump handle—the innovator and the wealthy first-adopter—the water is clearly coming in spurts. But to the person at the end of the pipe—the average consumer, and, more importantly, the investor—the water is flowing evenly.

To illustrate the point, I've plotted the real gross domestic product (GDP) of the United States and Britain since 1820 on a semilog scale in Figure 5-1. Recall that the slope of a semilog plot at any point shows the true rate of growth. Note how relatively smooth and constant the rates of growth are in the two countries. The American plot slopes upward at 3.6% per year, and the British at about 1.9% per year. (Incidentally, this plot places the eclipse of the British empire in 1871, when its GDP was exceeded by that of the U.S.—about a quarter of a century earlier than suggested by the plot of consol interest rates.) About two-thirds of the difference in GDP growth between the two nations can be accounted for by the higher American population growth, and the other third by our increasing edge in labor efficiency.

The United States and Britain have been at the forefront of world technological progress for the past two centuries. What you are look-ing at is its flesh-and-blood track; it is also the engine of increasing stock prices.

On occasion, other nations have had even more rapid growth. For example, in the 50 years following World War II, Japan's economy grew at an astonishing 6.65% real rate. However, little of this was the result of technological innovation, but rather to "catch up" to the level of the rest of the world. Even today, labor productivity in Japan is far below that of the United States and western Europe. It is not a coinci-dence that Figures 5-1 and 1-1 have nearly the same appearance, as they are driven by the same factors.

Now things start to get interesting. Recall that technological progress comes in spurts, but that the economic and investment rewards driv-en by economic activity occur relatively evenly. The *capitalization* of technological ideas is as uneven as the innovative process itself, how-ever. This is because investment in new technologies is driven by the first blush of excitement surrounding their discovery. And it is almost uniformly a bad business. For example, investors in almost all of the early automobile companies did very poorly. Similarly, although RCA pioneered the young radio industry, most of its investors got taken to the cleaners in the wake of the 1929 crash.

Generations before academic research proved that investing in young tech companies yielded low returns, J.P. Morgan grasped this fact. Consequently, he almost always avoided unseasoned companies. He made only one exception—Edison's invention of the electric light bulb in 1879. Both Morgan and Edison realized the transformative nature of this device. Edison lacked the enormous capital required to build the bulb factories and power plants necessary to exploit it, but

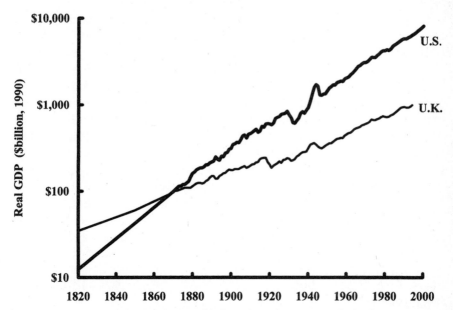

Figure 5-1. U.S. and U.K. real GDP ($billion, based on 1990 value). *(Source:* Angus Maddison, *The World Economy.)*

a consortium led by Morgan provided it. And, as almost always occurs, the lion's share of the ultimate reward did not fall to the original inventor. Unfortunately, Edison Electric, with its direct current technology, steadily lost ground to Westinghouse's more efficient alternating current system. When the two companies finally merged, Edison sold out in disgust, depriving himself of a great fortune. And, as he almost always did, Morgan prospered.

The key point is this: the funding, or capitalization, of transformative inventions is an intensely seductive activity. After all, who doesn't want to get in on the ground floor of the next General Motors, IBM, or Microsoft? From time to time, certain technologies capture the public imagination, and huge amounts of capital are hurled at companies promising to exploit them. In other words, the flow of capital to new technologies is driven not so much by demand from the innovators as by supply from an impressionable investing public.

This cycle has been occurring in fits and starts for the past three centuries, and an examination of the process demonstrates three things: First and foremost, the capitalization of the nation's great companies occurs largely during brief periods of public enthusiasm. Second, our society owes its success and prosperity to both the inventors and the financial backers of the technological process. And last, the returns to technology's investors are low.

Let's get a bit of nomenclature out of the way. When you and I purchase shares of stock or a mutual fund, according to strict economic
definition, we are not *investing*. After all, the money we pay for our
shares does not go to the companies, but, instead, to the previous
owner of the shares. In economic terms, we are not investing; we are
saving. (And, contrary to popular opinion, the overall economic effect
of saving is often negative.) Only when we purchase shares at a so-
called "initial public offering" (IPO) are we actually providing capital
for the acquisition of personnel, plant, and equipment. Only then are
we truly investing. Most of the time, we are buying and selling shares
in the "secondary market"; the company usually has no interest in the
flow of funds, since such activity does not directly impact it.

Here's the punch line: The returns on "real investing"—that is, the
purchase of IPOs—are ghastly. In 1991, academician Jay Ritter objec-
tively confirmed what most experienced investors have known for
generations—that the shares of new companies are a raw deal for
everyone but the underwriters. He found that from 1975 to 1984, IPOs
returned 10.37%—just 3% more than inflation—while the market
returned 17.41%. He concluded, in a triumph of academic understate-
ment, "Investors become periodically overoptimistic about the earnings potential of young growth companies." Ritter's conclusions have
since been confirmed by others and are also consistent with the sorry
showing by small-growth stocks discussed in Chapter 1, as most IPOs
fall into this category.

IPO investors thus deserve an honored place in our economic system—they are capitalism's unsung, if unwitting, philanthropists, bearing poor returns so that the rest of us may prosper. The spasmodic history of these philanthropic orgies is perhaps the most critical part of
any investor's (excuse me, *saver's*) education.

Diving For Dollars

Recall that the first stock exchanges were started in Paris, Amsterdam,
and London. The English "stock exchange" consisted of a cluster of
coffeehouses in the neighborhood of Change Alley. By the late seventeenth century, these coffeehouses became the most active and
advanced exchanges in the world. The average "stock jobber," as brokers were known, would have little trouble understanding the action
on the floors of the New York Stock Exchange or Chicago Mercantile,
although ordering a proper brew at Starbucks might strike them as
overly complex.

This revolution in financial engineering quickly found its way into
the era's emerging technologies. In 1687, William Phipps, a New

England sea captain, docked in England with 32 tons of silver raised from a Spanish pirate ship, enriching himself, his crew, and his backers beyond their wildest dreams. This captured the imagination of the investing public and before long, numerous patents were granted for various types of "diving engines," followed soon after by the flotation of even more numerous diving company stock issues. Almost all of these patents were worthless, submitted for the express purpose of creating interest in their company's stock. The ensuing ascent and collapse of the diving company stocks, culminating about 1689, could be said to be the first tech bubble. Daniel Defoe, of Robinson Crusoe fame, was the treasurer of one of those companies. His insider knowledge of their workings did not prevent his bankruptcy—one of the most spectacular of the age.

The diving companies never developed any credible operations, let alone earnings. This quickly became apparent to investors, and the madness was soon over. We don't have any records of exact prices and returns, but it's a sure bet that the eventual result of investment in all of these companies was total loss. It was very similar in this regard to the dot-com craze. Aside from Phipps' enterprise, no diving company had actually ever turned a profit, and it was not immediately clear how any of these companies could ensure access to a steady stream of treasure-laden wrecks. In modern parlance, all they had was a dubious business model.

For a few months, the shares of these companies rose dramatically. There was nothing unusual, *per se,* even three centuries ago, about the raising of capital for enterprises with questionable prospects. There was even nothing untoward about the shares of those enterprises rising temporarily in price. This is, after all, how capital markets work.

If you have trouble with the concept that such highly dubious enterprises can command a rational price, consider the following example: Assume that your neighbor Fritz tells you he thinks that sitting under his property is a huge reservoir of oil. He estimates that it is worth $10 million, but in order to produce it, he requires capital to pay for drilling equipment. He's willing to let you in for half the profits. How much would you be willing to stake him for?

Fritz has always been a bit dotty, but he's also a retired petroleum engineer, so there's a remote chance he is not blowing smoke. You estimate there is a one-in-a-thousand chance he's onto something. The expected payoff of your investment is thus $5 million (your half of his $10 million reservoir) divided by 1,000, or $5,000. Add in another factor of ten as a "risk premium," and you calculate that it might be reasonable to give your neighbor $500 for a piece of the action.

This is another way of saying that Fritz's adventure carries with it a low chance of success coupled with a high discount rate to compensate for its risk. Since you are applying such a high discount rate to the low expected cash flow, the share is worth very little. Further, subsequent reevaluation of your risk tolerance and of Fritz's chances of success will cause your estimation of the value of your share to fluctuate.

So it was not unusual that the shares of companies with dubious chances of success should have some value, or that this value should fluctuate. It's not unusual now (can you spell "biotech?"), and it was certainly not unusual 300 years ago. But from time to time, for reasons that are poorly understood, investors stop pricing businesses rationally. Rising prices take on a life of their own and a bubble ensues.

Monetary theorist Hyman Minsky comes as close to a reasonable explanation of bubbles as any. He postulates that there are at least two necessary preconditions. The first is a "displacement," which, in modern times, usually means a revolutionary technology or a major shift in financial methods. The second is the availability of easy credit—borrowed funds that can be employed for speculation. To those two, I would add two more ingredients. The first is that investors need to have forgotten the last speculative craze; this is why bubbles occur about once per generation. And second, rational investors, able to calculate expected payoffs and risk premiums, must become supplanted by those whose only requirement for purchase is a plausible story. Sadly, during bubbles, not a few of the former convert into the latter.

The last two conditions can be summarized in one word: euphoria. Investors begin purchasing assets for no other reason than the fact that prices are rising. Do not underestimate the power of this contagion. Listen to hedge fund manager Cliff Asness' observations on online trading in the late 1990s:

> I do not know if many of you have played video poker in Las Vegas. I have, and it is addicting. It is addicting despite the fact that you lose over any reasonable length period. Now, imagine video poker where the odds were in your favor. That is, all the little bells and buttons and buzzers were still there providing the instant feedback and fun, but instead of losing you got richer. If Vegas was like this, you would have to pry people out of their seats with the jaws of life. People would bring bedpans so they did not have to give up their seats. This form of video poker would laugh at crack cocaine as the ultimate addiction.

Or a somewhat dryer perspective, from economic historian Charles Kindleberger: "There is nothing so disturbing to one's well-being and judgment as to see a friend get rich." In the past several years, to lack this sense of exhilaration is to have been asleep. To recap, the necessary conditions for a bubble are:

- A major technological revolution or shift in financial practice.
- Liquidity—i.e., easy credit.
- Amnesia for the last bubble. This usually takes a generation.
- Abandonment of time-honored methods of security valuation, usually caused by the takeover of the market by inexperienced investors.

But whatever the underlying conditions, bubbles occur whenever investors begin buying stocks simply because they have been going up. This process feeds on itself, like a bonfire, until all the fuel is exhausted, and it finally collapses. The fuel, as Minsky points out, is usually borrowed cash or margin purchases.

The South Sea Bubble

The diving company bubble was, in fact, simply the warm-up for a far greater speculative orgy. Most bubbles are like Shakespeare's dramas and comedies: the costumes, dialect, and historical setting may be foreign, but the plot line and evocation of human frailty are intimately familiar to even the most casual observer of human nature.

The South Sea Bubble's origins were complex and require a bit of exposition. For starters, it was not one bubble, but two, both beginning in 1720: the first in France, followed almost immediately by one in England. As we saw in the first chapter, government debt was a relatively late arrival in the investment world, but once the warring nation-states of the late Middle Ages got a taste of the abundant military financing available from the issuance of state obligations, they could not get enough. By the mid-seventeenth century, Spain was hopelessly behind on its interest payments, and France was also rather deep in the hole to its debtors.

Into the financial chaos of Paris arrived a most extraordinary Scotsman: John Law. After escaping the hangman for killing a man in a 1694 duel, he studied the banking system in Amsterdam and eventually made his way to France, where he founded the Mississippi Company. He ingratiated himself with the Duke of Orléans, who, in 1719, granted the company two impressive franchises: a monopoly on trade with all of French North America, and the right to buy up rentes (French government annuities, similar to prestiti and consols) in exchange for company shares. The last issue was particularly attractive to the Royal Court, since investors would exchange their government bonds for shares of the Mississippi Company, relieving the government of its crushing war debts.

Law's so-called "system" contained one remarkable feature—the Mississippi Company would issue money as the price of its shares increased. Yes, the company issued its own currency, as did all banks of that time. This practice was one of the central mechanisms of pre-twentieth century finance. If the bank was sound and located nearby, its banknotes would usually be worth their face value. If it was unsound or further away, then its banknotes would trade at a considerable discount. (Of course, modern banks also print money when their loans are made in the form of a bank draft, as they almost always are.)

Now, all of the necessary ingredients for a bubble were present: a major shift in the financial system, liquidity from the company's new banknotes, and a hiatus of three decades from the last speculation. In 1720, as the Mississippi Company's shares rose, it issued more notes, which purchased more shares, increasing its price still more. Vast paper fortunes were made, and the word *millionaire* was coined. The frenzy spilled over the entire continent, where new ventures were floated with the vast amounts of capital now available.

There was even a fashionable new technology involved: the laws of probability. Fermat and Pascal had recently invented this branch of mathematics, and, in 1693, Astronomer Royal Edmund Halley developed the first mortality tables. Soon the formation of insurance companies became all the rage; these would figure prominently as the speculative action moved to London.

The ancien régime was not the only government deep in hock. By 1719, England had incurred immense debts during the War of the Spanish Succession. In fact, a decade before, in 1710, the South Sea Company had actually exchanged government debt held by investors for its shares and had been granted the right to a monopoly on trade with the Spanish Empire in America. The government, in exchange for taking over its debt, also paid the South Sea Company an annuity.

But neither the Mississippi Company nor the South Sea Company ever made any money from their trade monopolies. The French company never really tried, and war and Spanish intransigence blocked British trade with South America. (In any event, none of South Sea's directors had any experience with South American trade.) The Mississippi Company was just a speculative shell. The situation of the South Sea Company was a bit more complex, as it did receive an income stream from the government.

Unfortunately, its deal with the government was structured in a most peculiar manner. The South Sea Company was allowed to issue a fixed number of shares that could be exchanged for the government debt it bought up from investors. In other words, investors would exchange their bonds, bills, and annuities for stock in the company. The higher the share price of the company, the fewer the shares it had to pay investors, and the more shares that were left over for the directors to sell on the open market.

So it suited the South Sea Company to inflate its price. The liquidity sloshing through the European financial system in 1720 allowed it to do so. At some point, the share price took on a life of its own, and investors were happy to exchange their staid annuities, bonds, and bills for the rapidly rising shares. The directors took advantage of the meteoric price increase to issue several more lots of stock to the public: first for government debt, then for money. The later purchasers were allowed to purchase on margin with a 20% down payment, the remainder being due in subsequent payments. In the case of the South Sea Company, even this was a fiction, as many of the down payments were themselves made with borrowed money. In the summer of 1720, share values peaked on both sides of the channel; the last subscription was priced at £1,000 and was sold out in less than a day. (The stock price was about £130 at the start of the bubble.) The South Sea Company involved itself in a fair amount of skullduggery. The government became alarmed at the rapidly rising share price—there were still some gray heads remaining who had lived through the diving company debacle—and parliament proposed limiting the share price. In the process of blocking this, the company provided under-the-table shares (which in fact were counterfeit) to various notables, including the king's mistress, and the price limitation was scotched.

The most fantastic manifestation of the speculation was the appearance of the "bubble companies." With the easy availability of capital produced by the boom, all sorts of dubious enterprises issued shares to a gullible public. Most of these enterprises were legitimate but just a bit ahead of their time, such as one company to settle the region around Australia (a half century before the continent was actually discovered by Cook), another to build machine guns, and yet another that proposed building ships to transport live fish to London. A lesser number were patently fraudulent, and still others lived only in later legend, including a famous mythical company chartered "for carrying on an undertaking of great advantage but no one to know what it is." Interestingly, two of the 190 recorded bubble companies eventually did succeed: the insurance giants Royal Exchange and London Assurance.

The South Sea Company grew anxious over competition for capital from the bubble companies, and, in June 1720, had parliament pass the Bubble Act. This legislation required all new companies to obtain parliamentary charters and forbade existing companies from operating beyond their charters. Paradoxically, this was their undoing. Since many of the insurance companies, which helped sustain the frenzy by lending substantial amounts to the South Sea Company and its share-holders, started out in other lines of business, they were forced to cease operation. Prime among them was the Sword Blade Company, which, naturally enough, was chartered only to make swords. When the Bubble Act forced the withdrawal of their credit from the market, the effect was electric: the bubble was pricked. By October, it was all over.

The South Sea episode was a true mania, enveloping the populace from King George on down. Jonathan Swift best summarized England's mood at the time:

> I have enquired of some that have come from London, what is the religion there? They tell me it is the South Sea stock. What is the policy of England? The answer is the same. What is the trade? South Sea still. And what is the business? Nothing but South Sea.

A foreign visitor to Change Alley was more succinct, stating that it looked "as if all the lunatics had escaped out of the madhouse at once."

Neither the Mississippi Company nor the South Sea Company had any real prospects of foreign trade. While the former had no revenues at all, the latter had at least a stream of income from the government. Contemporary observers, eyeballing this cash flow, estimated the fair value of South Sea Company at about £150 per share, precisely where it wound up after the dust had settled.

Let's reflect on the four conditions necessary for the blowing of a bubble. First, Minsky's "displacement," which, in this case, was the unprecedented substitution of public debt with private equity. The sec-ond was the availability of easy credit, particularly the self-perpetuat-ing output of paper money from the Mississippi Company. Third was the 30-year hiatus following the diving company episode. The last con-dition was the increasing domination of the market by nonprofession-als clueless about asset valuation.

Although Fisher's discounted dividend method lay two centuries in the future, for centuries, investors had an intuitive working grasp of how to value an income stream, in the same way that ball players are able to catch fly balls without knowing the ballistic equations. Reasonable investors might debate whether the intrinsic value of South Sea Shares was £100 or £200, but no one could make a rational case for £1,000. And the more speculative bubble companies, which in nor-mal times might be valued like your neighbor Fritz's oil well, saw their prices go through the roof.

This, then, is the essence of a bubble: a brief period of rising prices and suspended disbelief, which, in turn, supplies large numbers of investors willing to invest in dubious enterprises at absurdly low discount rates and high prices. Bubbles streak across the investment heavens, leaving behind financial destruction and disillusionment, respecting neither intelligence nor social class. Probably the most famous dupe of the South Sea episode was none other than Sir Isaac Newton, who famously remarked, "I can calculate the motions of the heavenly bodies, but not the madness of people."

The Duke's Failed Romance

The first technological marvel that can be properly said to have transformed modern life was the development of large-scale canal transport. In 1758, the Duke of Bridgewater, heartbroken by an unsuccessful romance, concocted the radical notion of building a canal to bring coal from his mines to a group of textile mills 30 miles away. Completed nine years later and financed to the brink of his estate's financial ruin, this eventually proved enormously profitable, and within 20 years, more than 1,000 miles of canals laced the English countryside.

The initial returns on the first canal companies were highly agreeable, and their shares soared. Naturally, the profits made by early investors aroused a great deal of attention and set into motion the by now familiar process. Large amounts of capital were raised from a gullible public for the construction of increasingly marginal routes. Dividends, which were as high as 50% for the first companies, slowly disappeared as competing routes proliferated.

Bubbles are pricked when liquidity dries up. In this particular case, it was the disappearance of easy credit brought on by the French Revolution that produced a generalized price collapse. By the turn of the century, only 20% of the companies paid a dividend.

The canal-building bubble was the first of its kind, involving a business that not only provided healthy profits but also transformed and benefited society in profound and long-lasting ways. Although the average speed of canal transport was only a few miles per hour, it was a vast improvement over road conveyance, which was much slower, more dangerous, and less reliable. Until the canals, sea transport was far more efficient. Travel from, say, London to Glasgow, was many times cheaper, faster, and safer by sea than by land, although it was by no means a sure thing, either. For the first time, thousands of inland villages were brought into contact with the outside world, changing England forever.

The canal building episode is also an object lesson for those who become enthusiastic over the investment possibilities of new technology. Even if it is initially highly profitable, nothing attracts competition like a cash cow. Rest assured, if you have identified a "sure thing," you will not keep it a secret for long; you will attract competitors who will rapidly extinguish the initial flow of the easy profits.

The canals established a pattern that has held to this day—of transformative inventions that bring long-run progress and prosperity to society as a whole, short-run profits to an early lucky few, and ruin to most later investors.

A Very Profitable Clock

The canal episode also established another pattern in the finance of innovative technologies: it is the users, not the makers, who benefit. Over the long run, the canal operators did not profit nearly as much as the businesses that used the new method of transport, particularly the building and manufacturing trades that thrived in the newly prosperous inland towns.

The best example of this is a device invented about the same time as the blowing of the canal bubble: the marine chronometer. Profitable sea trade requires accurate navigation. This, in turn, demands the precise measurement of latitude (north/south position) and longitude (east/west position). The determination of latitude is a relatively easy task, and by the mid-eighteenth century, had been practiced for hundreds of years—a sea captain simply needs an accurate midday measurement of the sun's elevation.

But longitude is a much tougher nut. By the eighteenth century, seafarers realized that the most likely route to success lay in the development of a highly accurate timepiece. If a navigator could determine the local solar noon—the maximum elevation of the sun—and also know the time in London at the same moment, he then would know just how far east or west of London he was.

This required a timepiece that could keep time to within one-quarter of a second per day over a six-week journey—at sea. Master craftsman John Harrison finally accomplished this amazing feat in 1761. His clock—the so-called "H4," is considered a technological marvel even today; two and a half centuries ago, it was the equivalent of the space shuttle. But the key point is this: neither Harrison, nor his heirs, nor his professional successors ever made very much money from this crucial invention. In fact, the clock industry has no real investment history. Until Swatch and Rolex, no great timekeeping boodles were made. But the users of this technology—the East India

Company and the other great trading corporations of England and Holland—made vast fortunes with it. This is another early demonstration of the basic rule of technology investing: it is the *users,* and not the *makers,* who profit most.

Queen Victoria and Her Subjects Get Taken for a Ride

The reason why the invention of the marine chronometer did not produce an investment bubble was that its effects were not immediately visible. But if any technological marvel was both visible and revolutionary at the same time, it was the invention of the railway steam engine. Until the advent of steam power in the nineteenth century, long-distance overland travel was almost exclusively the province of the rich. Only they could afford the exorbitant fares of the coach companies, or if truly wealthy, their own coach-and-six. And even then, the poor quality of the roads and public safety made travel a dangerous, slow, and extremely uncomfortable endeavor.

At a stroke, the railroads made overland travel cheap, safe, rapid, and relatively comfortable. Even more importantly, the steam engine was undoubtedly the most dramatic, romantic, and artistically appealing technological invention of any age (aside from, perhaps, the clipper ship). Fanny Kemble, a famous actress of the period, captured the mood precisely after her first trip at the footplate of George Stephenson's *Rocket*. She found it:

> . . . . a snorting little animal which I felt inclined to pat. It set out at the utmost speed, 35 miles per hour, swifter than the bird flies. You cannot conceive what that sensation of cutting the air was; the motion as smooth as possible. I could either have read or written; and as it was I stood up and with my bonnet off drank the air before me. When I closed my eyes this sensation of flying was quite delightful and strange beyond description. Yet strange as it was, I had a perfect sense of security and not the slightest fear.

The public sensation surrounding rail travel was unimaginable to the modern reader—it was the jet airliner, personal computer, Internet, and fresh-brewed espresso all rolled into one. The first steam line was established between Darlington and Stockton in 1825, and in 1831, the Liverpool and Manchester Line began producing healthy dividends and soaring stock prices. This euphoria carried with it a bull market in railroad stocks, followed by a sharp drop in prices in the bust of 1837.

However, a second stock mania, the likes of which had not been seen in Britain before or since, ensued when Queen Victoria made her first railway trip in 1842. Her ride ignited a popular enthusiasm for rail travel that even modern technology enthusiasts might find difficult to fathom. Just as people today speak of "Internet time," in the 1840s "railway time" was the operative phrase. For the first time, people began to talk of distances in hours and minutes, instead of days and miles. Men were said to "get up a head of steam."

By late 1844, the three largest railway companies were paying a 10% dividend, and by the beginning of 1845, 16 new lines were planned and 50 new companies chartered. These offerings usually guaranteed dividends of 10% and featured MPs and aristocrats on their boards, who were generally paid handsomely with under-the-table shares. Dozens of magazines and newspapers were devoted to railway travel, supported by hundreds of thousands of pounds in advertising for the new companies' stock subscriptions. Nearly 8,000 miles of new railways were planned—four times the existing trackage.

By late summer 1845, with existing shares up 500%, at least 450 new companies were registered. Foreign lines were being projected around the globe, from the Bengal to Guyana. More than 100 new lines were planned for Ireland alone. In the latter part of the bubble, lines were planned literally from nowhere to nowhere, with no towns along the way. The Minsky "displacement" here was obvious. Credit was equally abundant: In the 1840s, it took the form of the subscription mechanism of purchase, in which an investor "subscribed" to the issue for a small fraction of the purchase price and was subject to "calls" for the remaining price as construction capital was needed. And, as in all bubbles, the sudden contraction of credit punctured it. By 1845, with building underway, investors sold existing shares to meet the calls for the capital necessary. By mid-October 1845, it was all over. Reporting the fiasco, the *Times of London* introduced the word "bubble" into popular financial lexicon when it proclaimed:

"A mighty bubble of wealth is blown away before our eyes."

The rapid contraction of liquidity cascaded through the British financial world in the following years, almost taking the Bank of England with it. Even consols fell; only gold provided a safe haven.

Until last year, it was commonly remarked that since so many thought the tech stock scene a bubble, it must not, in fact, be one. And yet, in the summer of 1845, it was apparent to anyone with an IQ above room temperature that railway shares would end badly. Much was also written in the press as to just how it would all end. No less than Prime Minister Robert Peel warned, "Direct interference on our part with the mania of railway speculation seems impracticable. The only question is whether public attention might not be called to the impending danger, through the public press." In short, Britain's most brilliant prime minister did everything but shout "irrational exuberance!" at the top of his lungs in Parliament.

The United States underwent its own railway mania in the post-Civil War period. But even taking into account the clocklike regularity of railroad bankruptcy and the Credit Mobilier scandal (in which this construction arm of Union Pacific plundered the parent company, not unlike the recent Enron scandal), things were a bit tamer here than in England. This was because U.S. companies were mainly financed with bonds, which are not as prone to bubbles as equity.

Nonetheless, the experience of the U.S. railway companies is instructive. Because of murderous competition from the scourge of railways and canals—competing parallel routes—these companies frequently went bankrupt, and returns to investors were low. On the other hand, the societal benefit of the railroads was immeasurable, allowing the settling and growth of the breadth of the continent. The financial rewards from the railroads went to the businessmen, builders, and particularly real estate brokers in places like Omaha, Sacramento, and a small junction town called Chicago.

"Wall Street Lays an Egg"

So quipped the headline of the entertainment newspaper *Variety* on the morning of Tuesday, October 30, 1929. Worse, the most famous of all market crashes was just the opening act of the longest and most painful episode in American financial history. Actually, the market rebounded nicely soon after the crash, erasing much of the pain. By early 1930, it was at a higher level than at the beginning of 1929. But for the next two years, the market relentlessly fell, reducing stock prices to a fraction of their former value and taking the rest of the economy with it.

The bubble in stock prices which preceded it was equally legendary, and, of necessity, inseparable from it. Once again, the "displacement" was technological. The early twentieth century saw a rate of innovation second only to that of the post-Napoleonic period. The aircraft, automobile, radio, electrical generator, and the devices it powered—most importantly Edison's light bulb—all burst upon the scene within a few decades. And once again, an expansion of credit loosened the investment floodgates.

Ironically, if blame can be assigned anywhere, it probably belongs to Winston Churchill, who, as Chancellor of the Exchequer, reinstated the gold standard and fixed the pound sterling at its prewar value of $4.86. Because of Britain's wartime inflation, this was a gross overvaluation, making British goods overly expensive abroad and foreign goods correspondingly cheap. The result was a gross trade imbalance that rapidly depleted the British Treasury of gold. The traditional solution for trade imbalance is to get your trading partners to reduce their interest rates; because low rates make investing in your partners unattractive, money flows out of those countries back to yours, solving the problem.

Unfortunately, low interest rates in the U.S. also made it easier to borrow money. In 1927, the U.S. was in the middle of an economic boom, and the last thing it needed was easier credit brought about by the lowered American interest rates sought by the British. Most American financial authorities realized that this was an awful idea. Unfortunately, Benjamin Strong, the chairman of the Federal Reserve Bank, and Montagu Norman, the Governor of the Bank of England, were close personal friends. Strong, who dominated the Fed, got his way and interest rates were lowered. This was the equivalent of throwing gasoline onto a fire.

Also in place was the third bubble ingredient. It had been more than a generation since the last great railroad enthusiasm, and there were not enough gray heads left to warn that the path led straight over a cliff. At about the same time, the final component of the mix was added as millions of ordinary citizens, completely ignorant of the principles of asset valuation, were sucked into the market by the irresistible temptation of watching their friends and neighbors earning effortless profits. They were joined by tens of thousands of professionals who should have known better. Over the subsequent two and a half years, stock prices rose more than 150%.

Of all history's great bubbles, the 1920s bull market was the most "rational." Between 1920 and 1929, real GDP rose almost 50%, seemingly confirming the optimists' predictions of a "new era" born of scientific progress. Further, by today's standards, stocks were positively cheap. Until 1928, they sold at approximately ten times earnings and yielded about 5% in dividends. Even at the peak, in the summer of 1929, stocks fetched just 20 times earnings, and dividends fell only to 3%. Again, tame by today's standards.

The great bull market of the Roaring Twenties was recognized as a bubble only in retrospect. How else do you explain a price drop of 90%? Of course, there were plenty of individual stocks that were ridiculously overpriced, some the result of rampant speculation and others of outright fraud. But the history of the 1920s bubble is better told with descriptive history than with numbers.

The signature characteristic of the era was the stock pool, which consisted of a group of wealthy speculators who would get together with the exchange's specialist (the floor trader charged with providing a market for the chosen stock) to drive up a stock's price. They would begin by slowly accumulating a sizeable block of a particular stock at low prices, then commence trading with each other in carefully choreographed fashion, driving the price up and down on gradually increasing volume. As this artificial activity flashed across the ticker tape, the investing public would become aware that something was afoot, or, in the parlance of the day, that the stock was "being taken in hand." If executed properly, the stock price would be lifted on a frenzy of speculative buying by the public, at which point the pool operators would "pull the plug" and sell.

The execution of a proper pool was a high art form, its most accomplished impresario being none other than Joseph P. Kennedy, Sr. Naturally enough, a few years later, he was appointed first commissioner of the Securities and Exchange Commission (SEC). Roosevelt famously justified his appointment of the old rogue by saying, "It takes a thief to catch a thief."

In fact, until the passage of the Securities Act of 1934, which established the SEC, the pools were perfectly legal. The most famous pools of all involved Radio Corporation of America, fondly known back then simply as "Radio." The names of Radio pool participants still astound the modern reader: Walter Chrysler; Charles Schwab, the distinguished head of U.S. Steel; Mrs. David Sarnoff, wife of Radio's president and founder; Percy Rockefeller; Joseph Tumulty, former aide to President Wilson; and last but not least, John J. Raskob, who we've already encountered, and, by the time of the pool, was head of the Democratic National Committee.

The second unique institution of the 1920s was the "investment trust." Like the modern mutual fund, it had professional managers operating large portfolios of both stocks and bonds. The key difference was that the investment trusts were themselves traded as stocks and touted to small investors as a way of obtaining diversified portfolios managed by experts. In most regards, they were identical to today's closed-end funds, and a few still survive (General American Investors, Tri-Continental, Adams Express, and Central Securities are examples). In fact, investment trusts had been a feature of the English and Scottish financial landscape for several decades, allowing small investors to diversify across a wide range of investments with just a few dozen pounds.

At first these trusts were conservatively run, but as the Roaring Twenties progressed, they began to pyramid themselves using borrowed capital similar to the "margin purchases" used by individual plungers. These "leveraged trusts" would magnify small changes in the levels of individual stocks into wild swings in the trust's price.

The Götterdämmerung was supplied by Goldman Sachs, which did not get into the trust business until late 1928. The Goldman Sachs Corporation sponsored the Goldman Sachs Trading Corporation to the tune of $100 million. Two months later, in February 1929, it merged with another trust sponsored by its parent company, the Financial and Industrial Securities Corporation. By a few days later, the merged trust was selling for twice its assets under management.

Most securities firms would have been happy with this agreeable showing, but Goldman was just getting warmed up. The merged trust began buying shares of itself, boosting its value still more. It then unloaded these inflated shares on the public. William Crapo Durant, a well-known former official of General Motors like Mr. Raskob, played a highly visible role in this fraud. More, the Trading Corporation itself sponsored another huge trust, the Shenandoah Corporation. Then, just 25 days later, the Shenandoah Corporation sponsored the Blue Ridge Corporation. Both of the new companies had on their boards a young lawyer named John Foster Dulles. (John Kenneth Galbraith, in his 1954 history of the crash, was barely able to conceal his glee over the past indiscretions of Dulles, who was by then the arch-conservative Secretary of State.) Finally, in August, the Trading Corporation acquired an enormous structure of nested West Coast trusts.

Goldman Sach's timing, of course, could not have been worse. Black Thursday was just several weeks away. The trusts collapsed pretty much in the reverse order of their creation, consistent with their increasing leverage: first Blue Ridge, then Shenandoah, and finally, the Trading Corporation. Shenandoah, which had been trading at 36 soon after its formation, fell to 3 by the end of October and touched 50 cents in 1932.

The crash of 1929 and its aftermath scarred the psyche of a generation of American investors, providing them with a particularly expensive lesson in Fisher's rules of capital value. It would take the passage of that generation before the ground would again become fertile for the seeds of financial speculation.

The Go-Go Market and the Nifty Fifty

The speculative binge spanning the years 1960 to 1972 was unlike any other in the history of finance, encompassing not one, but three different bubbles. No sooner would one burst than the next was inflated. As the stock market gradually went sour in the early 1970s, more and more investors crowded into the supposed shelter of the "safe" large-cap growth stocks, until finally they, too, collapsed of their own weight, beginning the descent into the awful bear market of 1973–74.

It should not surprise any of you by now that the first stirrings of speculative fever began in the late 1950s, almost exactly 30 years from 1929. For almost three decades, prudent investors bought only bonds and avoided common stocks at all costs. Then the generational Wall Street waltz finally took yet another pass in front of the band, and things began to pick up again.

Minsky's "displacement" this time around was the space race, and the magic words were "sonics" and "tronics." The company names seem dated, almost laughable today: Videotronics, Hydro-Space Technology, Circuitronics, and even Powertron Ultrasonics. (Although not nearly as ridiculous as the names of today's dot-coms will sound a few decades hence.) The initial public offerings of these companies were spectacular affairs, with typical first-day price rises of 50% to 100% followed by a rapid ascent, culminating in the inevitable price collapse as investors realized that earnings would not be forthcoming in the foreseeable future. The Tronics boom was a relatively small footnote in market history, significant mainly for its entertainment value (unless you happened to be one of the pigeons holding stock in those companies).

More serious was the acquisition frenzy that followed, which swallowed up large swaths of the nation's productive assets into increasingly inefficient, unwieldy conglomerates. For the better part of a century after the passage of the Sherman Antitrust Act in 1890, corporate America had looked for a way to achieve economies of scale without bringing down the government's wrath. Frustrated by the legal restrictions forbidding the acquisition of companies in the same industry, companies hit upon the notion of conglomeration—the building of huge multi-industry companies.

What happened next was completely unexpected. The conglomerates began to rise in value as the investing world perceived that their acquisitions would dramatically increase overall profitability. These companies could then use their overvalued stock to buy yet more companies. As more and more companies were gobbled up, the earnings of the consumed companies were added to the balance sheets of the conglomerates. Naïve investors were then presented with apparently rapidly increasing corporate earnings, mistaking this for increased efficiency. Prices ballooned even further, allowing the conglomerate to purchase even more companies. The banal nature of the industries under their wings was dressed up with impressive jargon: a zinc mine became a "space minerals division," shipbuilding became "marine systems," and meatpacking became "nutritional services."

At its height, the four biggest conglomerates—A-T-O, Litton, Teledyne, and Textron—sold for 25 to 56 times earnings. Pretty heady stuff for what were essentially collections of smokestack companies. Finally, in 1968, the music stopped when Litton announced an earnings disappointment, and the whole house of cards collapsed, with the Four Horsemen falling over 60% each.

Worse was to come. There comes a point when the efficiencies of scale bought by increasing size are outweighed by the more subtle disadvantages of sheer bureaucratic weight. Even companies in industries that benefit most from economies of scale—aircraft and automobiles, for example—eventually suffer when they grow too large, as happened recently with DaimlerChrysler. (And in some industries, such as medical care, the optimal company size is quite small—perhaps as few as a hundred employees—a fact belatedly recognized by the recent executives and shareholders of most HMO corporations.)

So by the mid-1960s, corporate America found itself blessed not by efficient multi-industry juggernauts, but rather cursed by stumbling behemoths with rapidly falling profitability.[1] And by 1970, investors had had it. They were fed up with flaky tech companies and corporate investors who could wheel and deal with the best but who couldn't operate a profitable company if their lives depended on it. They wanted safety, stability, and excellence—established companies that dominated their industry and had the proven ability to generate genuine growth.

Thus was born the "one decision stock": buy it, forget about it, and hold on to it forever. So investors loaded up on the bluest of the blue chips—IBM, Xerox, Avon, Texas Instruments, Polaroid—great companies all, at least in the early 1970s. Even in normal times, these companies were not cheap, selling at 20 to 25 times earnings with minuscule dividends. But these were not normal times. By 1972, McDonald's and Disney had risen to over 70 times earnings, and Polaroid to nearly 100.

The whole group of 50 stocks sold at 42 times earnings. What does a ratio of price-to-earnings (P/E) of 42 mean? Doing the same sort of calculation we did in Table 2-1, we discover that in order for a stock to increase in price by 11% per year (i.e., obtain the market return), it must increase its earnings by about 20% per year for a period of ten years. Now, it is not usual for individual companies to do this. *But it*

---

[1]This nightmare played out in reverse in the 1980s with leveraged buyouts, in which the formerly acquired companies were spun back off with the use of debt of varying quality, and the investing public became rapidly acquainted with the meaning of "junk bonds." These companies, in hock up to their eyeballs, often wound up in Chapter 11, damaging not only individual bondholders but imperiling the banks and insurance companies that held the defaulted bonds issued by these companies.

is impossible for the biggest of the nation's companies to all do so at the same time. As you saw in Figure 2-4, the long-term growth rate of corporate earnings and dividends is only 5% per year.

Almost all of these companies eventually disappointed, some more than others. The results for the stockholder were highly disagreeable.

Professor Jeremy Siegel makes the point that the Nifty Fifty were not bad long-term investments, with subsequent long-term returns nearly identical to the market. This is true, as far as it goes. The only trouble was that along the way most of these stocks lost between 70% and 95% of their value, and many never came back. A portfolio of stocks with market return and greater-than-market risk is not a blessing. Very few of the original shareholders calmly held on for the long run.

The Nifty Fifty provided another moral as well. The seven most recognizable tech names on the list—IBM, Texas Instruments, AMP, Xerox, Burroughs, Digital Equipment, and Polaroid—had truly awful returns—just 6.4% per year for the 25 years following 1972. But the cheapest 25 of the group by P/E had a return of 14.4% versus a return of 12.9% for the S&P 500. These "cheap" stocks, generally selling at P/Es of 25 to 40, were consumer companies—Phillip Morris, Gillette, and Coke. They did not produce the era's technology, but they certainly used it to advantage. So history once again demonstrated that the spoils went not to technology's makers, but to its users.

Yahoo!

A small confession. I could never decide which part of speech this corporate moniker was supposed to represent. Was it an interjection, reflecting the technological and economic ebullience of the time, or was it simply a noun, meant to describe the company's shareholders?

Since the definitive history of this sorry era in investing has yet to be written, you will be stuck with my fragmentary impressions. But there are a few things that can already be said about the Great Internet Bubble. First, in the past few years, we have all had bestowed upon us a morbid historical privilege, not unlike being present at the 1906 San Francisco earthquake. I can remember the sheer wonder of my first reading of Mackay's *Extraordinary Popular Delusions and the Madness of Crowds,* which described the Dutch Tulip, South Sea, and Mississippi Company episodes. What must it have been like to live in such a time, I wondered? Now you and I know. Not since the diving and bubble companies of the seventeenth and eighteenth centuries have entities with so little substance commanded such high prices. If we were not personally touched by these shooting stars, we all knew people who were.

The April 2000 edition of the Morningstar Principia Pro stock module occupies an honored spot on my hard drive, and from time to time I sift through the names with awe: Terra Networks, selling at 1,200 times *sales;* Akamai Technologies, 3,700 times *sales;* Telocity, 5,200 times *sales*. Not a one with *earnings*. What were we thinking?

My all-time favorite is Internet Capital Group. On August 5, 1999, it went public at $6 per share, rose to $212, then fell back to under a buck. Nothing unusual, really. What made it such an enchanted soul was that it was the direct descendant of the 1920s leveraged investment trusts—its holdings were small, private companies operating in the most wild and wooly part of the Internet scene—business-to-business (B2B). It actually issued *bonds,* which were of the same quality as those issued by my butcher at Safeway, if only the SEC would allow him to do so. The frosting on the cake was that it sold at an estimated ten times the value of the companies it held. So it not only owned just fluff, but was valued at ten times the fluff it held.

Again, all the ingredients were in place: First, Minsky's "displacement," this time in the guise of yet another revolutionary invention. Second, liquidity in the form of a Federal Reserve as accommodating as any red-light district house of pleasure. Third, yet another generation under the bridge since the last smashup. And, finally, one more joyous abandonment of Fisher's iron laws.

These stories of financial excess, from the diving company bubble to the dot-com mania, are not just entertaining yarns, they are also a mortal warning to all investors. There will always be speculative markets in which the old rules seem to go out the window. Learn to recognize the signs: technological or financial "displacement," excessive use of credit, amnesia for the last bubble, and the flood of new investors who swallow plausible stories in place of doing the hard math.

When this happens, keep a close hold on your wallet and remember John Templeton's famous warning: The four most expensive words in the English language are, "This time, it's different."

6

Bottoms: The Agony and the Opportunity

I'll admit that the last chapter is a bit disingenuous. You can only identify a bubble after it bursts. This was particularly true of the 1920s. From January 1920 to September 1929, the market's total return (dividends included) was an astonishing 20% per year. As sure as night follows day, should not a bust follow such a boom? And yet, as we've already seen, the market's precipitous rise was accompanied by strong economic fundamentals, suggesting a sound basis for the run-up. Further, similar near-20% returns have also occurred during other ten-year periods: from 1942 to 1952, 1949 to 1959, and 1982 to 1992. But none of these was followed by a crash.

Just as markets periodically suffer bouts of mania and gross over-valuation, so too do they regularly become absurdly despondent. Just as investors must deal rationally with irrational exuberance, they must also be able to handle pervasive gloom. The Great Internet Bubble will not be the last of its kind, but if history is any guide, we should not see anything approaching it until the next generation of investors takes leave of its senses, sometime around the year 2030. If the current generation gets caught out again, we should be very disappointed, as no previous generation has been so dense as to have been fooled twice. But then again, the Boomers have shown a singular talent for gullibility, and there is still plenty of time.

Of more immediate relevance to the long-term investor is the possibility of a period of low returns and pervasive pessimism. We've implicitly dealt with this in the second chapter when we examined the low estimate of future stock returns calculated from the Gordon Equation. On a more basic level, it is a simple mathematical fact that high past returns reduce future returns. In general, a high purchase price is not a good thing. And if expected returns are low, then the laws of statistics tell us that a severe downturn becomes more likely. In other words, if the expected return is 6% instead of 11%, normal variation about a lower average return will make the bad years look even worse.

One concept that is ignored by even the most sophisticated financial players is that over the long haul, risk and return become the same thing. Optimists will point out that there has never been a 30-year period in which stocks returned less than bonds. But this is simply because stocks have averaged 6% more return than bonds. Given this yearly advantage, it is almost impossible to string together 30 years in which stocks will not win. In other words, the long-term apparent safety of stocks was due to a combination of high stock returns, powered partially by 5% dividends, and low bond returns, due to unexpected inflation. Neither of these factors is likely to be present in the future. If the expected return of stocks is only 1% or 2% more than bonds, then because of random variability, the 30-year dominance of stocks over bonds is no longer a sure thing.

And even if stocks do maintain their 6% advantage over bonds—an extremely unlikely event, in my view—they can still underperform safer assets for very long periods, as happened from 1966 to 1983 when they underperformed both Treasury bills and inflation. Imagine: 17 years with zero real stock returns.

What we'll do in this short chapter is to take a look at what it's like to live and invest through such a period. Unless you were actively investing in stocks in 1966, you will benefit from a description of what the investment equivalent of 40 miles of bad road felt like. And even if you were around then, it doesn't hurt to be reminded.

Although each of the bubbles described in the last chapter was followed by a terrible bear market, we're only going to cover some of them, and not in exact sequence. We will, however, deal with the look and feel of these grim periods in a general way, exploring the reasons why they occur. We'll even formulate a set of "reverse Minsky criteria" for busts, which are the mirror image of those required for a bubble. And, finally, we'll muse over the societal and legislative reactions to these periods.

"The Death of Equities"

Readers of *BusinessWeek* were greeted with a cover story titled "The Death of Equities" in August 1979, and few had trouble believing it. The Dow Jones Industrial Average, which had toyed with the 1,000 level in January 1973, was now trading at 875 six and a half years later.

Worse, inflation was running at almost 9%. A dollar invested in the stock market in 1973 now purchased just 71 cents of goods, even allowing for reinvested dividends. With the kind permission of McGraw-Hill, I quote extensively from this morbid portrait of a market bottom:

> The masses long ago switched from stocks to investments having higher yields and more protection from inflation. Now the pension funds—the market's last hope—have won permission to quit stocks and bonds for real estate, futures, gold, and even diamonds. The death of equities looks like an almost permanent condition—reversible someday, but not soon.

The contrast in the mood evoked above with today's investment mindset cannot be more divergent. Diamonds, gold, and real estate? Most certainly. The price of the yellow metal had risen from $35 per ounce in 1968 to more than $500 in 1979 and would peak at over $800 the following year. Just as today, everyone's neighbors have gotten rich in the stock market, 20 years ago the wise and lucky had purchased their houses for a song with 6% mortgages and by 1980 were sitting on real capital wealth beyond their wildest dreams. Stocks and bonds? "Paper assets," sneered the conventional wisdom. The article continued:

> At least 7 million shareholders have defected from the stock market since 1970, leaving equities more than ever the province of giant institutional investors. And now the institutions have been given the go-ahead to shift more of their money from stocks—and bonds—into other investments. If the institutions, who control the bulk of the nation's wealth, now withdraw billions from both the stock and bond markets, the implications for the U.S. economy could not be worse. Says Robert S. Salomon Jr., a general partner in Salomon Brothers:
> "We are running the risk of immobilizing a substantial portion of the world's wealth in someone's stamp collection."

This excerpt refers to an interesting phenomenon. In the late 1960s, more than 30% of households owned stock. But by the 1970s and early 1980s, the number of stockholding families bottomed out at only 15%. It began to rise again, slowly at first, and then with the stock market's increasing popularity, more rapidly. Currently, it stands at more than 50% of all households.

Next, the very idea that stocks might themselves be a wise investment was attacked:

> Further, this "death of equity" can no longer be seen as something a stock market rally—however strong—will check. It has

persisted for more than 10 years through market rallies, business cycles, recession, recoveries, and booms. The problem is not merely that there are 7 million fewer shareholders than there were in 1970. Younger investors, in particular, are avoiding stocks. Between 1970 and 1975, the number of investors declined in every age group but one: individuals 65 and older. While the number of investors under 65 dropped by about 25%, the number of investors over 65 jumped by more than 30%. Only the elderly who have not understood the changes in the nation's financial markets, or who are unable to adjust to them, are sticking with stocks.

After reading the last chapter, you should be able to grasp the sublime irony of this passage. Did the elderly stick with stocks in 1979 because they were out of step, inattentive, or senile? No! *They were the only ones who still remembered how to value stocks by traditional criteria, which told them that stocks were cheap, cheap, cheap. They were the only investors with experience enough to know that severe bear markets are usually followed by powerful bull markets.* A few, like my father, even remembered the depths of 1932, when our very capitalist system seemed threatened and stocks yielded near 10% in dividends.

The opposite generational phenomenon occurred in 2001. The Internet Bust hit the singles apartments much harder than it did the retirement centers. The 1979 article ended by adding insult to injury:

> Today, the old attitude of buying solid stocks as a cornerstone for one's life savings and retirement has simply disappeared. Says a young U.S. executive: "Have you been to an American stockholders' meeting lately? They're all old fogies. The stock market is just not where the action's at."

The point of this exercise is not just to point out how markets can go to extremes (a valuable lesson in and of itself) but to demonstrate several more salient points. First, it is human nature to be unduly influenced by the last 10 or even 20 years' returns. It was just as hard to imagine that U.S. stocks were a good investment in 1979 as it is to imagine that precious metals, emerging markets, and Pacific Rim stocks are now.

Second, when recent returns for a given asset class have been very high or very low, put your faith in the longest data series you can find—not just the most recent data. For example, if the *BusinessWeek* article had explored the historical record, it would have found that nominal stock returns from 1900 to 1979 were 6% more than inflation.

Third, be able to estimate returns for yourself. At the time that the article was written, stocks were yielding more than 5% and earnings were continuing to grow at a real rate of 2% per year. Anyone able to add could have calculated a 7% expected real return from these two numbers. The subsequent real return was actually 11% because of the extraordinary increase of valuations typical of recoveries from bear markets.

Finally, do not underestimate the amount of courage it takes to act on your beliefs. As I've already mentioned, human beings are profoundly social creatures, and buying assets that everyone else has been running from takes more fortitude than most investors can manage. But if you are equal to the task, you will be well rewarded.

Ben Graham Goes Out on a Limb

The 1920s and its aftermath left Benjamin Graham deeply perplexed: How could so many have been so wrong for so long? After the cataclysm, why should any reasonable investor ever buy stocks again? And if so, what criteria should she use for their selection? The result was his manuscript, *Security Analysis*, a dense, beautifully written brick of a book, produced during the depths of the Depression. In it, Graham put his finger on just what went wrong and how a reasonable person should approach both stocks and bonds in the future. It is still considered a classic. (It went through many later editions. If you ever get bitten by the Graham bug and decide to read it, make sure you purchase McGraw-Hill's reproduction of the original 1934 edition, unless, of course, you can afford several thousand dollars for an original copy. Later editions were increasingly influenced by his co-authors David Dodd, Sidney Cottle, and Charles Tatham, who did not write nearly as well.)

By the time *Security Analysis* was published, the investing public had almost completely abandoned stocks. Most agreed with the leading economist of the time, Lawrence Chamberlain, who, in his widely read book, *Investment and Speculation*, flatly stated that only bonds were suitable for investment. This attitude persisted for nearly three decades. As late as 1940, a survey by the Federal Reserve Board found that 90% of the public expressed opposition to the purchase of common stocks.

Graham, as he always did, approached things from first principles. What was investing?

> An investment operation is one which, upon thorough analysis promises safety of principal and an adequate return. Operations not meeting these requirements are speculative.

Was Graham able to find suitable stock investments in 1934? Most definitely. Graham introduced a wonderful amoral relativism to invest-

ing: there were no intrinsically "good" or "bad" stocks. At a high
enough price, even the best companies were highly speculative. And
at a low enough price, even the worst companies were a sound investment.

Graham recommended that even the most conservative investors
hold at least 25% of their portfolios in common stocks, with the most
aggressive investors holding no more than 75%. The implication was
that the average investor should hold a 50/50 split between stocks and
bonds. Although tame by today's standards, in the depths of the
depression, recommending any stock ownership at all was a startling
piece of advice.

What did the market look like in 1932? Prices were so low that the
dividend yield was nearly 10%, and remained above 6% for more than
a decade. Almost all stocks sold for less than their "book value"
(roughly, the total value of their assets), and fully one-third of all
stocks sold for less than one-tenth of their book value! (By comparison, today, the average S&P 500 stock sells at about six times book
value.) In short, stocks could not be given away, even at these prices.
Anyone paying good money for them was considered certifiable.

The aftermath of the Nifty Fifty and the bear market of 1973–1974 is
equally instructive. By the end of 1974, the average stock sold at seven
times earnings, and fully one-third of those companies could be
bought at cheaper than five times earnings. Even the high-fliers of the
Fifty themselves—the crown jewels of American industry—were on
fire sale. McDonalds, which had been selling at a P/E of 83 in 1972,
could be bought at a P/E of 9 as late as 1980. During the same period, the P/E of Disney had fallen from 76 to 11; Polaroid, from 90 to
16; and Hewlett-Packard, from 65 to 18.

The rewards of fishing in such troubled waters are staggering. For
the 20 years following the 1932 bottom, the market returned 15.4%
annually, and for the 20 years following the 1974 bottom, 15.1%
annually.

We don't have such precise data on the aftermath of the earlier bubbles, but it was no doubt just as dramatic. South Sea shares, for example, fell about 85% from their peak. Although the other great public
companies were not as badly hit, stock prices still dropped significantly. Shares in the East India Company fell about 60%, while those
of the Bank of England fell 40%. The later collapse in prices of the
English railroad and canal companies was even more severe.

The societal effects of the collapses varied from episode to episode.
Certainly, aside perhaps from a bit of "malaise," to use President
Carter's unfortunate wording, the 1973–1974 decline had relatively lit-
tle long-term impact on the U.S. On the other hand, the Federal

Reserve's mishandling of the liquidity crunch brought on by the 1929 crash magnified its effects, resulting in the Great Depression, which scarred the national psyche for decades.

The collapse of railroad shares in 1845 was equally catastrophic; a worldwide depression nearly swept away the Bank of England. Only hard money retained its value. The most long-lasting effect of the railway mania is that Britain, to this day, is cursed with a disorganized bramble of a rail network. Even casual visitors cannot help but notice the contrast with France's more efficient layout, which was first surveyed by military engineers and then let out for private construction bids.

Minsky's criteria for bubbles work just as well in reverse with busts. A generalized loss in the faith of the new technologies to cure the system's ills is usually the triggering factor. A contraction of liquidity almost always follows, with the losses of faith and liquidity reinforcing each other. The third criterion is an amnesia for the recoveries that usually follow collapses. And finally, investors incapable of doing the math on the way up do not miraculously regain it on the way down. Cheap stocks excite only the dispassionate, the analytical, and the aged.

But by far, the most fascinating aftermath of crashes is the political and legal kabuki that often follows. Financial writer Fred Schwed astutely observed that, "The burnt customer certainly prefers to believe that he has been robbed rather than that he has been a fool on the advice of fools." History shows that when an entire nation has acted unwisely on bad advice, the rules of the game are likely to change drastically, and that the sources of that advice should beware.

The political reaction to the South Sea Bubble was violent. Many of the company's directors, including four MPs, were sent to the Tower. Most of their profits were confiscated, despite the fact that such a seizure of assets was a violation of common law. No one cared about such niceties, and the directors were lucky to escape with their lives. The legislative repercussions from the South Sea episode haunted the English capital markets for nearly two centuries thereafter. The Bubble Act, which had actually precipitated the collapse, required a parliamentary charter for all new companies.

Aside from wasting Parliament's time and energy, the Bubble Act mainly served to hinder the formation of new enterprises. Parliament almost outlawed stockbrokering and made illegal short sales, futures, and options. These devices serve to make the capital markets more liquid and efficient, and their absence undoubtedly served to make subsequent crises more difficult to manage. The railway mania itself is a case in point; had investors been able to sell short railway shares, the bubble and subsequent collapse would likely have been much less violent.

A similar reaction occurred in the United States in the wake of the 1929 crash that should give pause to many involved in the most recent speculative excess. At the center of this titanic story was a brilliant attorney of Sicilian origin, Ferdinand Pecora. Just before the market bottom in 1932, with embittered investors everywhere demanding investigation of Wall Street's chicanery, the Senate authorized a Banking and Currency Committee. It promptly hired Pecora, then a New York City assistant district attorney, as its counsel. In the following year, he skillfully guided the committee, and via it the public, through an investigation of the sordid mass of manipulation and fraud that characterized the era. The high and mighty of Wall Street were politely but devastatingly interrogated by Pecora, right up to J.P. "Jack" Morgan, scion of the House of Morgan and a formidable figure in his own right.

But the real drama centered around New York Stock Exchange President Richard Whitney. Tall, cool, and aristocratic, he symbolized the "Old Guard" at the stock exchange, who sought to keep it the private preserve of the member firms, free of government regulation.

In the drama of the October 1929 crash, Whitney was the closest thing Wall Street had to a popular hero. At the height of the bloodshed on Black Thursday—October 25, 1929—he strode to the U.S. Steel post and made the most famous single trade in the history of finance: a purchase of 10,000 shares of U.S. Steel at 205, even though at that point it was trading well below that price. This single-handedly stopped the panic.

But Dick Whitney was a flawed hero. His arrogance in front of the committee alienated both the legislators and the public. He was also a lousy investor, with a weakness for cockamamie schemes and an inability to cut his losses. He wound up deeply in debt and began borrowing heavily, first from his brother (a Morgan partner), then from the Morgan Bank itself, and finally from other banks, friends, and even casual acquaintances. In order to secure bank loans, he pledged bonds belonging to the exchange's Gratuity Fund—its charity pool for employees. This final act would be his downfall.

Under almost any other circumstances, he would not have been treated harshly for this transgression. But Whitney had found himself at the wrong place at the wrong time. In 1938, he went to Sing Sing. He was not the only titan of finance who found himself a guest of the state, however, and many of the most prominent players of the 1920s met even more ignominious ends.

The moral for the actors in the recent Internet drama is obvious. When enough investors find themselves shorn, scapegoats will be sought. Minor offenses, which in normal times would not attract notice, suddenly acquire a much greater legal significance. The next Pecora Committee drama already seems to be shaping up in the form of congressional inquiries into the Enron disaster and brokerage analyst recommendations. It is likely that we are just seeing the beginning of renewed government interest in the investment industry.

On the positive side, four major pieces of legislation came out of the Pecora hearings. Unlike the post-bubble English experience, the committee's effect was positive; three new laws were introduced that still shape our modern market structure. The Securities Act of 1933 made the issuance of stocks and bonds a more open and fair process. The Securities Act of 1934 regulated stock and bond trading and established the SEC. The Investment Company Act of 1940, passed in reaction to the investment trust debacle, allowed the development of the modern mutual fund industry. And finally, the Glass-Steagall Act separated commercial and investment banking. This last statute has recently been repealed. Sooner or later, we will likely painfully relearn the reasons for its passage almost seven decades ago.

This legislative ensemble made the U.S. securities markets the most tightly regulated in the world. If you seek an area where rigorous government oversight contributes to the public good, you need look no further. The result is the planet's most transparent and equitable financial markets. If there is one industry where the U.S. has lapped the field, it is financial services, for which we can thank Ferdinand Pecora and the rogues he pursued.

How to Handle the Panic

What is the investor to do during the inevitable crashes that characterize the capital markets? At a minimum, you should not panic and sell out—simply stand pat. You should have a firm asset allocation policy in place. What separates the professional from the amateur are two things: First, the knowledge that brutal bear markets are a fact of life and that there is no way to avoid their effects. And second, that when times get tough, the former stays the course; the latter abandons the blueprints, or, more often than not, has no blueprints at all.

In the book's last section, we'll talk about portfolio rebalancing—the process of maintaining a constant allocation; this is a technique which automatically commands you to sell when the market is euphoric and prices are high, and to buy when the market is morose and prices are low.

Ideally, when prices fall dramatically, you should go even further and actually increase your percentage equity allocation, which would require buying yet more stocks. This requires nerves of steel and runs the risk that you may exhaust your cash long before the market finally touches bottom. I don't recommend this course of action to all but the hardiest and experienced of souls. If you decide to go this route, you should increase your stock allocation only by *very small* amounts—say by 5% after a fall of 25% in prices—so as to avoid running out of cash and risking complete demoralization in the event of a 1930s-style bear market.

Bubbles and Busts: Summing Up

In the last two chapters, I hope that I've accomplished four things.

First, I hope I've told a good yarn. An appreciation of manias and crashes should be part of every educated person's body of historical knowledge. It informs us, as almost no other subject can, about the psychology of peoples and nations. And most importantly, it is yet one more demonstration that there is really nothing new in this world. In the famous words of Alphonse Karr, *Plus ça change, plus c'est la même chose*: The more things change, the more they stay the same.

Second, I hope I have shown you that from time to time, markets can indeed become either irrationally exuberant or morosely depressed. During the good times, it is important to remember that things can go to hell in a hand basket with brutal dispatch. And just as important, to remember in times of market pessimism that things almost always turn around.

Third, it is fatuous to believe that the boom/bust cycle has been abolished. The market is no more capable of eliminating its extreme behavior than the tiger is of changing its stripes. As University of Chicago economics professor Dick Thaler points out, all finance is behavioral. Investors will forever be captives of the emotions and responses bred into their brains over the eons. As this book is being written, most readers should have no trouble believing that irrational exuberance happens. It is less obvious, but equally true, that the sort of pessimism seen in the markets 25 and 70 years ago is a near certainty at some point in the future as well.

And last, the most profitable thing we can learn from the history of booms and busts is that at times of great optimism, future returns are lowest; when things look bleakest, future returns are highest. Since risk and return are just different sides of the same coin, it cannot be any other way.

PILLAR THREE

The Psychology of Investing

The Analyst's Couch

The biggest obstacle to your investment success is staring out at you from your mirror. Human nature overflows with behavioral traits that will rob you faster than an unlucky nighttime turn in Central Park.

We discovered in Chapter 5 that raw brainpower alone is not sufficient for investment success, as demonstrated by Sir Isaac Newton, one of the most notable victims of the South Sea Bubble. We have no historical record of William Shakespeare's investment returns, but I'm willing to bet that, given his keen eye for human foibles, his returns were far better than Sir Isaac's.

In Chapter 7, we identify the biggest culprits. I guarantee you'll recognize most of these as the face in the looking glass. In Chapter 8, we'll devise strategies for dealing with them.

7

Misbehavior

The investor's chief problem—and even his worst enemy—is likely to be himself.
Benjamin Graham

Dick Thaler Misses a Basketball Game

The major premise of economics is that investors are rational and will always behave in their own self-interest. There's only one problem. It isn't true. Investors, like everyone else, are most often the hapless captives of human nature. As Benjamin Graham said, we are our own worst enemies. But until very recently, financial economists ignored the financial havoc wreaked by human beings on themselves.

Thirty years ago, a young finance academic by the name of Richard Thaler and a friend were contemplating driving across Rochester, New York, in a blinding snowstorm to see a basketball game. They wisely elected not to. His companion remarked, "But if we had bought the tickets already, we'd go." To which Thaler replied, "True—and interesting." Interesting because according to economic theory, whether or not the tickets have already been purchased should not influence the decision to brave a snowstorm to see a ball game.

Thaler began collecting such anomalies and nearly single-handedly founded the discipline of behavioral finance—the study of how human nature forces us to make irrational economic choices. (Conventional finance, on the other hand, assumes that investors make only rational choices.) Thaler has even extended his research to basketball itself. Why, he wonders, do players usually go for the two-point shot when down by two points with seconds remaining? The two-point percentage is about 50%, meaning that your chance of winning is only 25%, since making the goal only serves to throw the game into overtime. A three-point shot wins the game and has a better success rate—about 33%.

At about the same time in the early 1970s that Thaler and his friend were deciding whether or not to brave the snowstorm, two Israeli psychologists, Daniel Kahneman and Amos Tversky, were studying the imperfections in the human decision-making process in a far sunnier clime. They published a landmark paper in the prestigious journal *Science*, in which they outlined the basic errors made by humans in estimating probabilities. A typical riddle: "Steve is very shy and withdrawn, invariably helpful, but with little interest in people, or in the world of reality . . ." Is he a librarian or mechanic? Most people would label him a librarian. Not so: there are far more mechanics than librarians in the world, and plenty of mechanics are shy. It is therefore more likely that Steve is a mechanic. But people inevitably get it wrong.

The Kahneman-Tversky paper is a classic, but it is unfortunately couched in an increasingly complex series of mind-twisting examples. Its relevance to investing is not immediately obvious. But Thaler and his followers were able to extend Kahneman and Tversky's work to economics, founding the field of behavioral finance. (Thaler himself dislikes the label. He asks, "Is there any other kind of finance?")

This chapter will describe the most costly investment behaviors. It is likely that at one time or another, you have suffered from every single one.

Don't Get Trampled by the Herd

Human beings are supremely social animals. We enjoy associating with others, and we particularly love sharing our common interests. In general, this is a good thing on multiple levels—economic, psychological, educational, and political. But in investing, it's downright dangerous.

This is because our interests, beliefs, and behaviors are subject to fashion. How else can we explain why men wore their hair short in the 1950s and long in the 1970s? Why bomb shelters were all the rage in the early 1960s, then fell into disuse in later decades, when the number of thermonuclear weapons was exponentially greater? Why the pendulum between political liberalism and conservatism swings back and forth to the same kind of generational metronome as stocks and bonds?

The problem is that stocks and bonds are not like hula hoops or beehive hairdos—they cannot be manufactured rapidly enough to keep up with demand—so their prices rise and fall with fashion. Think about what happens when everyone has decided that, as happened in the 1970s and 1990s, large growth companies like Disney, Microsoft, and Coca-Cola were the best companies to own. Their prices got bid to stratospheric levels, reducing their future return. This kind of price rise can go to absurd lengths before a few brave souls pull out their calculators, run the numbers, and inform the populace that the emperor has no clothes.

For this reason, the conventional investment wisdom is usually wrong. If everyone believes that stocks are the best investment, what that tells you is that everyone already owns them. This, in turn, means two things. First, that because everyone has bought them, prices are high and future returns, low. And second, and more important, *that there is no one else left to buy these stocks.* For it is only when there is an untapped reservoir of future buyers that prices can rise.

Everyone Can't Be Above Average

In a piece on investor preconceptions in the September 14, 1998, issue of *The Wall Street Journal,* writer Greg Ip examined the change in investor attitudes following the market decline in the summer of 1998. He tabulated the change in investor expectations as follows:

Expected Returns	Jun. 1998	Sept. 1998
Next 12 months, own portfolio	15.20%	12.90%
Next 12 months, market overall	13.40%	10.50%

The first thing that leaps out of this table is that the average investor thinks that he will best the market by about 2%. While some investors may accomplish this, it is, of course, mathematically impossible for the average investor to do so. As we've already discussed, the average investor must, of necessity, obtain the market return, minus expenses and transaction costs. Even the most casual observer of human nature should not be surprised by this paradox—people tend to be overconfident.

Overconfidence likely has some survival advantage in a state of nature, but not in the world of finance. Consider the following:

- In one study, 81% of new business owners thought that they had a good chance of succeeding, but that only 39% of their peers did.
- In another study, 82% of young U.S. drivers considered themselves in the top 30% of their group in terms of safety. (In self-doubting Sweden, not unsurprisingly, the percentage is lower.)

The factors associated with overconfidence are intriguing. The more complex the task, the more inappropriately overconfident we are.

"Calibration" of one's efforts is also a factor. The longer the "feedback loop," or the time-delay, between our actions and the results, the greater our overconfidence. For example, meteorologists, bridge players, and emergency room physicians are generally well-calibrated because of the brief time span separating their actions and their results. Most investors are not.

Overconfidence is probably the most important of financial behavioral errors, and it comes in different flavors. The first is the illusion that you can successfully pick stocks by following a few simple rules or subscribing to an advisory service such as Value Line. About once a week, someone emails me selection criteria for picking stocks, usually involving industry leaders, P/E ratios, dividend yields, and/or earnings growth, which the sender is certain will provide market-beating results.

Right now, if I wanted to, with a few keystrokes I could screen a database of the more than 7,000 publicly traded U.S. companies according to hundreds of different characteristics, or even my own customized criteria. There are dozens of inexpensive, commercially available software programs capable of this, and they reside on the hard drives of hundreds of thousands of small and institutional investors, each and every one of whom is busily seeking market-beating techniques. Do you really think that you're smarter and faster than all of them?

On top of that, there are tens of thousands of professional investors using the kind of software, hardware, data, technical support, and underlying research that you and I can only dream of. When you buy and sell stock, you're most likely trading with *them*. You have as much chance of consistently beating these folks as you have of starting at wide receiver for the Broncos.

The same goes for picking mutual funds. I hope that by now I've dissuaded you from believing that selecting funds on the basis of past performance is of any value. Picking mutual funds is a highly seductive activity because it's easy to find ones that have outperformed for several years or more by dumb luck alone. In a taxable account, this is especially devastating, because each time you switch ponies you take a capital gains haircut.

There are some who believe that by using more qualitative criteria, such as through careful evaluation and interviewing of fund heads, they can select successful money managers. I recently heard from an advisor who explained to me how, by interviewing dozens of fund managers yearly and going to Berkshire shareholder meetings to listen to Warren Buffet, he was able to outperform the market for both domestic and foreign stocks. The only problem was that his bond, real

estate, and commodities managers were so bad that his overall portfolio results were far below that of an indexed approach. Take another close look at Figure 3-4. If the nation's largest pension plans, each
managing tens of billions of dollars, can't pick successful money managers, what chance do you think you have?

Most investors also believe that they can time the market, or worse,
that by listening to the right guru, they will be able to. I have a fanta-
sy in which one morning I slip into the Manhattan headquarters of the
major brokerage firms and drop truth serum into their drinking water.
That day, on news programs all over the country, dozens of analysts
and market strategists, when asked for their prediction of market direction, answer, "How the hell should I know? I learned long ago that my
predictions weren't worth a darn; you know this as well as I. The only
reason that we're both here doing this is because we have mouths to
feed, and there are still chumps who will swallow this stuff!"

At any one moment, by sheer luck alone, there will be several
strategists and fund managers who will be right on the money. In
1987, it was Elaine Garzarelli who successfully predicted the crash.
Articulate, well-dressed, and flamboyant, she got far more media
attention than she deserved. Needless to say, this was the kiss of
death. Her predictive accuracy soon plummeted. Adding insult to
injury, her brokerage house put her in charge of a high-profile fund
that subsequently performed so badly that it was quietly killed off several years later.

The most recent guru-of-the-month was Abby Joseph Cohen, who
is low-key, self-effacing, and, for a market strategist, fairly scholarly.
(Her employer, Goldman Sachs, which emerged from the depths of
ignominy in 1929 to become the most respected name in investment
banking, makes a habit of hiring only those with dazzling math
skills.) From 1995 to 1999, she was in the market's sweet spot, recommending a diet high in big growth and tech companies.
Unfortunately, she didn't see the bubble that was obvious to most
other observers, and for the past two years, she's been picking the
egg off her face.

Remember, even a stopped clock is right twice a day. And there are
plenty of stopped clocks in Wall Street's canyons; some of them will
always have just shot a spectacular bull's-eye purely by accident.

There are really two behavioral errors operating in the overconfidence playground. The first is the "compartmentalization" of success
and failure. We tend to remember those activities, or areas of our portfolios, in which we succeeded and forget about those areas where we
didn't, as did the advisor I mentioned above. The second is that it's far
more agreeable to ascribe success to skill than to luck.

The Immediate Past Is Out to Get You

The next major error that investors make is the assumption that the immediate past is predictive of the long-term future. Take a look at the data from the table at the beginning of the chapter and note that in September 1998, after prices had fallen by a considerable amount, investors' estimates of stock returns were *lower* than they were in June.

This is highly irrational. Consider the following question: On January 1, you buy a gold coin for $300. In the ensuing month the price of gold falls, and your friend then buys an identical coin for $250. Ten years later, you both sell your coins at the same time. Who has earned the higher return? Most investors would choose the correct answer— your friend, having bought his coin for $50 less, will make $50 more (or at worst, lose $50 less) than you. Viewed in this context, it is astonishing that any rational investor would infer lower expected returns from falling stock prices. The reason for this is what the behavioral scientists call "recency"; we tend to overemphasize more recent data and ignore older data, even if it is more comprehensive.

Until the year 2000, with large growth stocks on a tear, it was very difficult to convince investors not to expect 20% equity returns over the long term. Blame recency. Make the recent data spectacular and/or unpleasant, and it will completely blot out the more important, if abstract, data.

What makes recency such a killer is the fact that asset classes have a slight tendency to "mean-revert" over periods longer than three years. Mean reversion means that periods of relatively good performance tend to be followed by periods of relatively poor performance. The reverse also occurs; periods of relatively poor performance tend to be followed by periods of relatively good performance. Unfortunately, this is not a sure thing. Not by any means. But it makes buying the hot asset class of the past several years bad odds.

Let's look what happens when you fall victim to recency. In Table 7-1, I've picked six asset classes—U.S. large and small stocks, as well as U.K., continental European, Japanese, and Pacific Rim stocks—and analyzed their performance at five-year intervals during the period from 1970 to 1999.

From 1970 to 1974, the top performer was Japan; but in the next period, from 1975 to 1979, it ranked fourth. In those years, the best performer was U.S. small stocks, which actually did best from 1980 to 1984. But during the next period, from 1985 to 1989, it ranked last. The best performer from 1985 to 1989 was again Japanese stocks, but from 1990 to 1994 it ranked last. In that period, the best performer was Pacific Rim stocks, which ranked next to last from 1995 to 1999. The

Table 7-1 Subsequent Performance of Prior Best-Performing Asset Classes

Time Period	Best Asset Class	Rank (1 to 6) in Next Five-Year Period
1970–1974	Japan	4
1975–1979	U.S. Small	1
1980–1984	U.S. Small	6
1985–1989	Japan	6
1990–1994	Pacific Rim	5
1995–1999	U.S. Large	??

best asset class in the late 1990s was U.S. large-cap stocks, and, if the past two years is any indication, it seems likely to be near the bottom of the heap next time around.

We've previously discussed how the recency illusion applies to single asset classes. For example, from 1996 to 2000, the return of Japanese stocks was an annualized *loss* of 4.54%, but over the 31 years from 1970 to 2000, it was 12.33%. Both inside and outside Japan, investors have gotten very discouraged with its stock market in recent years. But which of these two values do you suppose is a more accurate indicator of its expected future return?

Likewise, the 1996 to 2000 return for the S&P 500 was 18.35%, but the very long-term data show a return of about 10%. Again, which of these two numbers do you think is the better indicator?

Entertain Me

If indexing works so well, why do so few investors take advantage of it? Because it's so boring. As we discussed in Chapter 3, at the same time that you're ensuring yourself decent returns and minimizing the chances of dying poor, you're also giving up the chance of striking it rich. It doesn't get much duller than this.

In fact, one of the most deadly investment traits is the need for excitement. Gambling may be the second-most enjoyable human activity. Why else do people throng to Las Vegas and Atlantic City when they know that, on average, they'll return lighter in the wallet?

Humans routinely exchange large amounts of money for excitement. One of the most consistent findings in behavioral finance is that people gravitate towards low-probability/high-payoff bets. For example, it's well known among professional horse race bettors that it is much easier to make money on favorites than on long shots. The reason is that the amateurs tend to prefer long shots, making the odds for the remaining favorites more advantageous than they should be. After all, it is much more exciting to bet at fifty-to-one odds than at two-to-five. On a more obvious level, why does anyone buy a lottery ticket when the average payoff is about fifty cents on the dollar?

As we saw in the discussion of initial public offerings (IPOs) in Chapter 5, the same thing happens in the investment world, where small long shot companies attract too much capital, leaving less capital for duller, more established companies. This depresses the prices of the more established companies and increases their returns. And, as we've already seen, IPOs are a lousy business. (This is also the main reason why the returns of small cap growth stocks are so low, as we saw in Figure 1-18.)

I've formulated my own model, called the "investment entertainment pricing theory" (INEPT), which describes this phenomenon. For each bit of excitement you derive from an investment, you lose a compensatory amount of return. For example, a theater ticket may be thought of as a security with a high entertainment value and a zero investment return. At the opposite end of the scale, a portfolio full of dull value stocks—USX, Caterpillar, Ford, and the like—is the most liable to have higher returns.

The Wrong Risk

As we discussed in the first chapter, there are really two kinds of risk: short term and long term. Short-term risk is the knot we get in our stomachs when our portfolios lose 20% or 40% in value over the course of a year or two. It is a fearsome thing. Frank Armstrong, a financial advisor, writer, and ex-military pilot, observes he has known men who routinely faced death in the sky with equanimity but became physically ill when their portfolios declined 5%.

The fear of short-term loss drove investors out of stocks for a generation after the Great Depression, penalizing their returns by several percent per year. We can estimate that because of their fear of short-term loss, their portfolios were underexposed to stocks to the point where they lost 3% of return annually over the next three decades. Compounding 3% of underperformance over 30 years means that their final wealth was 59% less than it should have been. In other words, their fear of a 20% to 40% loss cost them 59% of their assets. In academic finance, this is called "myopic loss aversion"—focusing on short-term dangers and ignoring the far more serious long-term ones.

Why do we do this? Human beings experience risk in the short-term. This is as it should be, of course. In the state of nature our ancestors inhabited, an ability to focus on the risks of the moment had much greater survival value than long-term strategic analytic ability. Unfortunately, a visceral obsession with the here and now is of rather less use in modern society, particularly in the world of investing.

In Chapter 1, after looking at the long-term superiority of stocks over fixed-income securities, you may have found yourself asking the question, "Why doesn't everybody buy stocks?" Clearly, in the long term, bonds were actually *more* risky than stocks, in the sense that in every period of more than 30 years, stocks have outperformed bonds.

In fact, many academicians refer to this as "The Equity Premium Puzzle"—why investors allowed stocks to remain so cheap that their returns so greatly and consistently exceeded that of other assets. The answer is that our primordial instincts, a relic of millions of years of evolution, cause us to feel more pain when we suddenly lose 30% of our liquid net worth than when we face the more damaging possibility of failing to meet our long-term financial goals. How bad is the problem? Richard Thaler, in an immensely clever bit of research, examined the interaction of the risk premium and investor preference. He estimated the risk horizon of the average investor to be about one year. Myopic indeed!

Trees Don't Grow to the Sky

One of the most dangerous of all investment illusions is the great company/great stock fallacy. During the Nifty Fifty market of the early 1970s and the more recent mania over Internet and tech stocks, the importance of earnings growth was overemphasized. The only companies worthy of purchase were the well-run multinational firms, with strong growth arising from commanding market strength—Coca Cola, Disney, Microsoft, and the like. It certainly was a compelling story.

This is where the market separates the winners from the losers. Serious investors do the math; amateurs listen to stories. Here's the math, that most forgot to do:

In the free market system, the life of even the largest of corporations is positively Hobbesian—nasty, brutish, and short. Less understood is that company glamour is even more ephemeral. A glamorous company is one with strong growth, usually selling at a very high multiple of earnings. For example, at the height of the market froth in the spring of 2000, the three companies mentioned in the last paragraph sold at 48, 84, and 67 times earnings, respectively—from three to four times the valuation of a typical company. This means the market expected these companies to eventually increase their earnings *relative to the size of the market* to three or four times their current proportion.

This is a tricky concept. Let us assume that the stock market grows its earnings at 5% per year. This means that over a 14-year period, it will approximately double its earnings. (This is according to the "Rule of 72," which states that the earnings rate times the doubling time equals 72. In the above example, 72 divided by 5% is approximately 14. Or, alternatively, at a 12% growth rate, it takes only six years to double earnings.) If a glamorous growth company is selling at four times the P/E ratio of the rest of the market—say, 80 times earnings versus 20 times earnings—then the market is saying that during this same 14-year period, its earnings will grow by a factor of eight (4 × 2 = 8). This requires a growth rate of 16% per year sustained over the 14-year period. While a very few companies are able to turn this trick, the vast majority do not.

How long does the high growth of the most glamorous companies actually persist? On an economic scale, not much longer than a heartbeat. In a 1993 landmark study of earnings growth persistence, Thaler protégé Russell Fuller and his colleagues looked at the popular growth stocks—the top fifth of the market in terms of their P/E ratio. Their data showed that these very expensive companies increased their earnings about 10% faster than the market in year one, 3% faster in year two, 2% faster in years three and four, and about 1% faster in years five and six. After that, their growth was the same as the market's.

In other words, you can count on a growth stock increasing its earnings, on average, about 20% more than the market over six years. After that, nothing. Let's assume that the 20% excess growth found by Fuller occurs immediately in a company selling at 80 times earnings. If the price does not react to the 20% bump in earnings, it is now selling at 64 times earnings and *has only the growth potential of the rest of the market.* What do you suppose the market does to a stock selling at 64 times earnings when it finds out that it has only ordinary growth potential? In the hackneyed words of the market strategist, it is "taken out and shot." Sooner or later (and, experience shows, sooner—in about two to three years), this happens to almost all growth stocks; this is the main reason why they have lower returns than the market.

Even most professionals are unaware of just how ephemeral earnings growth is. If you simply look at stocks with high prior earnings growth, you discover that their future earnings growth is exactly the same as the market's, a phenomenon referred to as "higgledy piggledy growth" by its discoverer Richard Brealey. Market participants have better methods to find stocks with higher future growth than simply looking at past growth (although screening for raw past growth is a favorite neophyte technique) and assign those stocks high P/E ratios.

It's just that they don't do a very good job; these stocks wind up getting grossly overpriced relative to their actual future growth.

If you find this a bit confusing, don't despair; it's not an easy concept. Let's examine things in yet another way, by imagining two companies, Smokestack Inc., selling at 20 times earnings, and Glamour Concepts Inc., selling at 80 times earnings. This means that for every $100 of stock, Smokestack produces $5 of earnings ($100/20 = $5) and Glamour, $1.25 ($100/80 = $1.25). This is because the market expects Glamour to grow its earnings much more rapidly. If Smokestack grows its earnings at a rate of 6% per year, then after six years, it will increase its earnings by 48%—from $5 per share to $7.40 per share. So far, so good. How does Glamour do? The data from Fuller and his colleagues show that over the same six-year time frame, it will grow its earnings by 20% more than the market—in other words, by 78% ($1.48 \times 1.20 = 1.78$). This means that its earnings will grow from $1.25 per share to $2.23 per share. After that, it will have the same earnings growth as Smokestack, which, as we just calculated, is earning $7.40 per share. Somewhere in this sequence of events, usually just as its earnings growth is slowing down, the market sees that Glamour is grossly overpriced and clobbers its shareholders.

That's not to say that growth stocks always underperform value stocks. For the five years between 1995 and 1999, large growth stocks outpaced large value stocks by 10.7% *per year*, only to blow all of that lead in the next 15 months. As you might imagine, results are best and enthusiasm is greatest for growth stocks during tech-driven bubbles, while value stocks tend to do best in their aftermath.

The Faces in the Clouds

If there is one skill that separates us from both computers and the rest of the animal kingdom, it is our ability to recognize highly abstract patterns. Newton's intuition of the gravitational equation from a falling apple and Darwin's extrapolating the theory of evolution from observing gardeners and farmers select for favorable plant characteristics are two spectacular examples of this ability. We all rely on pattern recognition in our everyday lives, from complex professional tasks down to things as mundane as the route we take to work or the way we organize our closets.

But in investing, this talent is usually counterproductive. The simple reason is, for the most part, the pricing of stocks and bonds at both the individual and market level is random: *there are no patterns*. In such a chaotic world, the search for patterns is not only futile, it is downright dangerous. For example, after the 1987 market crash, the financial page of most newspapers printed a plot of the pre-crash stock rise and fall in the 1925–1933 period, superimposed with that of the 1982–1987 period. The implication was that, since the plots matched so closely before both crashes, a further catastrophic fall in stock prices similar to that of 1929–1933 was all but certain.

For a whole host of reasons, starting with the fact that the Fed managed the 1987 crash with far more skill than in 1929, no such thing happened. The point is that there are no repeatable patterns in security prices. If there were, the world's wealthiest people would be librarians.

I don't envy financial journalists. These benighted folks have to come up with fresh copy every week, and in some cases, every day. There is no way that the average journalist can produce the requisite number of column inches without resorting to interviews with market strategists and active money managers. The business pages are therefore filled with observations that go something like this: "We've found that on the nine previous occasions that widget inventories rose above the past six months' sales, stock prices fell more than 20%." This was no doubt true in the past. The problem is that sifting through numerous pieces of economic and financial data will produce some strong associations purely by chance, just like the Bangladesh butter production/S&P 500 correlation we previously discussed.

There are certainly pieces of data that are predictive of future economic activity, the best known being the monetary policy of the Fed and "leading indicators" such as housing starts or the length of the average industrial working week. The problem is that everyone knows, watches, and analyzes these statistics, and the results of such analysis have already been factored into stock and bond prices. You say that the Fed will be easing interest rates and this will be good for stocks? Well, the rest of the world knows this too, and stocks have *already* risen because of it. Acting on this information is thus likely to be of no value. Remember Bernard Baruch's famous dictum:

Something that everyone knows isn't worth knowing.

And lastly, even when patterns are well established, they can change. The classic example of this is the relationship between stock and bond yields. Before 1958, each time stock dividend yields fell below bond yields, stock prices fell. Before 1958, each time the stock yield fell below the bond yield, had you sold your stocks and waited for stock yields to rise again before repurchasing them, you'd have done handsomely. Until 1958. That year, stock yields fell below bond yields and never looked back. Had you sold your stocks then, you'd still be waiting to get back in. And you'll be waiting a good while longer.

Regrettable Accounting

Human beings are not very good at taking losses or admitting failure. For example, the most consistent bit of irrational investment behavior is the commonplace observation that we are less likely to sell losers than winners. This is known in behavioral finance circles as "regret avoidance." Holding onto a stock that has done poorly keeps alive the possibility that we will not have to confront the finality of our failure.

I don't find this one particularly troublesome. If you believe that the markets are efficient, then the performance of a fallen stock should not be any different than a successful one. Yes, a stock that has done poorly is quite likely to go bankrupt. But enough of these companies will rebound in price, making up for the ones that fail. In fact, Thaler has found that stocks that have recently fallen have, on average, higher expected returns than the market. This should not surprise anyone, since these tend to be value stocks.

But it highlights a much more serious problem, which is known as "mental accounting." This refers to our tendency to compartmentalize our successful and unsuccessful investments, mentally separating our winners and losers. This is particularly dangerous because it distracts us from what should be our main focus: the whole portfolio. A perfect example was the advisor I mentioned earlier who was extremely proud of his "ability" to pick successful active domestic and foreign stock managers but who ignored the fact that his overall portfolio performance was poor.

If you ask the average investor how his investments are performing, you will likely find out that he is doing quite well. How does he know? Because he owns some stocks and funds that have made a lot of money. Has he calculated his overall investment return? Well, no. (The most recent example of this phenomenon was that of the infamous Beardstown Ladies, who did not realize that deposits didn't count as investment return, thus grossly overestimating the results they trumpeted in their best-selling *The Beardstown Ladies' Common-Sense Investment Guide*.) What has happened is the all-too-human strategy of treasuring our successes and burying our failures. In the world of investing, this is much more than a harmless foible; it enables us to ignore the overall failure of our portfolio strategy. As a consequence, we suffer miserable long-term returns for the simple reason that we are not aware of just how bad they are.

The Country Club Syndrome

This is the peculiar affliction of the very wealthy. If you have your own jet, vacation in tony resorts, and send your children to the most exclusive private schools, then surely you can't use the same money managers as the little folks. You're above all that. *You* must engage investment firms and apply techniques available only to the elite. After all, telling the swells at the country club that you send your checks to Vanguard simply will not do.

So you use the best private money managers. Hedge funds. Limited partnerships. Offshore vehicles. And, because you're too busy and important, you don't keep track of the expenses incurred or your overall returns.

The problem with all of these vehicles is that there is scant public information available on their performance. But what we do know is not encouraging. Private managers are easiest to dispose of. They come from exactly the same pool of folks that run the pension funds. If the pension funds of GM, GE, and Disney, with tens of billions to invest, cannot beat the indexes, what chance do you have of attracting a skilled manager with your piddling $500 million? There are good theoretical reasons why this should be so, which we've already covered: expenses and tracking error. Even the rich can't avoid them. In fact, the biggest indexers are already busy in this playpen. If you have the $100 million ante, Vanguard will index the S&P 500 for just 0.025% per year. Now *that's* a club I'd like to join.

Hedge funds attract a lot of interest because of their exclusivity. Hedge funds are investment companies, similar to a mutual fund. But because of the small number of investors allowed—no more than 99— they are free of the constraints of the Investment Company Act of 1940 and are able to hold concentrated positions, extensively hedge or leverage their holdings, and employ other exotic strategies forbidden ordinary mutual funds. (From a legal point of view, hedge fund investors are assumed to be highly sophisticated and have little protection when things turn sour.)

Sunlight here is scarce. In the first place, since most of these funds are "hedged," that is, their market exposure is limited by the employment of futures and options, their returns are quite low. When you adjust for risk, their performance looks better, but their compensation structure alone should give pause—managers are often paid a hefty percentage of returns, and in some years, total fees can easily exceed 10%. These are the kinds of margins that even Lynch and Buffett in their heydays would have trouble overcoming.

Lastly, there is the risk of picking the wrong hedge fund. The list of institutions and wealthy investors shorn by Long-Term Capital Management's flameout in 1998, which almost single-handedly devastated the world economy, constituted the cream of the nation's A List. If it could happen to them, it could happen to anybody.

My experience is that the wealthier the client, the more likely he is to be badly abused. Brokerage customers are judged by their ability to generate revenues for the firm. Small clients are naturally not accorded the time and effort given to larger ones (or "whales," as the biggest are known in the brokerage business). This actually works in the small client's favor, as he or she is likely to be put into a load fund or a few stocks and forgotten about. On the other hand, the high-net-worth client is the ultimate brokerage firm cash cow and is likely to be traded in and out of an expensive array of annuities, private managers, and limited partnerships.

The wealthy *are* different than you and I: they have many more ways of having their wealth stripped away.

Summing It Up

In the words of Walt Kelly, "We have met the enemy, and he is us." I've described the major behavioral mistakes made by investors—the herd mentality, overconfidence, recency, the need to be entertained, myopic risk aversion, the great company/great stock illusion, pattern hallucination, mental accounting, and the country club syndrome. This shopping list of maladaptive behaviors will corrode your wealth as surely as a torrential rain strips an unplanted hillside.

8

Behavioral Therapy

In the last chapter, we examined the many sins to which the frail investment flesh is heir. In the next pages, we'll formulate strategies for defeating the enemy in the mirror. As always, the execution is a good deal harder than the planning, since we are attempting to vanquish some of the most primeval forces of human nature. In most cases, this will be the financial equivalent of "stop smoking," "lose weight," and "try not to get upset." But with enough effort and attention, you can at least tone down many of these damaging behaviors. Even modest improvements can greatly augment your bottom line.

Corral the Herd

As we've already seen, an investment that has become a topic of widespread conversation is likely to be overpriced for the simple reason that too many people have already invested in it. This was true of real estate and gold in the early 1980s, Japanese stocks in the late 1980s, the Tiger nations in the early 1990s, and most recently, technology companies in the late 1990s. In each case, disaster followed. So when all your friends are investing in a certain area, when the business pages are full of stories about a particular company, and when "everybody knows" that something is a good deal, haul up the red flags. In short, identify current conventional wisdom so that you can ignore it.

What I find most disturbing about the present market environment is that "everyone knows" that stocks have high long-term returns. The most optimistic interpretation of this situation is that there is almost no one left to buy stocks, suggesting that further price rises will be much harder to come by. A less sanguine outlook is that when everyone owns a particular asset class, many of these investors will be inexperienced "weak hands" who will panic and sell at the first sign of real trouble.

This suggests two strategies that I have found to be extremely helpful. First, as we've already mentioned, identify the era's conventional wisdom and assume that it is wrong. At the present time, the most prevalent belief is that stock returns are much higher than bond returns. While this statement may have been true in the past, it may not necessarily be true going forward.

The second strategy is to realize that the asset classes with the highest future returns tend to be the ones that are currently the most unpopular. This means that owning the future best performers will not provide you with a sense of investment solidarity with your more conventional friends and neighbors. In fact, they may actually express disapproval. (As anyone who has recently bought precious metals and Japanese stocks, or who bought junk bonds in the 1990s, experienced.) Although some people enjoy shocking others, most do not.

If you do not like being set apart from your friends by your investment habits, then my advice is to treat your investments as a bit of personal dirty linen that you do not discuss in public. When asked about your financial strategy, simply wave it aside with a blithe, "My advisor handles all that; I never look at the statements." Then change the subject.

Don't Let it Go to Your Head

The first step in avoiding overconfidence is to learn to recognize it. Do you think that you have above average driving ability, social skills, and physical good looks? The odds that you have all three are only one in eight! If you believe that your stock picking prowess will enable you to beat the market, ask yourself if you are really smarter than the folks on the other side of your trades. These are almost always savvy professionals whose motivation far exceeds yours. Further, they will have resources at their command that are simply out of your league.

Do you think that you can successfully pick market-beating fund managers? I hope that the data in Chapter 3 on fund performance has convinced you otherwise. If you actually were able to do so, then you would have a lucrative career as a pension fund consultant ahead of you, since the nation's largest corporations would pay you handsomely to identify superior money managers to shepherd their employees' retirement assets.

How do you avoid overconfidence? By telling yourself at least a few times per year, "The market is much smarter than I will ever be. There are millions of other investors who are much better equipped than I, all searching for the financial Fountain of Youth. My chances of being the first to find it are not that good. If I can't beat the market, then the very best I can hope to do is to join it as cheaply and efficiently as possible."

The most liberating aspect of an indexed approach is recognizing that by obtaining the market return, you can beat the overwhelming majority of investment professionals who are trying to exceed it.

Ignore the Past Ten Years

This peccadillo is a reasonably easy one to avoid. You need to constantly remind yourself of two things. The first is that purchasing the past five or ten years' best-performing investment invariably reflects the conventional wisdom, which is usually wrong. The second is that, more times than not, the purchase of last decade's *worst*-performing asset is a much better idea.

We've briefly discussed why this is the case. There is a weak tendency for asset classes to mean revert over periods of longer than a year or two—the best performers tend to turn into the worst, and vice versa. This is only a statistical trend, not a sure thing. Recognize that the returns data for an asset class of less than two or three decades are worthless—the fact that a particular market or market sector has done well over the past decade tells the intelligent investor nothing. (Recall from the first chapter that even the performance of bonds over the 50-year period before 1981 was highly misleading.)

Dare to Be Dull

Understand that in investing there is an inverse correlation between the sizzle and the steak—the most exciting assets tend to have the lowest long-term returns, and the dullest ones tend to have the highest. If you want excitement, take up skydiving or Arctic exploration. Don't do it with your portfolio. I'd even go one step further than that. If you find yourself stimulated in any way by your portfolio performance, then you are probably doing something very wrong. A superior portfolio strategy should be intrinsically boring. Remember, we are trying wherever possible to reduce portfolio volatility—the zigs and the zags—while retaining as much return as possible. Recall also that exciting investments are those that have attracted the most public attention and are thus "over-owned," that is, they have garnered excess investment dollars because of their publicity. This drives up their price, thus lowering future returns.

In most cases, the ultimate object of a successful investment strategy is to minimize your chances of dying poor—to obtain portfolio returns that will allow you to sleep at night. In other words, to be . . . boring.

If you still crave financial thrills or feel compelled to have exciting investments to talk about with folks at parties, then designate a very small corner of your portfolio as mad money, to be deployed in "exciting" investments. Just make sure to promise yourself that when it's gone, it's gone.

Get Your Risks Straight

Myopic risk aversion—our tendency to focus on short-term losses—is one of the most corrosive psychological phenomena experienced by the investor. It is best demonstrated by this apocryphal story: An investor places $10,000 in a mutual fund in the mid-1970s and then forgets about it. Shocked by the October 19, 1987, market crash, she panics and calls the fund company to inquire about the state of her account. "I'm sorry madam, but the value of your fund holdings has fallen to $179,623."

When you take risk, you should be earning a "risk premium," that is, an extra return for bearing the ups and downs of the market. Or you can turn the risk premium around and call it a "safety penalty," the amount of return you lose each year when you avoid risk. Let's be on the conservative side and assume that the safety penalty is just 3% per year. That means that for each dollar you make by investing in perfectly safe assets, you could have made $1.34 in risky assets after 10 years, $1.81 after 20 years, and $2.43 after 30 years. (Realize that these figures represent *expected* returns; there's an outside chance that after 30 years you might have as little as $1.20 or as much as $5.00. If you were guaranteed $2.34, there would be no risk.) You would have forgone those higher returns all because you were afraid of having a few bad months or, at worst, losing one-third or one-half of your money in a severe bear market (from which the markets usually, but not always, recover).

Combating myopic risk aversion is the most difficult emotional task facing any investor. I know of only two ways of doing this. The first is to check on your portfolios as infrequently as possible. Behavioral finance experts have found both in the research lab and in the real world that investors who never look at their portfolios expose themselves to higher risk and earn higher returns than those who examine their holdings frequently. Think about your house. It's a good thing that you can't check on its value every day, or even every year. You happily hold onto it, oblivious to the fact that its actual market value may have temporarily declined 20% on occasion.

Ben Graham observed this effect when he noted that during the Depression, investors in obscure mortgage bonds that were not quoted in the newspaper held on to them. They eventually did well because they did not have to face their losses on a regular basis in the financial pages. On the other hand, holders of corporate bonds, which had sustained less actual decrease in value than the mortgage bonds, but who were supplied with frequent quotes, almost uniformly panicked and sold out.

The other way to avoid myopic risk aversion is to hold enough cash so that you have a certain equanimity about market falls: "Yes, I have lost money, but not as much as my neighbors, and I have a bit of dry powder with which to take advantage of low prices."

At the end of the day, the intelligent investor knows that the visceral reaction to short-term losses is a profoundly destructive instinct. He learns to turn it to his advantage by regularly telling himself, each and every time his portfolio is hit, that low prices mean higher future returns.

There Are No Great Companies

This is really just another variant of "Dare to Be Dull." It is relatively easy to make the great company/great stock mistake. Everyone wants to own the most glamorous growth companies, when in fact history teaches us that the dullest companies tend to have the highest returns. In the real world, superior growth is an illusion that evaporates faster than you can say "earnings surprise." Yes, in retrospect it is possible to find a few companies like Wal-Mart and Microsoft that have produced long-term sustained earnings increases, but the odds of your picking one of these winning lottery tickets *ahead of time* from the stock pages are slim.

Instead, you should consider overweighting value stocks in your portfolio via some of the index funds we'll describe in the last section. Unfortunately, we'll find out in Chapter 13 that this isn't always possible, either for reasons of tax efficiency or because of your employment situation. But at a minimum, beware the siren song of the growth stock, particularly when people begin talking about a "new era" in investing. To quote my colleague Larry Swedroe, "There is nothing new in the markets, only the history you haven't read."

Relish the Randomness

Realize that almost all apparent stock market patterns are, in fact, just coincidence. If you dredge through enough data, you will find an abundance of stock selection criteria and market timing rules that would have made you wealthy. However, unless you possess a time machine, they are of no use. The experienced investor quickly learns that since most market behavior is random, what worked yesterday rarely works tomorrow.

Accept the fact that stock market patterns are a chimera: the man in the moon, the face of your Aunt Tillie in the clouds scudding overhead. Ignore them. When dealing with the markets, the safest and most profitable assumption is that there are no patterns. While there are a few weak statistical predictors of stock and market returns, most of the financial world is totally chaotic. The sooner you realize that no system, guru, or pattern is of benefit, the better off you will be.

Most importantly, ignore market strategists who use financial and economic data to forecast market direction. If we have learned anything over the past 70 years from the likes of Cowles, Fama, Graham, and Harvey, it's that this is a fool's errand. Barton Biggs's job is to make Miss Cleo look good.

Unify Your Mental Accounting

I guarantee you that each month, quarter, year, or decade, you will have one or two asset classes that you will kick yourself for not owning more of. There will also be one or two dogs you will wish you had never laid eyes on. Certain asset classes, particularly precious metals and emerging markets stocks, are quite capable of losing 50% to 75% of their value within a year or two. This is as it should be. Do not allow the inevitable small pockets of disaster in your portfolio to upset you. In order to obtain the full market return of any asset class, you must be willing to keep it after its price has dramatically fallen. If you cannot hold onto the asset class mutts in your portfolio, you will fail. The portfolio's the thing; ignore the performance of its components as much as you can.

Do not revel in your successes, and at least take note of the bad results. *Your overall portfolio return is all that matters.* At the end of each year, calculate it.[1] If your math skills aren't up to the task, it's well worth paying your accountant to do it.

---

[1] Here's how. If there are no additions to or withdrawals from you portfolio, simply divide the end value by the beginning value and subtract 1.0. For example, if you started the year with $10,500 and ended with $12,000, your return was (12,000/10,500) −

Don't Become a Whale

Wealthy investors should realize that they are the cash cows of the investment industry and that most of the exclusive investment vehicles available to them—separate accounts, hedge funds, limited partnerships, and the like—are designed to bleed them with commissions, transactional costs, and other fees. "Whales" are eagerly courted with impressive descriptions of sophisticated research, trading, and tax strategies. Don't be fooled. Remember that the largest investment pools in the nation—the pension funds—are unable to beat the market, so it is unlikely that the investor with $10 million or even $1 billion will be able to do so.

My advice to the very wealthy? Swallow your pride and make that 800 call to a mutual fund specializing in low-cost index funds. Most fund families offer a premium level of service for those with seven-figure portfolios. This is probably not exclusive enough for your tastes but should keep you clear of most of the unwashed masses and earn you returns higher than those of your high-rent-district neighbors.

CHAPTERS 7 AND 8 SUMMARY

1. Avoid the thundering herd. If you don't, you'll get trampled and dirty. The conventional wisdom is usually wrong.
2. Avoid overconfidence. You are most likely trading with investors who are more knowledgeable, faster, and better equipped than you. It is ludicrous to imagine that you can win this game by reading a newsletter or using a few simple selection strategies and trading rules.
3. Don't be overly impressed with an asset's performance over the past five or ten years. More likely than not, last decade's loser will do quite well in the next.
4. Exciting investments are usually a bad deal. Seeking entertainment from your investments is liable to lead you to the poorhouse.

1.0 = 0.143 = 14.3%. If you had inflows or outflows during the year, this must be adjusted for. (This is the mistake made by the Beardstown Ladies, who did not make this correction.) This is done by first calculating the net inflow. In the above example, if you added $1,000 and then took out $700 during the year, your net inflow was $300. You subtract half of this, or $150, from the top of the fraction, and add one-half to the bottom. So, (12,000 − 150)/(10,500 + 150) = 1.113; your return was 11.3%. If you had a net *outflow* of $300, then you do the reverse—add to the top, subtract from the bottom. So, (12,000 + 150)/(10,500 − 150) = 1.174; your return was 17.4%.

5. Try not to worry too much about short-term losses. Focus instead on avoiding poor long-term returns by diversifying as much as you can.
6. The market tends to overvalue growth stocks, resulting in low returns. Good companies are not necessarily good stocks.
7. Beware of forecasts made on the basis of historical patterns. These are usually the results of chance and are not likely to recur.
8. Focus on your whole portfolio, not the component parts. Calculate the whole portfolio's return each year.
9. If you are very wealthy, realize that your broker will likely do his best to bleed you with vehicles featuring excessive expenses and risks.

PILLAR FOUR

The Business of Investing

The Carny Barkers

Unless you are going to be trading stock and bond certificates with your friends, you will be forced to confront the colossus that bestrides the modern American scene: the financial industry. And make no mistake about it, you are engaged in a brutal zero-sum contest with it—every penny of commissions, fees, and transactional costs it extracts is irretrievably lost to you.

Each leg of this industry—the brokerage houses, mutual funds, and press—will get its own chapter. Their operations and strategies are somewhat different, but their ultimate goal is the same: to transfer as much of your wealth to their ledger books as they can. The brokerage industry is the most dangerous and rapacious, but also the easiest to deal with, since it can be bypassed completely. You *will* have to deal with the fund industry, and we'll discuss the lay of the land in this vital area.

More than seven decades ago, journalist Frederick Allen observed that those writing the nation's advertising copy wielded more power than those writing its history. Ninety-nine percent of what you read in and hear from the financial media is advertising cloaked as journalism.

In our modern society, it is impossible to avoid newspapers, magazines, the Internet, and television. You will need to understand how the financial media works and how it plays a central role in the survival of the brokerage and fund industries.

9

Your Broker Is Not Your Buddy

*A broker with a clientele full of contented customers was—and is—a broker who will soon be looking for a new job. Brokers need **trades** to make money.*
Joseph Nocera, from *A Piece Of The Action*

Imagine for a moment that you're a businessman who's been assigned by your company to a small country in eastern Europe. Let's call it Churnovia. (It neighbors Randomovia, which you heard about earlier.) Although you find the climate, culture, and cuisine to your liking, you do wonder about the nation's legal system. After all, Churnovia has only recently emerged from the shadow of the former Soviet Union, and legal concepts such as property and contractual obligation are not as well developed as they should be.

One day, you feel a belly pain and, by the time you are rushed to the hospital, you are in agony. You are whisked into surgery where your appendix is removed. You seem to recover rapidly and are quickly discharged home. But your spouse notices something curious while you're asleep: your abdomen seems to be *ticking*. Sure enough, you go into a quiet room and are able to detect a faint, regular noise emanating from your midsection.

You return to your surgeon and report this unusual observation. After replacing the stethoscope into his white coat, he nonchalantly replies, "Oh yes, it's not unusual for bellies to tick after a bout of appendicitis." You are not impressed, and your concern increases as your pain gradually returns, this time accompanied by high fever.

Your faith in Churnovian medicine shaken, you fly home, where doctors remove a wristwatch surrounded by a sack of infected tissue. This time, your recovery is not as rapid, and you are confined to the hospital for many weeks of antibiotic therapy. It is months before you can return to work. You begin to wonder about legal recourse and consult an expert in international law.

His report is not sanguine. "You see, there's a big difference between Churnovian and American medicine. For starters, doctors there have no firm educational requirements. You don't even have to go to medical school. Some, in fact, have never completed high school. All you have to do is cram for a multiple-choice exam, which you can take as many times as you need in order to pass. And as soon as you pass, you can hang out a shingle. What's worse, Churnovian doctors owe no professional duty to their patients. They can easily get away with performing unnecessary surgeries for financial gain. Also, when things go wrong, they aren't held to a particularly high standard. And here's the *pièce de résistance*: upon entering the hospital you signed an agreement to submit all disputes to an arbitration board whose structure is mandated by the Churnovian Medical Association. I'm sorry, but I'd be a fool to take your case."

Sound farfetched? It isn't. Once you step inside the office of a retail brokerage firm, you might as well be in Churnovia. Consider:

- There are no educational requirements for brokers (or, as they're known in the business, registered reps). No mandatory courses in finance, economics, law, or even a high-school diploma are necessary to enter the field. Simply pass the pathetically simple Series 7 exam, and you're on your way to a profitable career. In fact, having gotten this far in the book, you know far more about the capital markets than the average broker. I have yet to meet any brokers who are aware that small-growth stocks have low returns, or who are familiar with the most basic principles of portfolio theory. I have never met a broker who was aware of the corrosive effect of portfolio turnover on performance. And I have yet to encounter one who is able to use the Gordon Equation to estimate returns.
- Brokers have no fiduciary responsibility toward their clients. Although the legal definition of "fiduciary" is complex, this basically means the obligation to always put the client's interests first. Doctors, lawyers, bankers, and accountants all owe their clients fiduciary responsibility. Not so stockbrokers. (Investment advisors do.)
- There are few other professions where the service provider's interest is so different from the client's. Not even HMO medicine contrasts the welfare of providers and consumers as starkly. While you seek to minimize turnover, fees, and commissions, it's in your broker's best interest to maximize these expenses. A hoary old broker adage expresses this objective perfectly: "My job is to slowly transfer the client's assets to my own name."

- Almost all brokerage houses have you agree, at the time of opening your account, to resolve any future legal disputes via arbitration before the New York Stock Exchange, Inc. or NASD Regulation, Inc., in other words, the brokers' own trade groups.

In the following pages, we'll survey the sorry story of the brokerage industry and how its interests and yours are diametrically opposed.

The Betrayal of Charlie Merrill

By any measure, Charles Edward Merrill was a spirited visionary. Yet he certainly did not fit the stereotype. Self-aggrandizing and overly fond of carousing, strong drink, and other men's wives, he nearly single-handedly pioneered the financial services industry in the period surrounding World War II. The rise and fall of his dream—the brokerage company as public fiduciary—is a story worth telling.

Born in 1885, Merrill entered the brokerage business after dropping out of Amherst and quickly built a successful investment banking and retail brokerage firm. Merrill was repulsed by the corrupt financial climate of the late 1920s, with its bucket shops and overt stock manipulation, and strove to be different. Wall Street then was the ultimate insider's poker game in which the investing public invariably played the sucker. The 1929 crash produced a wave of popular revulsion against the brokerage industry and resulted in the passage of the Securities Acts of 1933 and 1934, and the Glass-Steagall Act, which still shape the financial industry today. But for decades before this, Charlie Merrill knew there was something wrong, and he wanted to fix it. In 1939 he got his chance, accepting the leadership of a new firm: the merged Merrill, Lynch & Co. and E.A. Pierce and Cassatt, later renamed Merrill Lynch.

Merrill undertook the job with relish and made it his mission to restore public confidence in the brokerage industry—in short, to "bring Wall Street to Main Street." This was a tough row to hoe, and his methods were nothing short of revolutionary. First and foremost, he paid his brokers by salary, not commissions. Since the first "stock jobbers" began plying their trade in the coffeehouses of London's Change Alley in the late seventeenth century, brokers had made their living by "churning" their clients—encouraging them to trade excessively in order to generate fat fees.

Merrill wanted to send a message to the investing public that his brokers were different from the commission-hungry rogues of his competitors. By contrast, his salaried employees would act as the objective, disinterested stewards of the public's capital. He would not charge for collecting dividends, as did other "wirehouses" (as brokerage firms, which communicated over private phone lines, were known). Commissions would be the minimum allowed by the exchange. Although high by today's standards, a Merrill customer would get rates offered only the biggest clients at other firms. A Merrill broker would always disclose the company's interest in a particular stock, something that was not required by law and unheard of elsewhere in the industry (and rarely done even today). Hot tips were replaced by analytic research.

Merrill's revolution succeeded. By the time he passed away in 1956, Merrill Lynch had grown into the nation's largest wirehouse, with 122 offices, 5,800 employees, and 440,000 customers. Yet Merrill died an unhappy man.

First and foremost, although Merrill Lynch had made the mass market transition, the rest of Wall Street had not yet made it to Main Street. It gave the old man no satisfaction to be the leader of a failed, backward industry. But more importantly, the rest of Wall Street continued to treat the client as it always had: not as an object of respect, worthy of the most effective and efficient investment product, but instead as a "revenue center."

Worse was still to come. Donald Regan (who later became Treasury Secretary) took over the reins at Merrill in 1968. The markets were buoyant that year. Then, as now, tech stocks were all the rage and trading volume was high, at least by the standards of the day. Brokers at other firms, all of whom worked on a commission basis, were making money like it was going out of style. But there was no joy at Merrill, where the brokers were salaried. Defections mounted, and within a short time after assuming power, Regan was forced to join the rest of the industry and allow his troops a piece of the commission action.

Thus was Merrill's legacy betrayed, along with its clients. In the short run, Regan had saved the company; the defections stopped and profitability returned. Trading volume at Merrill skyrocketed as it became just like everyone else. At the same time, the company ceased treating its clients' interests as a sacred trust and turned them into cash cows to be methodically milked for commissions.

This was the end of the trail for the modern retail brokerage firm as a socially useful enterprise. It fell to others, notably Ned Johnson at Fidelity and Jack Bogle at Vanguard, to later champion inexpensive access to the markets for the average investor. We'll examine that story—the rise of the mutual fund industry—in the next chapter.

Stockbroking's Seamy Underside

Few industries are as opaque to serious study as retail brokerage. The most basic data pertaining to broker background and performance,

portfolio turnover, and expense simply do not exist. It is truly astonishing that the SEC, charged with protecting the public interest in the
capital markets, collects little information about the level of performance, fees, turnover, and other expenses in the industry. And it seems
to have little interest at all in the training and level of knowledge of
brokers as a group. It is a sad fact that you can pass the Series 7 exam
and begin to manage other people's accumulated life savings faster
than you can get a manicurist's license in most states.

The brokerage industry itself is extremely tight-lipped about fees,
performance, and corporate practices. Because of this, we are forced
to look at the indirect evidence—anecdotal descriptions of the qualifi-
cations, training, incentives, and culture at the big wirehouses. Even
the most cursory study reveals that there is very good reason for the
secrecy.

The first observation is the most obvious. As we've already discussed, your investment return, on average, will be the market return
minus your expenses. Does it have to be said that your broker has an
incentive to keep those expenses—the nearly exclusive source of his
income—as high as possible? For proof, just look at what brokers do
and don't recommend to their clients. Rarely are Treasury securities
recommended, because they carry minuscule commissions. And you
will almost never see a broker suggest a no-load fund.

Principal Transactions Are Not Principled Transactions

There is a lot of confusion about one source of a broker's income—
spreads. A stock or bond does not have one price, but two: the lower
"bid" and the higher "ask." You buy at the higher ask price and sell at
the lower bid price. The difference between the two is small for heavily traded stocks, typically less than 1% of the purchase price, and large
for thinly traded stocks—as much as 6% of the price. Thus, every time
the investor buys, then later sells a stock or bond, he loses the spread
between the bid and the ask price. The spread goes to the "market
maker," the person or company that at all times maintains an invento-
ry of the stock or bond, to allow for smooth trading.

In many cases, the broker is acting as an "agent," which means that
he and his company are *not* the market makers. Instead of getting the
spread, they trade with the market maker and collect a commission for
this service. But frequently the broker acts as "principal," meaning that
his firm is, in fact, the market maker, buying from and selling to its
own clients. In this case, they do collect the spread and are not
allowed to also charge a commission. (Although illegal, the charging
of a commission on a principal transaction—"double dipping"—is not

a rare occurrence.) This is usually noted on the trade confirmation as a "principal transaction." And here is where most of the skullduggery occurs.

Profit margins are quite high with principal transactions—the client almost never finds out that the stock or bond he just purchased was acquired from another of the firm's customers at a much lower price. Clients are told simply that "there is no commission" on principal transactions, as if they have just benefited from an unexpected bit of corporate largess.

Even worse, many wirehouses' principal transactions take the form of "specials"—undesirable stocks and bonds underwritten or purchased in quantity by the firm and passed off on clients via brokers touting glowing research reports from the company's crack analysts. Brokers who can unload large amounts of such toxic waste on their unsuspecting clients are rewarded with bonuses and prizes (typically exotic vacations). I have never seen a broker-run account that was not laced with obscure, illiquid stocks and bonds carrying high commissions and spreads; these securities have "special" written all over them. Sadly, clients are never told that such transactions involved a special.

Most brokerage houses also sell mutual funds. These almost always carry a sales fee, or "load." As we'll see in the next chapter, load funds do not perform any better than funds sold without a sales fee—known as "no-load funds." Yet, brokers almost never recommend no-load funds, for obvious reasons.

Have you ever wondered how your broker comes up with his recommendations? Do you think that he carefully analyzes the market, stock by stock, looking over each company's fundamental financial data, industry trends, and marketing data? Hardly. The average broker is a salesman, not an expert in finance. Your broker's stock picks come straight from the "squawk box," a loudspeaker that connects every branch to headquarters. Several times a day, the firm's industry analysts and strategists report their conclusions simultaneously to thousands of brokers around the country. Later that day, or that week, you get the hot tip from your broker.

The problem is that you, as a small retail customer, are last in line. The large institutional players—pensions, privately managed money, and mutual funds—have received the news long before you, and the price of the stock has already been bid up by the time your broker phones you with the recommendation. In this poker game, you're the patsy. But you're in good company, because the analyst's recommendations are already tainted. The world of brokerage stock analysis is a small, inbred one. At its center are the corporate officers who dole out financial information about their companies to the analysts. Not only are all of the analysts getting their information from the same place, but their access to it is exquisitely dependent on the good will of the company.

If analysts are too critical of the companies they are covering, that vital information—the lifeblood of their craft—could dry up in a heartbeat. So the recommendations parroted back to you via the analyst, through the squawkbox, to your broker, are likely to have had most of their punches pulled.

The analyst-to-broker-to-you flow of information is flawed in another serious way—the connection that the brokerage firms have with their investment-banking arms, which underwrite new issues of stocks and bonds. These operations are enormously profitable and are a minefield for the unsuspecting investor. We've already come across specials—often newly underwritten stocks and bonds that have not sold well. Less overt, and much more widespread, is the compromised relationship between the brokerage's analysts, who are telling the brokers what to recommend to the clients, and the firms they cover, that also stand to gain from a broker's recommendations.

The analysts feel immense pressure to recommend the stocks of companies that their firm underwrites, or whose underwriting business they are seeking. Analysts are frequently threatened with discipline, or worse, for making unfavorable recommendations about such companies, and their recommendations are laced with euphemisms such as "outperform," "accumulate," or "hold." Because it may anger a potential underwriting client, the word "sell" does not seem to be in their vocabulary. "Hold" is the worst it gets when it comes to recommendations.

The significance of this complex relationship is that you can't trust your broker's recommendations. Does the analyst who is feeding them to the broker really believe in his buy recommendations? Or is he simply trying to curry favor with the company for the sake of its investment banking business? Does the analyst believe that you should be selling some of your names but is afraid of offending the company involved because the brokerage firm wants to get or keep its investment banking business? These issues got completely out of hand in the latter stages of the dot-com mania a few years ago. During this period, enormous underwriting profits dangled before the investment bankers' eyes, and the interests of the retail clients were completely forgotten. Investors found out too late that the recommendations of the big wirehouses' most prestigious technology analysts were driven more by the desire to garner underwriting business than to serve the interests of the clients.

Given such perverse incentives, it should not surprise you that the result is systematic abuse. Seen from the inside, the brokerages appear geared almost entirely to excessive trading and the resultant fees and spreads. The most shocking aspect of the brokerage business is that brokers almost never actually calculate the investment results of their clients, let alone reflect on methods for improving them. In recent years, their *modus operandi* has changed somewhat. "Wrap accounts," in which a set fee is charged for portfolio management, including commissions, are gaining in popularity. Another innovation is the institution of accounts allowing unlimited trading, also for a fixed fee. But at the end of the day, most wirehouses operate on the "2% rule"—collect 2% in fees and commissions, overt or hidden, on your clients' assets, or you're out.

My experience is that the 2% figure is extremely conservative—it is not unusual to see accounts from which as much as 5% annually is extracted. You say 2% doesn't sound like much? If the real return of your portfolio over the next few decades is 4%, you're giving your broker half of that, leaving 2% for yourself. Compounded over 30 years, that means you are left with 55 cents for every $1 you should have had.

There are only two studies that have actually looked at the level of returns and turnover in the average brokerage account. The first, by Gary Schlarbaum and his colleagues at Purdue and the University of Utah, found that, superficially at least, the brokerage accounts they examined did seem to obtain the market return, even after expenses. Unfortunately, their study covered the period from 1964 through 1970. During these seven years, small stocks outperformed large stocks by 8% per year. Since small investors tend to hold small stocks more heavily than institutional investors, their returns should have been much higher. But because of the relatively unsophisticated methodology used at that time, the true amount of the shortfall is impossible to determine.

More disturbing was the amount of trading taking place in these accounts. A total of 179,820 trades were executed in 2,506 accounts over the course of seven years. On average, that meant 76 trades per account, or about 11 per year. At an average of $150 per trade, this amounts to $1,650 per year. Since the median account size was approximately $40,000, that's 4% skimmed off the top annually. Thirty years ago, trading was expensive and the average account usually did not hold many stocks. So these accounts were being turned over as much as 100% per year. An even better idea of the amount of turnover is provided by the number of accounts with no trading in the seven-year period: just 17 of the 2,506. Not many buy-and-holders in that crowd.

What does 4% per year in commissions mean? Theoretically, after a few decades, your broker could wind up with more of your money in

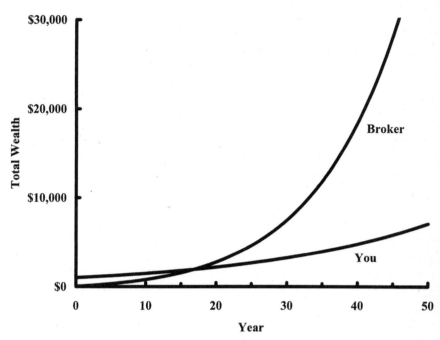

Figure 9-1. You and your broker: 8% return, 4% fees.

his bank account than you have in yours. This is demonstrated in Figure 9-1, in which it is hypothetically assumed that you and your broker can both earn 8% per year, but that he takes 4% of your portfolio each year, leaving you with a 4% return. Meanwhile, he can invest his commissions at 8%. After 17 years, he has accumulated more than you have, and after 28 years, he has twice as much.

The other major study, done by Brad Barber and Terrence Odean, at "a large discount broker" (think Charles Schwab) showed that the average portfolio turned over about 75% of its contents each year, and that the most active 20% of traders turned over an average of 258% of their stocks each year. (In other words, each position was traded, on average, every five months.) For every 100% of turnover, investors lost 4% of return. Please note that this was at a *discount* brokerage, where the commissions were much lower than at a typical full-service brokerage, and where brokers are not paid a slice of commissions.

Even the most casual of interactions with brokers and their current and former clients reveals several highly bothersome patterns:

- Brokers clearly occupy the lowest rung of investment sophistication and expertise. On the top rungs are the institutional money managers and brokerage house industry analysts; they are well-acquainted with the basics of modern finance. My experience is that many of these wirehouse aristocrats actually invest their personal portfolios in index funds. Unless you are a large client (or, as you would be known in the trade, a "whale"), you will never chat with one of these folks. And, of course, you will never actually have your money managed by them. The average broker, on the other hand, usually knows nothing about the relationship between turnover and return, how to build an efficient diversified portfolio, or the expected return of various asset classes. I have yet to meet a broker, for example, who is aware that value stocks historically have had higher returns than growth stocks. The plain fact is that they are not trained by the brokerage houses to invest—they are trained to sell.

- Brokers pay almost no attention to the returns their clients earn. It is rare to come across one who routinely calculates his clients' annual returns, let alone considers what these data might mean. In fact, the corporate culture at the major brokerage houses completely ignores what we've been doing in these pages—the objective, evidence-based scientific investigation of *what actually works.* If you catch a broker off-guard, particularly after a few drinks, and ask him how much time he spends discussing with his peers how to improve his clients' returns, you are likely to get a very blank look.

- Brokers do undergo rigorous training, sometimes lasting months—in sales techniques. All brokerage houses spend an enormous amount of money on teaching their trainees and registered reps what they really need to know—how to approach clients, pitch ideas, and close sales. One journalist, after spending several days at the training facilities of Merrill Lynch and Prudential-Bache, observed that most of the trainees had no financial background at all. (Or, as one used car salesman/broker trainee put it, "Investments were just another vehicle.") Although there were a few hour-long classes on the basics of stocks and bonds, these sessions were geared toward keeping the green recruits just one step ahead of their clients. Most of the training time was spent in a language lab-like setting, followed by role playing, in which sophisticated sales scripts were demonstrated and discussed. The modern broker is taught not to be pushy but, rather, to draw prospective clients into discussions of their worries and needs. Thirty years ago, a broker was taught to say, "AT&T is poised for a big move, and we at E.F. Hutton think you should buy 200 shares." Now, trainees are taught this approach:

"Mr. Smith, what is your most pressing concern?" In other words, the Zen of selling less, so that they can sell a lot more. At the final sessions, Merrill hopefuls were encouraged to get their real estate and insurance licenses and make a minimum of 180 cold calls per week.

- What do brokers think about almost every minute of the day? Selling. Selling. And Selling. Because if they don't sell, they're on the next train home to Peoria. The focus on sales breeds a curious kind of ethical anesthesia. Like all human beings placed in morally dubious positions, brokers are capable of rationalizing the damage to their clients' portfolios in a multitude of ways. They provide valuable advice and discipline. They are able to beat the market. They provide moral comfort and personal advice during difficult times in the market. Anything but face the awful truth: that their clients would be far better off without them. This is not to say that honest brokers who can understand and manage the conflicts of interest inherent in the job do not exist. But in my experience, they are few and far between. After all, what is best for the client is to keep investment costs and turnover as low as possible, which also minimizes a broker's income. Not infrequently, brokers become disenchanted and leave the business. Occasionally, they will even become fee-only advisors, whose compensation is not tied to trading. (For the record, I am a principal in a fee-only advisory business and will freely admit that the fees charged by many in the trade are as excessive as that seen at the brokerage houses.) But, by definition, you are not going to find such a person at a full-service brokerage house unless you happen to engage his services right before he quits.

Brokers will protest that in order to keep their clients for the long haul, they must do right by them. This is much less than half true. It's a sad fact that in one year a broker can make more money exploiting a client than in ten years of treating him honestly. The temptation to take the wrong road is more than most can resist.

The message of this chapter is the clearest of the book: Under no circumstances should you have anything to do with a "full service" brokerage firm. Unfortunately, this is frequently more easily said than done. Your broker is often your neighbor, fellow Rotarian, or even family. And eventually, by design, they all become your friend. Severing that professional relationship, although necessary to your financial survival, can be an extremely painful process.

Your journey through and beyond this book will allow you to manage your money without outside help. But if you do engage an advisor, make sure that he or she is compensated only through fees that you pay, and not from sales fees and payments by the funds or other investments they sell. The reason for this is simple: you do not want anyone near your money—advisor or broker—whose compensation is tied in any way to his choice of investment vehicles.

10

Neither Is Your Mutual Fund

We've just seen what treacherous territory the first leg of the investment business—the brokerage industry—is. The second leg, the mutual fund industry, provides less hostile terrain. Unlike the retail brokerage business, you actually have a chance of emerging intact from your dealings with the mutual fund business. While there are pitfalls a-plenty in this playground, they are much easier to see and avoid.

Loading the Dice Against You

As we've already discussed, the mutual fund—an investment product that makes highly diversified portfolios of stocks and bonds available to the smallest of investors—first began to transform the financial landscape in the 1920s. The excesses and imperfections of this early period were ironed out by the Investment Company Act of 1940, resulting in the creation of the relatively trouble-free, modern "open-end" fund, whose shares can be created or retired at will by the company to accommodate purchases and sales, as opposed to the "closed-end," or exchange-traded, 1920s investment trust, with shares that cannot be easily created or retired. But even the modern mutual fund scene is far from perfect.

The first and most obvious mutual fund trap to avoid is the load fund. These are usually sold by brokers or as insurance vehicles, carry a sales fee, and frequently also attach other ongoing charges designed to transfer wealth from you to whomever sold you the fund. These sales fees can be either front-loaded ("A-shares," paid upon purchase), back-loaded ("B-shares," paid upon sale), or be ongoing.

What do you get for the sales fee? Less than nothing. In Table 10-1, I've tabulated the ten-year returns for funds that have a sales fee (load

Table 10-1. Load Fund versus No-Load Fund Ten-Year Performance and Fees, April 1991 to March 2001

Category	Ten-Year Return	Expenses	Ten-Year Return	Expenses	12b-1
Large Growth	14.30%	0.98%	13.33%	1.70%	0.64%
Large Blend	14.07%	0.83%	13.58%	1.65%	0.63%
Large Value	13.98%	0.96%	13.66%	1.64%	0.63%
Mid Growth	14.21%	1.06%	13.53%	1.82%	0.67%
Mid Blend	13.76%	1.09%	12.83%	1.72%	0.66%
Mid Value	14.36%	1.12%	15.09%	1.84%	0.66%
Small Growth	14.67%	1.17%	11.86%	1.92%	0.66%
Small Blend	13.07%	1.07%	12.96%	1.84%	0.62%
Small Value	13.48%	1.17%	16.14%	1.82%	0.58%
Average	**13.95%**	**0.98%**	**13.47%**	**1.72%**	**0.64%**
	No-Load Funds		Load Funds		

(*Source*: Morningstar Inc., April 2001.)

funds) and those that have none (no-load funds) for each of the nine Morningstar categories. The average load fund return is 0.48% per year *less* than that of the average no-load fund. This is mostly accounted for by the 12b-1 fees added into the fund expenses. What are 12b-1 fees? They are an additional level of expense allowed by the SEC in order to pay for advertising. The theory is that this fee allows the fund to build up assets, thereby increasing its economy of scale, and reducing its fees. As you can see from Table 10-1, this is a fairy tale. Even after subtracting the 12b-1 fees from the expense ratios of the load funds, their expenses are still higher than those of the no-loads.

Even worse, the expenses and returns of load funds calculated in Table 10-1 do not take into account the load itself. These typically run about 4.75%. Amortize that over ten years, and you've lost yet another 0.46% of return per year.

Who buys this rubbish? Uninformed investors. Who sells it to them? Brokers, investment advisors, and insurance salesmen. Is it illegal? No. But it should be.

A close relative to the load mutual fund is the variable annuity. These are sold by insurance companies and carry an insurance feature. Like load funds, most come with high sales fees and ongoing insurance charges that are often higher than those of load funds. These products are not bought—they are sold. Their only advantage is that they compound free of taxes until they are redeemed. This tax advantage, however, is only rarely worth the cumulative cost of the fees. To add insult to injury, a large chunk of these are sold by insurance agents, financial planners, and brokers for retirement accounts, where the tax deferral is unnecessary. Consider a recent advertisement from Kemper Annuities & Life in *Financial Planning* magazine, a trade publication for investment advisors:

Now an annuity that keeps paying,
   and paying
   and paying
   and paying
   and paying
   and paying . . .

The advertisement goes on to explain how the product being pushed, the Gateway Incentive Variable Annuity, pays the salesman a 4% upfront commission plus a 1% "trail" fee each year. The ad urges the magazine's investment-professional readers to "Find out more about the annuity that keeps paying and paying and paying . . ."

A great deal, no doubt, for the salesman. But not for the person buying one of these beauties, who, after first paying a 4% sales fee, then keeps paying the 1% "trail fee" each and every year. My message here is obvious: steer clear of mutual funds and variable annuities with sales loads and fees. Buy only true no-load funds and annuities that do not carry fees of any type, including 12b-1 fees. The major no-load companies are Fidelity, Vanguard, Janus, T. Rowe Price, American Century, and Invesco.

Into the Sunlight, But Not Quite Out of The Woods

Get the load fund and variable annuity pitfalls out of the way, and you're almost home. The most obvious difference between the mutual fund and retail brokerage business is the amount of sunlight. The transparency of the fund industry is simply breathtaking. Just by opening your daily newspaper, you can compare the performances of thousands of stock and bond funds. With a little more effort, you can get a pretty good idea of the expenses incurred by each fund. (If you want to know everything there is to know about any given fund, treat yourself to a single issue of Morningstar's Principia Pro fund software for $105. A warning: This is a highly addictive package, and you may not be able to buy just one.) Imagine what would happen if you called your local brokerage and tried to get the performance and expense data on each of its brokers. If you were lucky, they would muffle their laughter and politely suggest that you mind your own business.

This availability of information means that the fund company's interests are much more closely aligned with yours. Given the ubiquity of fund performance information, fund investors are highly sensitive to

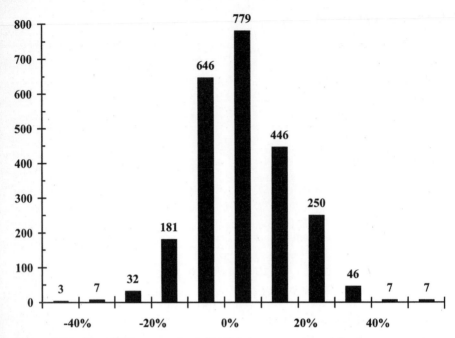

Figure 10-1. Year 2000 returns for 2,404 U.S. large-cap mutual funds.

short- and intermediate-term fund returns. Unlike the retail brokerage world, funds pay exquisite attention to investment performance.

But you and your fund company are still not quite on the same team. There is one key area where your interests and its diverge: management fees. In order to understand this, take a look at Figure 10-1. What I've plotted is the performance of the 2,404 domestic large-cap funds in 2000. Notice the enormous amount of scatter in fund performance for that year—310 funds gained more than 20%, and 223 funds *lost* more than 10%. The difference in annual performance among funds is so large that investors usually don't notice if the fund company slices off an extra half a percent in fees.

The companies understand this all too well: "You know, last year was a good one. The shareholders won't care if we raise our management fee a bit. Why not?" So fees creep upward; between 1981 and 1997, the expense ratio for the average stock fund rose from 0.97% to 1.55%. This slightly overstates the case, as a lot of small, inefficient funds are included in this statistic—the "dollar weighted" fee average has not risen as dramatically—but the upward trend is clear. Over the past decade, the explosion of assets under management should have *reduced* fees via economies of scale. This increasing fee trend is nothing short of scandalous.

Gunning the Fund

Consider Fidelity Investments, which currently has more than $600 billion in assets under management. The year 2000 was not a good one for "Fido." None of its stock funds was one of the 310 in the large-cap universe that returned more than 20%. In fact, only 22 of their 72 large-cap stock funds made any money at all. The best, its Dividend Growth Fund, gained 12.25%. Nothing to write home about, but still better than the performance of the average large-cap fund, which lost about 6%.

So what does Fido do with the bad hand dealt it in 2000? Advertise the Dividend Growth Fund to death. The average fund investor, not realizing that past performance does not persist, sees the ads and buys the fund, no matter what its fees. After all, if the fund beat its peers by 18% in a given year, what difference does a little extra expense make?

Inside the Fidelity organization, this tactic is known as "gunning the fund." The first and best-known example occurred almost two decades ago. Unlike 2000, 1982 and 1983 were good years for Fido, particularly for a 30-year-old manager named Michael Kassen. His Select Technology Fund returned an amazing 162% for the one-year period ending June 1983. Until that point, Fido's reclusive chief, Edward Crosby ("Ned") Johnson III, had been reluctant to use the press. But persuaded by one of his lieutenants, he instructed Kassen to cooperate for a cover story in *Money*, to the point of posing outdoors in the middle of a Boston February for several hours with shorts and squash racket.

This headline accompanied Kassen, his racket, and playing shorts in the next issue: "How to Invest in Mutual Funds. They're the Safest Surest Way to Invest in a Surging Market." What happened next exceeded Fido's wildest dreams. Within several weeks, new investors poured so much money into the fund that it tripled in size to $650 million, an enormous sum in those days.

Goosebumps aside, Kassen himself was somewhat less than ecstatic. It was nearly impossible for him to effectively deploy so much cash so fast in the relatively small companies on which his fund focused. Because of the subsequent collapse of the tech market, new shareholders got a very steep tuition bill from the College of the Capital Markets. Over the year following the peak inflow in mid-1983, the fund lost almost a quarter of its value.

This sequence highlights what I call the "mutual fund hierarchy of happiness." At the top of the pyramid is the fund family. Fidelity collected more than 1% in fees and 3% in front-end loads on Select Technology's $650 million in assets, no matter how it performed. The fund manager was less happy: he was now faced with the impossible job of attempting to invest a mountain of cash rapidly in a small corner of the market, a setup for incurring huge market impact costs, which we discussed in Chapter 3. Fortunately, his pain was eased by a high salary and the knowledge that as a newly minted superstar manager, he could demand even higher compensation, lest he peddle his scarce "talents" elsewhere.

At the bottom of this pyramid were, and are still . . . the shareholders. About the only thing performance-chasing investors have going for them is the faint glow of association with the soon-to-disappear notoriety of their fund manager. Weighing much more heavily on the other side of the scale is the possibility that the fund company might not be able' to resist piggybacking higher management fees on its new popularity, the likelihood that the new shareholders have invested in a sector or style that has just topped out, and the certainty that their assets will be invested with a maximum of market impact.

The subsequent history of Fidelity Select Technology is instructive. After garnering nearly $1 billion dollars in assets in 1983 and 1984, the tech market turned stone cold, underperforming the S&P 500 by an average of 20% in each of the next six years. By 1989, fund assets had fallen to just $71 million. At that point, the fund's performance turned around, and it gradually began to accumulate assets again, finally reaching the $1 billion mark in 1998. In that year, it beat the S&P 500 by 66%, and in 1999, as the dot-com mania heated up, by 96%. Within 12 months, assets quintupled to $5.2 billion, just in time for the tech collapse of 2000.

The story of Select Technology is emblematic of the nature of fund flows. First, they are most often contrary indicators—funds in high-performing sectors of the market tend to attract great piles of assets. In industry parlance, this is known as "hot money": assets thrown by naïve investors at high past performance. It is more often than not a sign that the top is near. And even if it isn't, it certainly serves as a drag on the performance of the funds, which are faced with deploying a large amount of capital in a fixed number of existing company shares.

Second, and most important, it highlights the conflict of interest between the investors and the fund company. Just as the brokerage firms exist to make clients trade as much as possible, the fund companies exist for one purpose: to collect assets, no matter how poorly their funds subsequently perform.

Most fund shareholders are "hot money" investors, buying high and selling low, as Select Technology's hapless plungers did in the 1980s. Ned Johnson's special genius is his ability to pander to the public's desire for an endless number of investment flavors-of-the-moment. You say Argentine and Turkish bonds are all the rage and you want a fund investing in emerging markets debt? You've got it. Southeast Asian Stocks? Coming right up. Wireless? Nordic? Biotech? No problemo. "We were in the manufacturing business. We manufactured funds," was how one Fido executive put it. (These were funds, by the way, that few of Fidelity's principals and employees would ever dream of owning themselves.)

Not only was this system wildly successful at garnering capital; it functioned as a veritable roach motel—money checked in, but it never checked out. After Fido shareholders had gotten burned by last year's hot fund, they would redeem their assets into a Fidelity money fund and eventually reinvest them in yet another one of Ned's 231 flavors.

Finally, I can't help but mention the Morningstar Unpopular Funds Strategy. Since Morningstar is located in Chicago and staffed by a sports-loving crowd, they have a special affinity for losers. Every year since 1987, they've used the fund money flows discussed above to identify the most popular and unpopular fund categories. They then follow the average performance of the three most popular and unpopular fund groups forward for three years. Eight out of nine times, the unpopular funds beat the popular funds, and seven out of nine times the unpopular funds beat the average equity fund. Most tellingly, the popular fund categories also lagged the average equity fund seven of nine times. I certainly don't recommend this as an investment strategy, but it's an excellent example of the dangers of chasing performance, because of the tendency for asset classes to "mean-revert," that is, to follow good performance with bad, and vice versa.

Watching the Cookie Jar

As you can see, the conflict of interest between you and your fund company is just as direct as that between you and your broker. You are engaged in a zero-sum game with both—every dollar in fees and commissions paid to a fund company or broker is a dollar irretrievably lost to you. But the brokerage industry has one big advantage over the fund industry; the river of cash flowing to the broker is much better hidden than the management fees paid to the fund company. A good analogy would be the difference between a cookie jar placed in your child's bedroom versus one sitting in the kitchen. The baked goods are going to disappear much more rapidly from the bedroom jar than from the one in the kitchen.

Whereas between 2% and 5% of the cookies are going to abscond from the average brokerage account each year, the fund companies can only get away with much less. Since their fees are published at regular intervals in the newspaper and in the annual reports they must send to you by law, there are few cookies (or fees) that can be hidden.

But you can still learn a lot about the relative integrity of the fund companies just by watching those jars. For example, almost all large fund companies offer an "equity income" fund, which specializes in large value funds sporting reasonable dividends. Vanguard's equity income fund charges 0.41%; Fidelity's, 0.67%; and Scudder's, 0.87%. Each company also offers a large international-growth fund: Vanguard charges 0.53% for its; Fidelity, 1.05%; and Scudder, 1.12%. Each has a small-cap growth fund: Vanguard charges 0.42% for its; Fidelity, 0.80%; and Scudder, 1.70%. Finally, each offers a precious metals fund. Vanguard charges 0.77%; Fidelity, 1.41%; and Scudder, 1.81%.

I picked these four classes at random, simply looking for equivalent funds offered by all three companies. What have we learned? That there are real cultural differences among fund families. Scudder just can't keep its hands out of the cookie jar. (It is no coincidence that Scudder, before it was recently sold to Deutsche Bank, belonged to the same corporate parent as Kemper Annuities & Life, producers of the annuity that keeps paying, and paying, and paying.) Fido is a bit more restrained, but not by much. And Vanguard seems to be very well behaved. (None of the Vanguard funds I mentioned, by the way, are index funds, which charge even lower expenses. In order to make the comparisons apples-to-apples, all of the fees quoted above are for actively managed funds.)

What accounts for the differences among the fund companies? Their ownership structures do. Nowadays, most fund companies are owned by large financial holding companies. In Scudder's case it was owned by Zurich Scudder Investments, and then by Deutsche Bank. (Scudder, in fact, after helping pioneer international and no-load investing along with Vanguard, has of late changed names multiple times and is in the process of committing corporate suicide by converting to a load-distribution mechanism and looking for merger partners.) As such, fund companies exist solely to generate revenues for the parent company. Their primary goal is the same as Louis XIV's famous directive to his tax collectors, "Extract the maximum amount of feathers from the goose, with the least amount of hissing." You, of course, star in this minor drama as the goose.

Fidelity's structure is unusual for a financial organization of its size, because it is privately owned, mainly by Ned Johnson and family. The Johnson family must be less greedy than their corporate brethren; their fees tend to be just a smidgen less. Vanguard's ownership structure, as we'll soon see, is actually designed to encourage *low* fees.

Journalist Jason Zweig captured this problem best in a speech given to an industry forum in 1997, in which he began by noting,

> This February, two portfolio managers, Suzanne Zak and Doug Platt, left IAI, a fund company based in Minneapolis. As Suzanne Zak told *The Wall Street Journal:* "It got to the point where I wanted to get back to the basics instead of being part of a marketing machine." And Doug Platt, whose father founded IAI, added: "My father retired over 20 years ago, and the firm's structure and focus are entirely different from what it was then. *IAI is basically a marketing company that happens to be selling investments.*"

Zweig then asked the participants to consider whether *they* were running an investment firm or a marketing firm. The differences, according to him, are many:

- A marketing firm advertises the track records of its hottest funds. An investment firm does not.
- A marketing firm creates new funds because they can sell them, not because they think they are good investments. An investment firm does not.
- A marketing firm turns out "incubator funds," kills off those that do not perform well, and advertises the ones that survive. An investment firm does not.
- An investment firm continually warns its clients that markets sometimes go down. A marketing firm does not.
- An investment firm closes a fund to new investors when it begins to incur excessive impact costs. A marketing firm does not.
- An investment firm rapidly reduces its fees and expenses with increasing assets. A marketing firm keeps fees high, no matter how large its assets grow.

By Zweig's definition, only about 10% of mutual fund companies are investment firms. The rest are marketing firms. Buyer beware.

The 401(k) Briar Patch

The nation's fastest growing investment pool is the employer-sponsored, defined-contribution structure. The centerpiece of this scheme is the 401(k) system, with more than $1.7 trillion under management. These plans are wildly popular with employers since they are inexpensive to fund and administer. Further, they effectively shield employers from multiple types of liability. Unfortunately, most plans pay scant attention to expenses; the typical plan has overt costs of at least 2% per year. And that's before we take into account the hidden

costs from commissions and spreads, much of which accrue eventually to the fund companies. Why is so little attention paid to 401(k)
expenses? Because the employers focus on the services provided by
the fund companies, particularly in the record-keeping area, without
considering or even caring about the true cost of these services to their
employees.

Worse, most of the stock funds offered by the fund companies are
heavily weighted with the large-cap glamour companies of the 1990s.
As a result, there is inadequate diversification into other asset classes.
Most plans have no index funds beyond the S&P 500.

The result of all this is breathtaking. Although it's difficult to get a
handle on the precise returns obtained by employees, the best available data suggest that 401(k) plans provide at least 2% per year less
return than those earned in traditional "defined-benefit" plans. And
these, as we've already seen in Figure 3-4, are no great shakes to begin
with. (In fairness, it should be noted that the return of a traditional
defined-benefit plan accrues to the employer, who, in turn, will be
paying their retirees a fixed benefit.)

The 403(b) plan structure, utilized by teachers, suffers from the same
flaws. Worst of all are 457 plans, provided to certain public employees, with average total costs well in excess of 3% per year. Until
recently, 457 funds could not even be rolled into IRA accounts at
retirement/termination, although the 2001 tax legislation makes this
possible for most 457 owners when they leave their employment.

What can you do if your employer has put you into one of these
dogs? You really only have two choices, neither of which may be
palatable or even possible: try to get the plan changed or quit and roll
it over into an IRA.

The ascent of self-directed, defined-contribution plans—of which
the 401(k) is the most common type—is a national catastrophe waiting to happen. The average employee, who is not familiar with the
market basics outlined in this book, is no more able to competently
direct his own investments than he is to remove his child's appendix
or build his own car. The performance of the nation's professional
defined-benefit pension management illustrated in Figure 3-4 may not
be spectacular, but at least the majority of managers delivered performance within a few percentage points of the market's. Because of
the substandard nature of most 401(k)s, the average employee is
already starting out 2% to 3% behind the market. He will almost certainly fall even further behind because of the participants' generalized
lack of knowledge of three of the four pillars—investment theory, history, and psychology. Toss in the inevitable luck of the draw, and
many will have long-term real returns of less than zero. It is possible

that, in the next few decades, we shall see a government bailout of this system that will make the savings and loan crisis of the 1990s look like a trip to Maui.

Jack Bogle Breaks Away From the Pack

If Fidelity's ownership structure is unusual, then Vanguard's is unique. The four mutual fund examples I provided above are not isolated cases. Within almost any asset class you care to name, and compared to almost any other fund company, Vanguard offers the lowest fees, often by a country mile. Why? Having told the stories of Charlie Merrill and Ned Johnson's Fidelity, the time has now come for the most remarkable saga of all—that of Jack Bogle and the Vanguard Group. For it was Mr. Bogle who finally realized Merrill's dream of bringing Wall Street to Main Street.

John C. Bogle did not exactly tear up the track in his early years at Princeton. He had a particularly shaky freshman start, but by his senior year had begun to impress his professors with his grasp of the investment industry. The choice for his senior thesis could not have been more fortuitous—"The Economic Role of the Investment Company." (Bogle had his interest piqued by a 1949 article about mutual funds in *Fortune*.) Bogle's thin tome was a snapshot of the nascent mutual fund industry in 1951 and, more importantly, a roadmap for its future. Graduating from Princeton magna cum laude, he set out to make his mark on the investment industry.

Walter Morgan, who worked for one of the few fund companies in existence at the time—Wellington Management Company—decided to hire this brash beginner. Bogle was an ambitious young man and was concerned that the tiny mutual fund industry might not offer a palette broad enough to support his aspirations. He needn't have worried. For in the process of almost single-handedly creating his vision of what the investment business *should* be, he forever raised the public's expectations of it.

Bogle rose rapidly at Wellington and within a decade became Morgan's heir apparent. Like everyone else, he got caught up in the excitement of the "Go-Go Era" of the mid-1960s and, in its aftermath, became *hors de combat*, fired from what he had begun to think of as "his" company—Wellington.

But Wellington Management had picked the wrong man to fire. Few managers knew the ins and outs of the fund playbook—the Investment Company Act of 1940—as well as Jack Bogle. Among other things, the Act mandated that the fund directorship be separate from that of the companies which provided their advisory service, in this case Wellington Management. Fortuitously, only a few of the fund's directors worked for the management company. After months of acrimonious debate, the Wellington *Fund* declared its independence from Wellington *Management*, and on September 24, 1974, with Bogle at the helm of the new company, Vanguard was born. At a stroke, he became his own man, free to let loose upon an initially unappreciative public his own private vision of the great investment company utopia—The World According to Bogle.

The new company's first order of business demonstrated Bogle's revolutionary genius by establishing a unique ownership structure— one never before seen in the investment industry. It involved creating a "service corporation" that ran the funds' affairs—accounting and shareholder transactions—and was owned by the funds themselves. *Since the service company—Vanguard—was owned exclusively by the funds, and the funds were owned exclusively by the shareholders, the shareholders were Vanguard's owners.* Vanguard became the first, and only, truly "mutual" fund company—that is, owned by its shareholders. There was, therefore, no incentive to milk the investors, as generally happened in the rest of the investment industry, because the funds' shareholders were also Vanguard's owners. The only imperative of this system was to keep costs down.

This structure, by the way, exists in a few other areas of commerce, most prominently in "mutual" insurance companies, in which the policyholders also own the company. This ownership structure is disappearing from the insurance industry scene, however, with existing policyholders receiving company stock. TIAA-CREF, the teachers' retirement fund, also offers mutual funds to the general public. While not mutually owned by its shareholders like Vanguard, it functions essentially as a nonprofit and offers fees nearly as low as Vanguard's.

In 1976 came the first retail index fund. By this time, Bogle had learned of the failure of active fund management from several sources: the study by Michael Jensen we mentioned in Chapter 3, the writings of famed economist Paul Samuelson and money manager Charles Ellis, and, of course, from his own painful experience at Wellington. (Incidentally, Samuelson's economics textbook was the source of Bogle's initial troubles at Princeton. Had he scored a few points lower in that introductory course, he'd have lost his scholarship and been forced out of school. The world would have never heard of the Vanguard Group.)

Bogle calculated by hand the average return of the largest mutual funds: 1.5% less than the S&P 500. In his own words, "Voilà! Practice confirmed by theory." His new company would provide the investor with the market return, from which would be subtracted the smallest possible expense. Thus did Bogle make available to the public the same type of index fund offered to Wells Fargo's institutional clients a few years before. The expense ratio was fairly small, even for those days—0.46%.

Last to go were sales fees. Realizing that these fees were inconsistent with indexing and keeping costs as low as possible, Bogle made all of his funds "no-load," that is, he eliminated sales fees, which had been as high as 8.5%. In this respect, Bogle was not quite a pioneer; several other firms, including, ironically, Scudder, had previously eliminated the load.

At the time, this series of actions was considered an act of madness. Many thought that he had lost his head and predicted the firm's rapid demise.

In a remarkable *tour de force*, less than two years after leaving Wellington, Bogle had assembled in one place the three essential tools that would forever change the investment world: a mutual ownership structure, a market index fund, and a fund distribution system free of sales fees.

Although Vanguard did not exactly set the fund business on fire during its first decade, it gradually grew as investors discovered its low fees and solid performance. And once fund sizes began increasing, the process became a self-sustaining virtuous cycle: burgeoning assets allowed its shareholders the full benefit of increasing economies of scale, reducing expenses, further improving performance, and attracting yet more assets. By 1983, expenses on Vanguard's S&P 500 Index Trust fell below 0.30%, and by 1992, below 0.20%.

Interestingly, it was with its bond funds that Vanguard's advantage first became most clearly visible. There were two main reasons for this. First, the Vanguard 500 Index Trust could not have picked a worse time to debut. During the late 1970s, small stocks greatly outperformed large stocks. Recall Dunn's Law, which states that the fortunes of indexing a given asset class are tied to the fortunes of that asset class relative to others. In other words, if large-cap stocks are doing terribly, so too will indexing them. Because of this, Vanguard's first index fund was in the bottom quarter of all stock funds for its first two full calendar years and did not break into the top quarter (where it has remained, more or less, ever since) for six more years.

Second, as we saw in Figures 3-1, 3-2, and 10-1, there is a great amount of scatter in the performance of stock funds. Over periods of a year or two, a 0.50% expense advantage is easily lost in the "noise" of year-to-year active stock manager variation. Not so with bonds—particularly government bonds. One portfolio of long Treasury bonds or GNMA (mortgage-backed) bonds behaves almost exactly the same as another. Vanguard's GNMA fund has a rock-bottom expense of 0.28%, while the competition's average is 1.08%.

In the bond arena, this 0.80% expense gap is an insurmountable advantage—even the Almighty himself is incapable of assembling a portfolio of GNMAs capable of beating the GNMA market return by 0.80%. Of 36 mortgage bond funds with ten-year track records as of April 2001, the Vanguard GNMA fund ranks first. Among all government bond funds, it is by far the largest—more than twice the size of the runner-up.

Initially, the competition was scornful, particularly given the poor early performance of the Vanguard Index Trust 500 Fund. But as Vanguard's reputation, shareholder satisfaction ratings, and, most importantly, assets under management grew, it could no longer be ignored. By 1991, Fidelity threw in the towel and started its own low-cost index funds, as did Charles Schwab. As of this writing, there are now more than 300 index funds to choose from, not counting the newer "exchange-traded" index funds, which we'll discuss shortly.

Of course, not all of the companies offering the new index funds are suffused with Bogle's sense of mission—fully 20% of index funds carry a sales load of up to 6%, and another 30% carry a 12b-1 annual fee of up to 1% per year for marketing. The most notorious of these is the American Skandia ASAF Bernstein (no relation!) series, which carries both a 6% sales fee and a 1% annual 12b-1 fee. Paying these sorts of expenses to own an index fund boggles the mind and speaks to the moral turpitude of much of the industry.

There are other fund companies besides Vanguard well worth dealing with. TIAA-CREF—the pension plan for university and public school teachers—functions much like Vanguard, with all "profits" cycling back to the funds' shareholders. If you employ a qualified financial advisor, Dimensional Fund Advisors does a superb job of indexing almost any asset class you might wish to own at low expense. There are a few for-profit fund companies, like Dodge & Cox, T. Rowe Price, and Bridgeway, that are known for their investment discipline, intellectual honesty, and shareholder orientation. If you just can't make the leap of faith to index investing, these are fine organizations to invest with. Finally, there's even one load fund company worthy of praise: the American Funds Group. Its low fees and investment discipline are head and shoulders above its load-fund brethren. And if you have $1 million to invest, you can purchase their family of funds without a sales fee.

Thus did Vanguard finally shame most of the other big fund companies into offering inexpensive index funds. The Fidelity Spartan series has fees nearly identical to Vanguard's, and Charles Schwab's are not unreasonable, either. But none has offered the breadth of asset classes offered by Vanguard. Until last year.

The recent explosion of "exchange-traded funds" (ETFs) has changed the landscape of indexing. ETFs are very similar to mutual funds, except they are traded as stocks, similar to the investment trusts of the 1920s and to today's closed-end funds. The best known of these vehicles are Spyders, based on the S&P 500, and Cubes that track the Nasdaq 100. (A bit of nomenclature. In this context, the traditional mutual fund is referred to as "open-ended.")

There are advantages and disadvantages to ETFs, all relatively minor. The advantages are that they can be run more cheaply than an open-ended mutual fund, since the ETF does not have to service each shareholder as an individual account. Also ETFs, because of the way they maintain their composition, can be slightly more tax efficient than regular mutual funds. They are also priced and traded throughout the day, as opposed to the single end-of-day pricing and trading of a regular fund. On the minus side, like any other stock, you will have to pay a spread and a commission. This can be a real problem with some of the more esoteric ETFs, which are very thinly traded, and thus can have high spreads and even high impact costs at small share amounts. This will dent your return a bit.

My other concern about ETFs is their institutional stability. It is highly likely, but not absolutely certain, that Vanguard and Fidelity will still be supporting their fund operations in 20 or 30 years. The same cannot be said for many other entities offering ETFs. The concern here is not so much that your assets will be at risk—the Investment Company Act of 1940 makes that a very unlikely event. Rather, given the corporate restructuring that is endemic in the industry, I would worry the companies may decide that poor-selling ETFs should be dissolved, incurring unwanted capital gains. So I would not hold any of the more obscure ETFs in a taxable portfolio.

But ETFs are extremely promising. The scene is still evolving rapidly and by the time you read this, there will likely have been further dramatic changes in this area. It is now easy to build a balanced global portfolio consisting solely of ETFs. However, at the present time, because of the above considerations, I'd still give the nod to the more traditional open-ended index funds.

CHAPTER 10 SUMMARY

1. Never, ever, pay a load on a mutual fund or annuity. And never pay an ongoing 12b-1 fee for a mutual fund or excessive annuity fees.

2. Do not chase the performance of active managers. Not only does past performance not predict future manager performance, but excellent performance leads to the rapid accumulation of assets, which increases impact costs and reduces future return.
3. Be cognizant of the corporate structure and culture of your fund company. To whom do its profits flow? Is it an investment firm or a marketing firm?

11

Oliver Stone Meets Wall Street

No matter how cynical you become, it's never enough to keep up.
Lily Tomlin

The third, and least obvious, leg of the financial industry stool is the press, for it is reporters, editors, and publishers who inform and drive the investment patterns of the public. The relationship between the fourth estate and the brokerage and mutual fund industries is subtle, complex, and immensely powerful. We've already touched on this issue with the story of Michael Kassen's 1983 vault to fame on the strength of a single *Money* magazine cover. Two decades ago, it astounded everyone that nearly a billion dollars in assets could be moved with a single article. Now, when a fund arrives at the top of the one-year or five-year rankings for its category and is showered with billions in new money, no one blinks.

The engine of retail brokerage and fund flows is the financial media. In the words of songwriter Paul Simon, we live in a world suffused with "staccato signals of constant information"; try as you may, there is no escape from *Money, The Wall Street Journal, USA Today*, and CNBC. Unless you don't subscribe to any newspapers or magazines, don't watch television, don't listen to the radio, don't surf the Internet, and have no friends, you cannot help but be influenced by the world of business journalism. And the better you are at dealing with it, the better off your finances will be.

The bread and butter of the finance writer is the "successful" fund manager, market strategist, or newsletter writer. Having read this far, the flaw in this style of journalism should be obvious to you. All "successful" market timers are simply very fortunate coin flippers. Almost all apparently successful managers are lucky, not skilled. You might as well be reading about lottery winners. They may be fascinating from a human interest perspective, but there's no need to send them large checks.

Newsweek personal finance columnist Jane Bryant Quinn labels this style of journalism "financial pornography"—alluring, but utterly lacking in redeeming value. So why do investors take it seriously and use it to influence their investment decisions? Because they know little of what you have now mastered. That there are no gurus. That there are no money masters. That even if such people did exist, they wouldn't be managing a mutual fund, writing a newsletter, or spilling that most precious of investment commodities—information—for nothing to Lou Rukeyser and his 20 million viewers.

More germane is the question, why do journalists continue to grind out this trash? The answer is complicated. At the bottom rungs of the profession, most reporters just don't get it. Journalism attracts people with exceptional linguistic talent, but I've found that very few have the mathematical sophistication to appreciate the difference between skill and luck. The language of finance is mathematics, and if you're going to do first-rate financial journalism, you have to be able to crunch your own numbers and understand what they're telling you. Not many writers can do that.

Secondly, a competent financial journalist should have a grasp of the scholarly literature pertaining to investing. By scholarly literature I mean journals that publish original academic research, usually produced by a profession's national organizations. For example, your doctor finds out about the latest advances in medicine from "peer-reviewed journals"—periodicals such as the *New England Journal of Medicine* and *Journal of the American Medical Association*, in which the articles are all carefully reviewed, vetted, and edited. You'd be very alarmed if your physician admitted that most of her continuing education came from *USA Today*, wouldn't you? Unfortunately, that's just where most financial journalists (and most finance professionals, for that matter) turn. They rely on their brethren in the popular financial press and ignore finance's scholarly peer-reviewed literature—*Journal of Finance, Journal of Portfolio Management*, and the like.

On the other hand, the folks at the top of the greasy pole—the regular columnists for the major national periodicals—are usually well-informed and smart enough to understand the futility of market timing and stock picking. But they do have one slight problem: they like to eat on a regular basis. You can only write so many articles that say, "buy the market, keep your costs down, and don't get too fancy," before it starts to get very old. Whereas there is a never-ending supply of fund-managers-of-the-month who can provide much-needed fodder for articles.

The picture becomes complete when we understand the sad fact that most investors pick their mutual funds and brokerage houses on the basis of press coverage. So the circle closes. The relationship between money managers and the financial press is usually not a "conspiracy" (although as we'll see shortly, sometimes it is), but it is clear that each party desperately needs the other. Without active managers, there are no stories; without glowing manager interviews, there are no patsies to invest in the managers' funds. (Or, in Keynes' aviary, "gulls.")

The symbiosis between money managers and the press is hardly unique; consider fashion, automobiles, and travel reportage. But it is hard to come up with another example with an economic impact as large as that of financial journalism. Just as many automobile purchasers will buy on the basis of a favorable review in *Car and Driver*, a glowing money manager story can move vast amounts of capital.

This is the most benign interpretation of the relationship between journalists and the financial industry. Unfortunately, in recent years there has been a trend towards an increasingly sinister alliance between the "watchdogs" of the press and the industry it is supposedly overseeing on our behalf.

For example, in the late 1980s it was revealed that *Money* had begun to conduct joint focus groups with a major fund company. Its rationale was that they were both, after all, in the same business. Really? The business of most fund companies is the extraction of fees from shareholders. Is that also part of *Money's* mission? Given that almost all financial periodicals increasingly benefit from a steadily rising stream of advertising revenue from the fund families, it seems likely that in many cases, they may indeed be on the same team.

Journalists tend to be a cynical lot, but it's hard to find many as hard-bitten as intelligent, successful financial writers. They know that what they're writing isn't good for their readers, but there are deadlines to meet and mouths to feed. In a 1999 issue of *Fortune*, an anonymous writer penned a notorious piece entitled, "Confessions of a Former Mutual Funds Reporter." Its writer admitted, "We were preaching buy-and-hold marriage while implicitly endorsing hot fund promiscuity." Why? Because, "Unfortunately, rational, pro-index-fund stories don't sell magazines, cause hits on Web sites, or boost Nielsen ratings." The article went on to admit that most mutual fund columnists invest in index funds. (As do an increasing number of brokers, analysts, and hedge fund managers.)

At the very top of the financial journalism heap are a select number of writers who are so popular and craft prose so well that they can get away with a regular output of unvarnished reality. As we've already seen, Jane Bryant Quinn is one of these. Scott Burns of the

Dallas Morning News, Jonathan Clements of *The Wall Street Journal,* and Jason Zweig of *Money* are three other compulsive truth tellers. (And mark you well: Jason is *no* relationship to Martin.) But they are a few faint points of light in what is otherwise a swirling professional cesspool. In general, you are better off ignoring the entire genre— print, television, and Internet.

Let's add some flesh to the topic with a few real-life examples. A representative attention-grabber was the headline from the August 1998 issue of *Worth* magazine: "Beat the S&P With Our Five Top-Ranked Funds." Their recommendations were Eclipse Equity, Barron Asset, Vanguard Windsor II, MFS Massachusetts Investors Growth Stock, and GAM International. These funds were picked not only because of their superb prior performance, but also because of the magazine's overall favorable impression of the managers and their techniques. During the next two years, two beat the S&P, three didn't, and the average return of the five they recommended was 23.17%, versus 33.63% for the S&P. This is exactly what you'd expect from simply tossing darts at the newspaper's fund tables—a few winners, but more losers, with sub-par performance overall.

The most prestigious of all fund ranking systems is the *Forbes* Honor Roll. This is one exclusive list. Not only must the fund have a long track record of excellent returns and consistent high-quality management, but it must also have above average returns in bear markets. Few periodicals have *Forbes's* depth of expertise and talent. If anyone can pick funds, it ought to be them.

So how have they done? Actually, not too badly. From 1974 to mid-1998, the average domestic Honor Roll fund returned 13.6%, versus 13.3% for average actively managed funds. So it appears that by using careful selection criteria, *Forbes* can pick mutual funds that will do slightly better than average. But, unfortunately, not better than the market, which returned 14.3%.

Now the bad news. First, many of the Honor Roll funds carried loads, which were not included in the calculation and would have reduced returns by about another 1% or so. Second, the turnover of these funds would have generated far more in taxable gains than simply holding an index fund. And last, the turnover of the funds on the Honor Roll is notable in and of itself. Only a small number of the funds stay on the list for more than a decade. What does that say for a fund selection system that results in such a rapid shuffling of names? If successful managers stayed successful, surely they would stay on the list year after year. And yet, as we see, that kind of performance—the kind that persists—doesn't exist.

To Whom Do I Listen?

If the popular media is at best worthless, and at worst a downright dangerous place to seek investment guidance, then to whom does the intelligent investor turn for information? The real epiphany of the markets is: *the market itself is the best advisor.* The reason is blindingly simple. When you buy the market, you are hiring the aggregate judgement of the most brilliant and well-informed minds in finance. (Recall the disappearance of the Scorpion. Even the smartest analysts didn't know exactly where the submarine had sunk, but their collective judgement was stunningly accurate.) By indexing, you are tapping into the most powerful intelligence in the world of finance—the collective wisdom of the market itself.

The only real guidance you'll need is in two areas:

- Your overall asset allocation. We've already begun to discuss this problem and we'll finish the job in the next chapter.
- Your self-discipline. That is, you'll need to keep your head while everyone else is losing his. No, you won't have to time the market, call the top or bottom, or leap tall buildings in a single bound. You'll only need to remember two things. First, that in the not too distant future, there will be exciting new technologies and once again, you will hear the siren song, "This time it's different; the old rules don't apply any more." Your neighbors and friends will get caught up in the frenzy, and they will earn higher returns than you. But only for a while. All you have to do is . . . nothing. Stand pat, keep to the plan. Do not exchange your boring old economy stocks and bonds for shares in the new tech companies. Second, there will come a time when the markets are in turmoil and you'll hear another song, this one in a sad minor key, "The end is near. Only a fool owns stocks." Again, all you'll have to do is . . . nothing. Or, if you're feeling brave, take some of your cash and buy more stocks.

Just because you don't have to pay too much attention to finance doesn't mean you shouldn't. Presumably, you're reading this book because you're at least vaguely interested in the topic. There is a world of useful investment information out there, and it's yours for the taking. The surprising thing is that the news you need to know is mostly old—sometimes very old. For example, if forced to make the choice, I would trade all of the financial research done in the last decade for the contents of Fisher's *The Theory of Interest*, which was written more than 70 years ago and formed the basis of Chapter 2.

So here's how I'd proceed. First, do not read any more magazine or newspaper articles on finance, and, whatever you do, do not watch *Wall Street Week, Nightly Business Report*, or CNBC. With the extra hour or two you'll gain each week from turning off the TV, I would start a regular reading program. Begin with two classics:

1. *A Random Walk Down Wall Street*, by Burton Malkiel, is an excellent investment primer. It explains the basics of stocks, bonds, and mutual funds and will reinforce the efficient market concept.
2. *Common Sense on Mutual Funds*, by John Bogle, will provide more information than you ever wanted to know about this important investment vehicle. Mr. Bogle has been an important voice in the industry for decades and writes beautifully. It is both opinionated and highly recommended.

Take your time. Read no more than 10 to 20 pages an evening, then do something recreational. After you're finished with these two books, you will know more about finance than 99% of all stockbrokers and most other finance professionals. You're then ready for the "postgraduate course" that will take you through the rest of your life. Remember, most of what you need to know is ancient history, sometimes literally.

As we learned in Chapters 5 and 6, there is nothing really new in finance; the recent events on Wall Street would not have surprised the denizens of the Change Alley coffeehouses of the late seventeenth century. The more history you learn, the better. This is where finance becomes fun, because the best financial historians tend to be gifted literary craftsmen. I can guarantee you that you won't be able to put most of the following books down:

- *A Fool and His Money*, by John Rothchild and *Where are the Customers' Yachts?* by Fred Schwed. Ground-level trips through Wall Street in the 1980s and 1930s, respectively, providing an eye-opening view of the capital markets in those eras.
- *Once in Golconda*, by John Brooks. The story of how things got nasty between New York and Washington in the aftermath of the Great Depression and how Uncle Sam finally got his hands on Wall Street, to the benefit of just about everybody.
- *Devil Take the Hindmost*, by Edward Chancellor. A history of manias and crashes over the centuries. If this book doesn't bulletproof you from the next bubble, nothing will.
- *Bernard Baruch, Money of the Mind, Minding Mr. Market*, and *The Trouble with Prosperity*, all by James Grant. This man has a better grasp of capital market history than anyone else I know,

and the quality of his prose is superlative to the point that it occasionally becomes distracting.

- *Capital Ideas*, by Peter Bernstein. An engaging history of modern financial theory and its far reaching influence on today's markets.
- *Winning the Loser's Game*, by Charles Ellis. A succinct look at the essence of money management by one of the country's most-respected wealth managers.

All of the above works are easily accessible to the average reader. If you're good with numbers and don't mind a bit of effort, I'd also recommend the following:

- *Global Investing*, by Gary Brinson and Roger Ibbotson. A panoramic view of stocks, bonds, commodities, and inflation the world over. Now more than a decade old, it's beginning to show its age but is still well worth it.
- *Asset Allocation*, by Roger Gibson. An excellent primer on portfolio theory and the mathematics of arriving at effective allocations.

But what about "keeping up" with progress in finance? I'm afraid that if someone were to publish a yearbook titled "Genuine Advances in Investing," it would be a very thin volume most years. If you're good at math and a glutton for punishment to boot, you can log onto the *Journal of Finance's* Web site (http://www.afajof.org/jofihome. shtml) to see what's new. You can even subscribe to the print journal for $80 per year.

Finally, in the day-to-day media there are two regular columns that, in addition to providing a good periodic review of practical finance, will also do an excellent job of keeping you up on the rare bits of useful news that occasionally trickle out of academia. The first is Jonathan Clements' "Getting Going" column each Wednesday in *The Wall Street Journal*. (The *Journal* is a superb national newspaper, but rely on it for news, not investment insight. Mr. Clements' columns aside, you won't learn much that's useful about investing from its contents.) The second is Jason Zweig's monthly column in *Money*.

What have we learned from our tour of the financial media? Two things. First, nearly all of what you will find in television, newspapers, magazines, and the Internet is geared to the care and feeding of the retail investment business and journalists, who depend on each other for their survival. It is of no use to you. And second, because there is little that is new in the basic behavior of the capital markets, the most useful way of developing investment expertise is to absorb as much market history as you can.

INVESTMENT STRATEGY

Assembling the Four Pillars

The Winner's Game

Our voyage through the theory, history, psychology, and business of investing finally pays off in this section. Here's where we assemble these four pillars into a coherent investment strategy that you can deploy and maintain with a modest amount of effort.

First we'll explore the retirement "numbers game": How much will I need to save to meet my goals? How much can I spend? How certain can I be of success? Then, in Chapter 13, we reach the book's "main event": What factors must I consider in the design of my portfolio? Just what should my portfolio look like? What funds do I buy?

Nuts and bolts and practicalities are finally laid out in Chapter 14. The first part is your portfolio's "assembly instruction booklet"; it illustrates a powerful method for the psychologically tough task of slowly building your stock exposure. The second section is the "maintenance manual"; it describes the periodic "tune-ups" necessary to maintain your portfolio's health.

To paraphrase Winston Churchill, by the end of this section you will not have reached your investment journey's end; you will not even reach the beginning of its end. But you will have ended its beginning. This section will provide that journey's roadmap.

12

Will You Have Enough?

Before we get our fingers dirty with real stocks, bonds, and mutual funds, it is important to consider just *why* we are saving. As pointed out by the late Professor Irving Fisher in Chapter 2, we save so that we may spend later. Investment is simply the execution of that deferral of consumption. At base, then, the pattern of that future consumption—when and how you spend your savings—is the single most important factor determining your asset allocation. To wit, are you saving for retirement? Emergencies? A house? A child's education? The benefit of future generations?

In most cases, you'll be saving and investing simultaneously for several of these things. For example, most young families will likely be saving for all except the last reason. It makes little sense to have separate programs for each, but, rather, to combine all of your goals into one portfolio. Having one overall investment policy for all your assets will greatly simplify your financial management, reduce expenses, and increase your chances of success.

Retirement is the paramount objective for most investing, so we'll attack that first. After we've mastered this area, saving for the other goals, both separately and together with retirement, is not much of a stretch.

The Immortal Retiree

The best way to understand retirement saving is to work backwards. We'll spend the first half of this chapter attacking the problem of how much money you'll need on the day you retire, and the second half discussing how to get there. Along the way we'll find out that various market scenarios affect young savers and older retirees in radically different ways.

Let's start with what at first seems a silly assumption—that you'll live forever. This is an extremely easy thing to plan for, as long as you remember to think in "real" (inflation-adjusted) terms. And it's not that silly an assumption; in financial terms, retirement essentially is "forever." Among annuity and insurance purchasers—admittedly a healthier-than-average group—15% of surviving spouses, usually the wife, live to at least age 97.

This means that many retirees will need to plan on more than 35 years of retirement. Financially, there's not much difference between living 35 years and living forever. To illustrate this, assume that all of your money is in a Roth IRA, meaning that you don't have to worry about taxes at any stage and that you'll need $40,000 per year in current spending power in retirement. If you earn a 4% real return, then you can withdraw that 4% of your nest egg each year without reducing your principal. You will be able to maintain this forever, since the nest egg's value will rise along with inflation. The 4% you withdraw from it each year for living expenses will also keep up with inflation. This means that you'll need $1 million (calculated by dividing $40,000 by 0.04).

Next, imagine earning the same 4% real return and dying on schedule after 35 years with *nothing* left over. In that case, since you will be spending down capital as well as earnings, you'll need only $746,585. (We'll discuss in a few paragraphs how this calculation is accomplished.) The key point is this—there's not a great deal of difference between living forever, which requires $1 million, and living for 35 years, which requires $746,585. Further, because of the uncertainties of the market and your own life, it's foolish to plan on dying on schedule with zero.

This "back of the envelope" method of calculating retirement is a superb one—simply estimate your living expenses, including any taxes you'll owe on your retirement withdrawals, and adjust for what you expect from Social Security (which may not be much). Then divide by your expected real rate of return, as we did above. Four percent is a reasonable estimate, given the expected returns for stocks and bonds we calculated in Chapter 2.

A more precise, but much more dangerous, technique uses the second example we described above—dying "on schedule" after 30 or 40 years with nothing. This method involves employing an amortization calculation, typically using a standard financial calculator, such as a Texas Instruments TI BA-35, which can be bought for about $20. This is an extremely common procedure among financial planners and is computed in exactly the same way as a mortgage (except that in this instance you are the bank, receiving monthly payments until the "loan" of your nest egg is paid off). This is how we arrived at the $746,585 figure mentioned above. To reiterate, amortization allows for no "margin of error." Make a few wrong assumptions, and you're eating Alpo in your golden years.

How much margin of error do you need? Unfortunately, a lot. You see, all of the calculations we've done so far contain an extremely perilous assumption—*that our return is the same each and every year.* For example, in the calculation above we assumed that you'll receive a fixed 4% return that never changes, year after year.

But in the real world, this does not happen. If you expect reasonable returns, then you have to bear risk. And by its very definition, the word "risk" means that you cannot expect to receive the same return each and every year. So you are going to have to live with the markets the way they are—good years and bad years, occurring in a completely unpredictable sequence.

The problem is that the precise sequence of the good and bad years is critical. This phenomenon was first brought to public attention by Philip L. Cooley, Carl M. Hubbard, and Daniel T. Walz of Trinity University. They looked at the success rate of various withdrawal strategies over numerous historical periods and came to the conclusion that only at a withdrawal rate of 4% to 5% of the initial portfolio value (i.e., $40,000–$50,000 of a $1,000,000 mixed stock-bond portfolio) do you have a reasonable expectation of "success." (Which they defined as dying without debt.) The scariest thing about their results was that the period they studied had real stock returns of 7%. Future stock returns are likely to be lower, which means that even their 4% to 5% withdrawal rate may be overly optimistic. An excellent summary of their work is available at http://www.scottburns.com/wwtrinity.htm.

On a more basic level, however, you can apply a much simpler acid test to your withdrawal strategy: What would happen if the day you retired at a market top, say on January 1, 1966, which marked the beginning of a long, brutal bear market, and you lived for another 30 years, until December 31, 1995? For the first 17 years (1966–1982), the real return of the S&P 500 was zero. The return for the last 13 years (1983–1995) was spectacular, bringing the real return for the whole 30-year period from 1966 to 1995 , up to 5.3%, not too far below the historical norm of 7%.

To study this, I assumed that you began the period with $1,000,000 and then calculated results of various withdrawal rates from the following mixes: 100% stock, 100% bond, and 75/25, 50/50, and 25/75 stock/bond mixes of both. I further assumed that the equity portfolio consisted of 80% S&P 500 and 20% U.S. small stocks with five-year Treasuries as the bond component. The results of 7%, 6%, 5%, and 4% withdrawal rates (that is, withdrawing $70,000, $60,000, $50,000, and $40,000 in real terms) are plotted in Figures 12-1 through 12-4. Again, it is important to realize that the amounts on the vertical scale are in *inflation-adjusted* 1966 dollars.

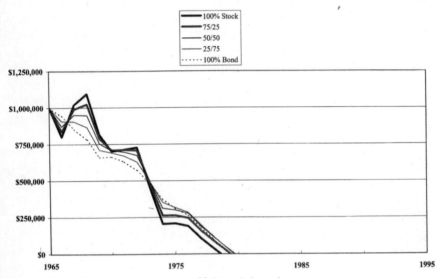

Figure 12-1. $70,000 annual real (1966 $) withdrawal.

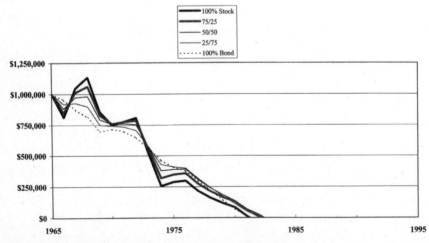

Figure 12-2. $60,000 annual real (1966 $) withdrawal.

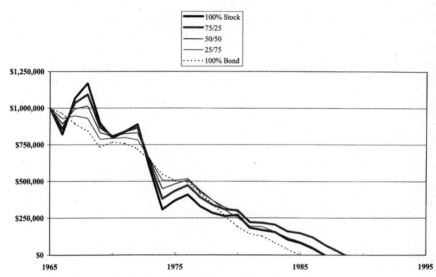

Figure 12-3. $50,000 annual real (1966 $) withdrawal.

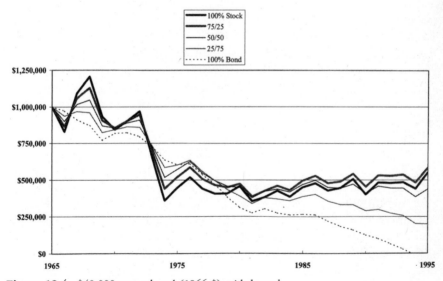

Figure 12-4. $40,000 annual real (1966 $) withdrawal.

These are profoundly disturbing results. Since real equity returns were 5.3% during the period, the conservative back-of-the-envelope method of withdrawing the real return every year should have allowed us to safely withdraw 5.3% annually and still have our real principal intact. In fact, such a withdrawal rate completely depleted all the portfolios, no matter what their stock/bond composition. The amortization method predicts that we should have been able to withdraw 6.7% per year if we were willing to completely deplete the portfolio in 30 years. As you can see from Figures 12-1 and 12-2, a 6.7% withdrawal rate would actually have depleted all the portfolios in about 15 years. This means that a "penalty" of about 1.5%–2% was extracted by "the luck of the draw." In other words, a particularly bad returns sequence can reduce your safe withdrawal amount by as much as 2% below the long-term return of stocks. Recall from Chapter 2 that it's likely that future real stock returns will be in the 3.5% range, which means that current retirees may not be entirely safe withdrawing more than 2% of the real starting values of their portfolios per year!

It's important to understand that in all of the above cases, we have been talking about withdrawing a constant real amount of the beginning portfolio value. For example, in Figure 12-1, we withdrew a real $70,000—7%—of a $1 million portfolio every year, increasing the initial $70,000 each year for inflation. This is *not* the same as spending 7% of the portfolio value each year. Were we to do that, we would withdraw less money each year as stock prices fell. For example, if stock prices immediately fell by 20%, we could only spend $56,000. Think about spending a quarter of your portfolio each year. You will never completely run out of money, although your portfolio value will vanish into insignificance after a decade or two. But if you can tolerate the fluctuations in withdrawal amounts inherent in a more reasonable constant-percentage withdrawal (say, 4% or 5% per year), then you will never completely run out of money.

This gets to the heart of financial risk. The odds are that you will *not* encounter the worst case of a prolonged and profound bear market at the beginning of your retirement. It is just as likely that the opposite may occur—a prolonged bull market at the beginning—and that you will be sitting in unexpected clover, able to withdraw 6% of your starting amount or more each year. But we cannot forecast the future. If you plan reasonable withdrawals (2 to 5% of the initial nest egg value, adjusted upwards for inflation in each year), there is the small risk of disaster, which you can lessen only by lowering your retirement living expenses.

The best way of performing a retirement calculation is with a so-called "Monte Carlo" analysis. This more sophisticated methodology runs thousands or even millions of "what if" scenarios and computes the percentage of times your strategy "succeeded" (that is, you didn't die poor). It uses the same three inputs as the amortization method: the initial nest egg amount, expected real rate of return, and length of retirement. It also needs a fourth bit of data, the "standard deviation" of the portfolio, which is a measure of portfolio risk. I've found that Monte Carlo gives results very similar to those obtained in the Trinity study, with the additional advantage that it allows you the flexibility of adjusting portfolio risk and return. Don't worry about having to do calculations manually; Efficient Solutions has written a simple and inexpensive Windows-based Monte Carlo tester.[1]

It's important to realize how the traditional amortization method and the more sophisticated methods relate (Trinity study, data in Figures 12-1 to 12-4, and Monte Carlo). The amortization method, which assumes that you earn the same return each year, computes the withdrawal rate or nest egg size at which the more sophisticated methods indicate a 50% chance of success. That's not enough margin of error for most investors. There's a simple way of estimating how much you can withdraw to get to 90% success: Subtract 1% from your withdrawal rate for a portfolio that is mostly bonds and 2% for one that is mostly equity. Say you think that your stock portfolio has an expected return of 5%. That means that to have a 90% chance of success, you can only withdraw 3% of the real initial nest egg each year.

Finally, Uncle Sam has provided a tempting way out of this dilemma. Treasury Inflation Protected Securities (TIPS) currently yield a 3.5% inflation-adjusted return. If you can live on 3.5% of your savings *and* you can shelter almost all of your retirement money in a Roth IRA (which does not require mandatory distributions after age 70 1/2), then you are guaranteed success for up to 30 years, which is the current maturity of the longest bond. For devout believers in the value of a well-diversified portfolio, this option is profoundly unappealing, as this is a poorly diversified portfolio—the financial equivalent of Eden's snake. (Although it's a very secure basket!) At a minimum, however, some commitment to TIPS in your sheltered accounts is probably not a bad idea.

At the end of the day, you can never be completely certain that your retirement will be a financial success. Further, you are faced with a tradeoff between the amount of your nest egg you can spend each year and the probability of success—the less you spend, the more likely you are to succeed. And certainly, any retiree who annually withdraws much more than 5% of their real initial nest-egg amount over the decades sorely tempts the fates.

---

[1]This software is available at a discount to readers of this book. You can find it at http://www.effisols.com. (Warning: This software does not come shrink-wrapped in a pretty box; you will need to be comfortable with Internet credit-card purchases and software downloads.)

Retirees: Pray for Rain

I apologize if the math in this section is a little steep. Even if you don't understand all of the numbers, there's one important concept I want to leave you with: the worst-case scenario for a retiree is to start out with a long period of poor returns. In this situation, the combination of poor returns and mandatory withdrawals for living expenses will devastate most retirement portfolios if the bear market lasts long enough. Even after the bad times have ended and returns improve, there just won't be enough capital left to benefit from those higher returns, and you'll run out. The only way out of this grim trap is to spend less and save more.

But at the end of the day, you also have to realize that it is impossible to completely eliminate risk. I'm amused when financial planners and academics talk about methods that predict a 40-year success rate of, say, 95%. If you think about it, this implies that our political and financial institutions will remain intact for about the next millennium (40 years divided by a failure rate of 5% equals 800 years). Considering the history of human civilization, this is a pretty heroic assumption. The only way most investors can drive their chance of success above 90% is to completely deprive themselves both before and after retirement. At some point, enough is enough—in order to live a little, you've got to bear some risk of failure.

The very best thing that can happen to a retiree is to have a run of good years right off the bat. In that case, you'll be sitting on a wad of assets that you likely won't be able to spend, no matter how low returns are later.

The Savings Game

The opposite is true for young savers: they should be praying for a bear market so that they can accumulate shares cheaply before they retire. The worst thing that can happen to savers is to have a prolonged period of high prices, which means that they will have acquired expensive shares that are likely to have poor returns in retirement. Again, to summarize:

	Bull Market	Bear Market
Retiree	Good	Bad
Saver	Bad	Good

By this point, we've done most of the heavy lifting—figuring out how much you'll need to have on hand the day you retire. Here, the precise sequence of good and bad years, although it does influence your outcome, is far less critical. The reasons for this are complex and have to do with the "duration" of your portfolio.

As we found out in the first chapter, if you own a bond that yields a nominal 5% and bond yields rise to 10%, that is bad. Bond yields and prices are inversely related. But at some point, you will break even because you can reinvest your interest at the higher rate. The "duration" of your bond is that point at which you break even.

Next, consider a bond from which you are siphoning off half the interest coupon to pay for living expenses. Because you are reinvesting less at the higher interest rate, you have now effectively lengthened its duration. Conversely, if you augment the interest payments with additional cash, you are shortening the effective duration.

In the same way, any portfolio from which withdrawals are being made has a very long duration. This statement seems paradoxical—if you're spending down a portfolio, shouldn't that *decrease* its duration? No. Because you are lessening the amount that can be reinvested at a higher yield, you are *increasing* duration—defined as the time it takes to break even after a price fall. Conversely, shouldn't savings increase duration? No. In the same way that augmenting a bond's interest shortens its duration by reinvesting more at higher yields, by saving you are *decreasing* duration. This is why a price fall early in retirement is such a bad thing. It is almost certain that your portfolio duration—the break-even point—is longer than your expected survival. On the other hand, a portfolio into which savings is flowing has a short duration. This is why a young person in the savings phase of her life will do better with falling prices.

For this reason, relatively simple calculations will work nicely for the savings phase. The easiest way to do this is with a financial calculator, such as the TI BA-35 I mentioned a few pages ago.[2] I've calculated some final real nest egg amounts per real $100 saved each month in

---

[2] If you decide to experiment with this (which I highly recommend), here's how you do it: On your TI BA-35, enter financial mode by hitting 2nd-FIN. Key in the number of years you'll be saving, then hit the N key. Enter your real rate of return as a percentage. For example, for a real return of 4%, hit "4" then the %i key. Enter the amount you'll be saving each year, change it to a negative number by hitting the +/− key, then hit the PMT key. Enter the amount of your current portfolio ("0" if you're starting from scratch), hit the PV key. Hit the CPT key, followed by the FV key, and your future nest egg will come up. It is slightly more accurate to do this computation with monthly data, but also more complicated—the PMT amount will have to be monthly savings, N will be the number of months (i.e., 360 for 30 years) and %i, the *monthly* interest rate. For example, for a 4% annual return this value is 0.327.

Table 12-1. Final Real (Inflation-Adjusted) Nest Egg Amounts per Real $100 Saved Each Month. (See text.)

	Portfolio Real Return					
Years	2%	3%	4%	5%	6%	7%
5	$6,302	$6,458	$6,618	$6,781	$6,949	$7,120
10	$13,260	$13,945	$14,670	$15,436	$16,247	$17,105
15	$20,942	$22,624	$24,466	$26,482	$28,691	$31,110
20	$29,423	$32,685	$36,384	$40,580	$45,344	$50,754
25	$38,787	$44,349	$50,885	$58,573	$67,629	$78,304
30	$49,126	$57,871	$68,527	$81,538	$97,451	$116,945
35	$60,541	$73,547	$89,992	$110,846	$137,360	$171,141
40	$73,144	$91,719	$116,106	$148,252	$190,768	$247,154

Table 12-1. For example, assume that you have 25 years until retirement and obtain a 4% real return for that term. If you save $100 per month, at the end of 25 years you'll have a real nest egg of $50,885. This is a *real* $100 you are saving: this means you'll have to increase the $100 initial savings with inflation. If you can save a real $500 per month, you'll have $254,420 (five times the amount indicated in the table). Using our back-of-the-envelope method, at a real return of 4%, this will provide you with $10,177 real income per year. (That is, $254,420 × 0.04 = $10,177.)

Let's approach this from the opposite end. Assume you've decided you want to retire on $50,000 per year. Our back-of-the-envelope method tells us that you'll need a $1.25 million nest egg to do this ($50,000/0.04 = $1.25 million). And remember, this method gives you almost no margin of error for a bad initial-return draw of the cards.

How much do you need to save to obtain $1,250,000 for retirement? If you have 20 years until retirement, you'll have to save a real $3,436 per month! We determine this by noting from Table 12-1 that saving a real $100 per month at a real rate of 4% produces $36,384 after 20 years. So, to produce a real $1,250,000 nest egg we will have to save ($1,250,000/$36,384) × $100 = a real $3,436 per month for 20 years.

By using a similar calculation, if you have 30 years until retirement, you'll need to save a real $1,824 per month; if you have 40 years, you'll need to save a real $1,077 monthly. In Table 12-2, I've tabulated the monthly savings requirement for each real rate of return and time until retirement to retire on $50,000 per year. If you wish to retire on more or less, adjust the required savings in Table 12-2 by the proportionate amount. So if you wish to retire on $100,000 per year, for example, multiply all the values in Table 12-2 by a factor of two.

Table 12-2. Monthly Savings Required to Retire on $50,000 per Year. (See text)

	Portfolio Real Return					
Years	2%	3%	4%	5%	6%	7%
5	$39,670	$25,808	$18,888	$14,747	$11,992	$10,032
10	$18,854	$11,952	$8,521	$6,478	$5,129	$4,176
15	$11,938	$7,367	$5,109	$3,776	$2,905	$2,296
20	$8,497	$5,099	$3,436	$2,464	$1,838	$1,407
25	$6,445	$3,758	$2,457	$1,707	$1,232	$912
30	$5,089	$2,880	$1,824	$1,226	$855	$611
35	$4,129	$2,266	$1,389	$902	$607	$417
40	$3,418	$1,817	$1,077	$675	$437	$289

If you find these calculations grim, well, they are. The message is loud and clear: If you want to retire comfortably, you must save a lot. And you must start very early. In fact, every decade you delay saving for retirement can more than double the amount you must save each month. Although this book's focus is on investing, its message is useless if you cannot save enough to invest.

Now for the only sermon of the book. Our consumer society propels the average person to spend far more than is necessary or healthy. If you find it difficult to save, then you may have a problem. For starters, I'd read Thomas Stanley and William Danko's *The Millionaire Next Door* to understand how most people become rich. Want to know the auto most commonly driven by the wealthy? No, not a Mercedes—it is a Ford F-150 pickup. Another interesting fact: The average plumber retires far sooner than the average lawyer, even though lawyers make more money than plumbers. Why? Because the attorney "must" drive a nicer car, live in a nicer part of town, buy more expensive clothes, and take more exotic vacations than the plumber. The message is obvious. The easiest way to get rich is to spend as little as possible.

Other Goals

This book is not intended as a financial planning guide; topics such as mortgages, debt management, insurance, and estate planning are well beyond its brief. But there are a few financial planning topics pertaining to basic portfolio mechanics and financial theory that are worth mentioning:

Emergencies. This falls under the mantra of the financial planner: "five years, five years, five years." That is, you should not put any money at risk that will be needed within five years. In addition, you should have at least six months of living expenses on hand in safe liquid assets—short-term bonds, CDs, money market, checking, and savings accounts. This doesn't mean that you need a separate account for this purpose—it can be part of your overall asset allocation.

Your emergency money, however, must be held in your taxable accounts. Holding liquid assets in a retirement account doesn't accomplish this, as tapping an IRA before age 59½ for an emergency will likely trigger an enormous combined tax bill/early-withdrawal penalty. Many retirement and 401(k) plans do allow borrowing in emergency situations. Doing so is a bad idea since defaulting on such a loan triggers a 10% early-withdrawal tax penalty.

House savings. Since you are unlikely to be saving for a house for much more than five years, you should also place this money into short-term bonds, CDs, and money market accounts. And, of course, it should be held in a taxable account.

College savings. This is an enormously complex area, and one that has recently undergone a revolution with the introduction of so-called 529 plans, which can be highly tax-advantaged. I'd recommend taking at look at www.collegesavings.org and also having a chat with your accountant about these plans, which come in many shapes and sizes.

From the asset management point of view, college savings is a very sticky wicket, since its time horizon is intermediate between that of emergency savings and retirement planning. You may be saving for as little as a few years to as long as two decades, depending on the age of your child and your available funds. Unfortunately, as we've seen, stocks can have poor returns for even 20 years. Worse, if you have a decade of very poor returns, you will then find yourself within the five-year bond-only window mentioned above. If you begin saving when your child is four and have nine years of bad returns, you now have five years left until he or she enters college. What do you do? With some trepidation I'd recommend placing a maximum of 30% to 40% of your child's college fund in stocks, then begin to shift that into bonds as matriculation approaches. When the college expenses come due, you can sell the residual stocks for tuition in the good years and sell the bonds in the bad years.

CHAPTER 12 SUMMARY

1. Manage all of your assets—personal savings, retirement accounts, emergency money, college accounts, and house savings—as one portfolio.
2. You or your spouse may live a lot longer than you think. You should plan on spending, at maximum, the expected real return of your portfolio each year—i.e., 3% to 4% of its value.
3. Even this assumption may not be conservative enough. Should you experience a prolonged period of poor returns early in your retirement, you may run out of money before the market can rebound.
4. You cannot start saving early enough. Most workers who begin their retirement savings after age 40 will find it impossible to retire when they want to.
5. You cannot save enough. The most successful prescription for a successful retirement is to get into the habit of curbing your material desires. Now.
6. Do not invest any money in stocks that you will need in less than five years.
7. Have available at least six months of living expenses in safe investment vehicles in a taxable account.

13

Defining Your Mix

The time has come to build your portfolio. Similar to the construction of a house, we will proceed methodically, examining each brick, timber, and shingle in turn, before assembling them into a whole.

The individual construction materials will be the investment vehicles we have discussed in previous chapters—for the most part, open-end mutual funds or exchange-traded funds, with the odd single Treasury security thrown in. The three main materials—the bricks, timbers, and shingles, if you will—are the three main kinds of investments—U.S. stocks, foreign stocks, and short-term bonds.

After we've examined these basic materials in some detail, we'll discuss which are most appropriate for the house you are building. Just as you would favor steel beams and concrete over wood for the construction of a large apartment house, so too are certain asset classes and mutual funds more appropriate for certain kinds of portfolios.

To complete the analogy, the ultimate purpose of your portfolio, just like your house, is to protect you from the unpredictability of the elements. When you build a house, it is often hard to predict exactly which force of nature will most threaten it. If you knew in advance whether flood, fire, or hurricane would strike, then you could design it more precisely. But often you cannot accurately forecast the precise nature of the risks it will face. So you compromise and design it so that it might withstand all three tolerably well within your construction budget.

In the same way, you will not know exactly what kinds of economic, political, or even military, adversity will befall your portfolio. If, for example, you knew for sure that inflation would be the scourge of the economy for the next generation, then you would emphasize gold, natural resources, real estate, and cash, as well as a fair amount of stocks. If you knew that we were to suffer a deflationary depression, similar to what occurred in the 1930s, you would hold only long-maturity government bonds. And if you knew that the world would suffer a loss of confidence in U.S. industrial leadership, you would want a portfolio heavy in foreign stocks and bonds.

In short, during the next 20 or 30 years, there will be a single, best allocation that in retrospect we will have wished we had owned. The only problem is that we haven't a clue what that portfolio will be. So, the safest course is to own as many asset classes as you can; that way you can be sure of avoiding the catastrophe of holding a portfolio concentrated in the worst ones.

Famed money manager and writer Charles Ellis, in a 1975 article in *Financial Analysts Journal,* observed that investing was like amateur tennis. The most common way of losing a match at this level is to make too many "unforced errors." That is, missing easy shots by trying to hit the ball too hard or nailing the corner. The best way to win a game with your friends is to simply make sure you safely return the ball each time. In other words, in amateur tennis, you don't win so much as you avoid losing—hence the title of Ellis's article, "Winning the Loser's Game."

Portfolio strategy is exactly the same as the Ellis version of tennis— *the name of the game is* not *losing.* In this chapter, what we'll strive to do is design portfolios that have the best likelihood of *not* losing.

Bricks

What do we mean when we say, "the U.S. market?" Most analysts start with the S&P 500. Contrary to popular perception, these are not the 500 biggest companies in the nation, but instead are 500 firms chosen by Standard & Poor's as *representative* of the makeup of the U.S. industry. It is a "capitalization-weighted" index. We've already come across this term, but it's worth reviewing again.

As this is being written, the total value of all outstanding U.S. stock—about 7,000 companies in all—is $13 trillion. This is also referred to as its "market capitalization," or "market cap" for short. Of this, the S&P 500 accounts for $10 trillion, or about three-quarters, of the market cap. The biggest company in the S&P 500 is General Electric (GE), with a market cap of about $400 billion, or 4% of the index. The smallest, American Greetings, has a market cap of $700 million, or 0.007% of the index—six hundred times smaller than GE. So an index fund which tracks the S&P 500 would have to own 600 times as much GE as American Greetings.

What happens if GE plunges in value and American Greetings zooms? Nothing. Since an index fund simply holds each company in proportion to its market cap, the amount of each owned by an S&P 500 index fund adjusts automatically with its market cap. In other words, an index fund does not have to buy or sell stock with changes in value (unlike Wells Fargo's ill-fated first index fund, which had to hold equal-dollar amounts of all 1,500 stocks on the New York Stock Exchange).

This raises some important semantic points. When most investors say the words "index fund," they are almost always referring to an S&P 500 fund. But the U.S. market consists of more than 7,000 publicly traded companies. So the S&P 500 is not a true "market index," since it only holds about 7% of the total number of companies in the market. However, these 7% of companies, because they are very large, make up 75% of the total U.S. market cap.

There are actually three true "market indexes." The most widely used is the Wilshire 5000, which, in spite of its name, consists of 7,000 publicly traded stocks. The second is the Russell 3000, which owns the 3,000 biggest companies. Even though it excludes the smallest 4,000 U.S. companies in the Wilshire 5000, these very small stocks amount to only 1% of the U.S. market capitalization. Finally, the Center for Research in Security Prices' (CRSP) "universe" index is of historical value only, as its returns can be followed back to 1926, when it held just 433 firms in cap-weighted fashion. It now holds thousands and behaves very similarly to the Wilshire 5000.

Here is where things start to get interesting. There are funds that track the Wilshire 5000 and Russell 3000, but they are not truly "index funds," because it would be too cumbersome to own all 7,000 or 3,000 stocks in the index. Instead, these funds own a representative sampling of the market. Thus, they do not track the indexes precisely. The exact term for such a fund is "passively managed"—that is, it owns some, but not all, of the stocks in an index, or those meeting certain criteria.

On the other hand, an S&P 500 fund is almost always a true "index fund," because it owns all 500 stocks in the index. But it is *not* passively managed. In fact, it is quite actively managed—by the Standard & Poor's selection committee—whose members determine the index's makeup! In practice, though, there is little real difference between "passively managed" and "index" mutual funds, and in common usage both terms are employed interchangeably.

As discussed in a previous chapter, we most certainly want to index, since doing so incurs minimal expenses, thereby beating the overwhelming majority of active-fund managers. So, we are faced with two basic choices—the S&P 500, which includes only the biggest compa- nies, or the more broadly based Wilshire 5000 and Russell 3000 total- market indexes, which include smaller stocks.

Owning the U.S. "market" means the whole shooting match—the Wilshire 5000. The granddaddy of all "total-market" funds is the Vanguard Total Stock Market Index Fund. With rock-bottom expenses of 0.20%, it is a superb choice. Since its inception in 1992, it has done an excellent job of tracking the Wilshire 5000, Wilshire actually best- ing it by a few basis points before expenses. (A basis point is one one- hundredth of 1%. For example, when Alan Greenspan cuts interest rates by 0.5%, he has cut the rate by 50 basis points.) Even more amaz- ingly, over the past five years, it has managed to beat the index by four basis points *even after expenses.*

This gets to an important issue, so-called "transactional skill." It is often said that a monkey could run an index fund. Nothing could be further from the truth. Precisely tracking an index requires a very high degree of market savvy, discipline, and nerve. The head of Vanguard's indexing shop, George U. ("Gus") Sauter, is the universally recognized master of the craft and is usually able to squeeze out a "positive track- ing error"—that is, actually beat the index by a slight amount, particu- larly with smaller, less-liquid stocks.

Transactional skill is one of investment's many ironies. Recall that in Chapter 3 we showed that investment managers demonstrated no evi- dence of *selection* skill—that is, they could not successfully pick stocks. But quite clearly, as Mr. Sauter and a few other practitioners have demonstrated year after year, there is skill—transactional skill—in the actual *execution* of stock purchases and sales.

There are multiple vehicles that enable you to buy the entire U.S. market in one fund. I've listed all of the players in the "total-market" playground in Table 13-1.

When and where do you own a total-market index fund? In two sit- uations. First, a total-market index fund is an ideal "core" equity hold- ing in a taxable account, because of its "tax efficiency." The Russell 3000 and the Wilshire 5000 have essentially no turnover. Stocks may leave the index via mergers and acquisitions, but these are often not taxable events. The only way a stock truly leaves these portfolios is feet first, by going bankrupt, in which case you don't have to worry about capital gains. Would you want to hold a total-market fund in a retirement account? Only, in my opinion, if you want to keep things extremely simple and not have to own more than a few funds. Otherwise, in a retirement account, you'll want to break the U.S. mar- ket into separate parts.

Table 13-1. U.S. Total Market Funds

Fund	Index	Type	Fees	Expense Ratio	Minimum Reg./IRA	Assets ($M)	Taxable/ Sheltered
Vanguard Total Stock Market Index	Wilshire 5000	Open-end	None	0.20%	$3,000/$1,000	14,689	Both
Fidelity Spartan Total Market Index	Wilshire 5000	Open-end	None	0.25%	$15,000/$15,000	1,046	Both
Schwab Total Stock Market Index	Wilshire 5000	Open-end	None	0.40%	$2,500/$1,000	260	Both
Schwab Total Stock Market Index Select	Wilshire 5000	Open-end	None	0.27%	$50,000/$500	257	Both
iShares Russell 3000 Index	Russell 3000	ETF	*	0.20%	*	1,303	Both

* Exchange-traded fund; incurs commissions and spreads. No minimum purchase.
(*Source:* Morningstar, Inc.)

Lumpers and Splitters

It's now time to tackle an extremely difficult issue—one that is so thorny that even experts occasionally disagree strongly about it. Namely, is it worthwhile to further break down the U.S. stock market into subclasses, such as small and large, or value and growth?

The naysayers (lumpers) have a very simple and powerful argument: because the market is ruthlessly efficient, there are no segments of the market that offer superior long-term expected returns. Breaking the market into subclasses is at best expensive and distracting and, at worst, will expose you to unnecessary risk.

The splitters say, "Look at the historical data. Value stocks have higher returns than growth stocks, and small stocks have higher returns than large stocks. It is logical to overweight value and small size." The reason why small stocks have higher returns is obvious— they are more risky. But the reason for the higher returns of value stocks is a bit of a mystery. Interestingly, the two possible reasons for this are mutually exclusive. The first is the behavioral reason we discussed in Chapter 7—investors overestimate the earnings growth of glamour stocks. The second possible reason is that value stocks are, in fact, riskier than growth stocks and therefore should have higher returns. My sympathies lie with the behavioral camp, but this controversy is far from settled.

We need to get a bit of nomenclature out of the way here. In Figure 13-1, I've diagrammed the relationship between the market and its segments. The most commonly accepted way of splitting the market is into four corners—large growth, large value, small growth, and small value. Large growth and large value together form the "large market," which is generally defined as the S&P 500. Small value and small growth together make up the "small market," defined by most as the Russell 2000 or the S&P 600. Since growth stocks have market caps that are much larger than value stocks, they overwhelm them in most indexes, so large growth and large market behave nearly identically. The same goes for small-cap stocks; the small-growth and small-market subsegments behave in nearly the same way.

As you have probably guessed by now, my sympathies lie with the splitters. Once you decide to split, you are faced with just how to do so. Where, for example, do you draw the line between a large company and a small company? The most commonly used U.S. small company index is the Russell 2000, which has a median market cap of about $1 billion. On the other hand, in academia the most commonly used small-stock index is the CRSP 9-10 Decile index; it has a median market cap of just $152 million. ("9-10 Decile" refers to the fact that

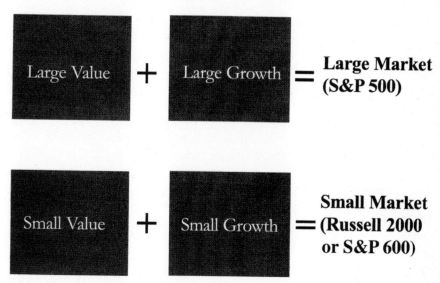

Figure 13-1. The four corners of the market.

these stocks are in the ninth and tenth deciles—that is, the bottom fifth—of market cap size. Many refer to these very small companies—in the $50–300 million market-cap range—as "microcap" stocks.) And, yes, there's a fund tracking this microcap index, although it isn't available to the general public.

How do you draw the line between a value company and a growth company? The most common approach splits the market by the ratio of price-to-book values by thirds, into value (bottom third) and growth (top third), with the middle third being called "blend."

Here things start to get a little confusing. The Barra/Vanguard method splits value and growth into halves according to market cap—the most expensive half of the market cap is designated as "growth," the other half as "value." Since growth stocks have higher market caps than value stocks, halving the S&P 500 by this method produces many more names on the value list (usually around 350) than on the growth list (usually around 150).

The point of all this is that whereas the Vanguard Growth Fund contains only growth stocks, the Vanguard Value Fund contains both value and blend. On the other hand, value index funds from some other companies contain only value stocks. (Vanguard/Barra similarly splits the S&P 600 Small-Cap Index into a small-growth index with about 200 stocks and a small-value index with about 400. This method suffers from the same problem of "blend contamination" of the large-value index.)

You can see that slicing the market into the four corners of the U.S. market—large value, large growth, small value, and small growth—can be very complicated, since we have to decide twice where to make the cuts. There's another factor to consider here as well. In Chapter 1, we discussed the fact that the stocks of small companies had higher returns than the stocks of large companies. In actual practice, you have to be exceptionally cautious about attempting to implement small-stock strategies, because these companies are very expensive to trade. Most actively managed mutual funds and small investors do not pay much attention to the costs of trading small stocks and wind up wiping out any possible small-stock advantage in this manner. Thus, for your small-stock exposure, it's critical to employ an index fund manager experienced in the techniques of small-stock trading, such as the Vanguard or DFA groups. John Montgomery of the Bridgeway Group is quite adept at this as well.

In Table 13-2, I've listed the major U.S. market-sector index funds available to the investor. Pay careful attention to the last column, which indicates whether or not each fund is appropriate for taxable accounts, sheltered accounts, or both. Note that three of the four "corner assets" (large value, small value, small growth) are *not suitable* for taxable accounts because of the high turnover necessary to maintain their characteristics. For example, a small-value fund may toss out a stock because it has become too large, turned into a growth stock, or both, triggering a large amount of capital gains. Even the Vanguard Value Index Fund, which invests only in large-cap stocks, distributes about 5% of its portfolio each year as capital gains, reducing your after-tax return accordingly. The REIT sector is also inappropriate for taxable accounts because most of its return comes from dividends, which are taxed as ordinary income.

Also note that several of the funds levy a "contingent redemption fee," again, payable to the existing shareholders, for shares held less than one to five years, to discourage trading. There's one other wrinkle at Vanguard that small investors should be aware of, and that's the $10 service fee on index fund accounts of less than $10,000. At $1,000 of assets, this amounts to 1% per year, and at just below $10,000 assets, 0.10% per year. Fortunately, most investors grow out of this problem, but it is an unpleasant annoyance.

It's worth discussing the difference between Mr. Montgomery's offering in Table 13-2—the Bridgeway Ultra-Small-Company Tax-Advantaged Fund—and the other small-company funds. The Bridgeway fund, which is aimed at taxable accounts, invests in much smaller companies than the other small company funds—typically in

Table 13-2. U.S. Stock Index Funds

Fund	Index	Type	Fees	Expense Ratio	Minimum Reg./IRA	Assets ($M)	Taxable/ Sheltered
Large-Cap Market:							
Vanguard 500 Index	S&P 500	Open-end	none	0.18%	$3,000/$1,000	74,796	Both
Vang. Tax-Managed Growth & Income	S&P 500	Open-end	*	0.19%	$10,000/NA	2,063	Taxable
Vang. Tax-Managed Cap. App.	Russell 1000	Open-end	*	0.18%	$10,000/NA	2,383	Taxable
Fidelity Spartan 500 Index	S&P 500	Open-end	none	0.19%	$10,000/$500	8,609	Both
USAA S&P 500 Index	S&P 500	Open-end	none	0.18%	$3,000/$2,000	2,987	Both
Schwab S&P 500	S&P 500	Open-end	none	0.36%	$2,500/$1,000	3,077	Both
Schwab 1000	Russell 1000	Open-end	none	0.47%	$2,500/$1,000	4,159	Both
iShares S&P 500 Index	S&P 500	ETF	***	0.09%	***	3,767	Both
iShares S&P 100 Index	S&P 100	ETF	***	0.20%	***	175	Both
SPDRs	S&P 500	ETF	***	0.11%	***	29,110	Both
iShares Russell 1000	Russell 1000	ETF	***	0.15%	***	450	Both
Small-Cap Market:							
Vanguard Small-Cap Index	Russell 2000	Open-end	none	0.27%	$3,000/$1,000	3,228	Sheltered
Vanguard Tax-Managed Small-Cap	S&P 600	Open-end	**	0.20%	$10,000/NA	589	Taxable
iShares S&P 600 Small-Cap Index	S&P 600	ETF	***	0.20%	***	812	Sheltered

Table 13-2. U.S. Stock Index Funds (Continued)

Fund	Index	Type	Fees	Expense Ratio	Minimum Reg./IRA	Assets ($M)	Taxable/ Sheltered
iShares Russell 2000 Index	Russell 2000	ETF	***	0.20%	***	2,257	Sheltered
Bridgeway Ultra Small Co. Tax Adv.	CRSP-10	Open-end	none	0.75%	$2,000	44	Taxable
Large-Cap Value:							
Vanguard Value Index	S&P 500/ Barra Value	Open-end	none	0.22%	$3,000/$1,000	3,287	Sheltered
iShares Russell 1000 Value Index	Russell 1000 Value	ETF	***	0.20%	***	631	Sheltered
iShares S&P 500/Barra Value Index	S&P 500/ Barra Value	ETF	***	0.18%	***	521	Sheltered
Large-Cap Growth:							
Vanguard Growth Index	S&P 500/ Barra Growth	Open-end	none	0.22%	$3,000/$1,000	9,061	Both
iShares Russell 1000 Growth Index	Russell 1000 Growth	ETF	***	0.20%	***	528	Both
iShares S&P 500/Barra Growth Index	S&P 500/ Barra Growth	ETF	***	0.18%	***	427	Both

Small-Cap Value:							
Vanguard Small-Cap Value Index	S&P 600-SC/ Barra Value	Open-end		0.27%	$3,000/$1,000	482	Sheltered
iShares Russell 2000 Value Index	Russell 2000 Value	ETF	***	0.25%	***	608	Sheltered
iShares S&P SC 600 Value Index	S&P 600-SC/ Barra Value	ETF	***	0.25%	***	332	Sheltered
Small-Cap Growth:							
Vanguard Small-Cap Growth Index	S&P 600-SC/ Barra Growth	Open-end		0.27%	$3,000/$1,000	310	Sheltered
iShares Russell 2000 Growth Index	Russell 2000 Growth	ETF	***	0.25%	***	412	Sheltered
iShares S&P SC 600 Growth Index	S&P 600-SC/ Barra Growth	ETF	***	0.25%	***	165	Sheltered
REIT:							
Vanguard REIT Index	Morgan Stanley REIT	Open-end	****	0.33%	$3,000/$1,000	1,081	Sheltered

* 2% redemption fee for shares held less than one year, 1% for shares held 1–5 years.
** 2% redemption fee for shares held less than one year, 1% for shares held 1–5 years.
*** Exchange-traded fund, incurs commissions and spreads. No minimum purchase.
**** 1% redemption fee for shares held less than one year

(*Source:* Morningstar, Inc.)

the $50-$100 million "microcap" range, versus about $1 billion for the others. It is thus riskier than the other small-company funds in Table 13-2, and, as a consequence, has a higher expected return. It should also be a better "diversifier" than the other funds, since smaller stocks tend to be less correlated with the rest of the market than larger ones. On the other hand, its expenses are higher, and it is also subject to greater "institutional risk"—the possibility that Bridgeway, or at least its investment culture, may not survive long-term.

Some of you will notice that the Nasdaq 100 Cubes fund is not listed. Yes, this is an efficient, inexpensive (0.18% annual fee) index exchange-traded fund, which we discussed in Chapter 10. But it is essentially a concentrated large-growth fund. Its average holding sells at more than 50 times earnings, and it is fearfully vulnerable to market declines, having lost more than 60% of its value during the recent downturn. In fact, I recommend completely avoiding the large-growth and small-growth categories.

As we've already seen in Chapter 1, small growth is a very bad actor in the long term, with the lowest return of any of the four corner portfolios and very high risk. Because of the way that large growth is defined, the Nasdaq 100 is very similar to the S&P 500, except that because of its much higher valuation, it has a relatively low expected long-term return.

I recommend using a small-market fund in place of a small-growth fund, and a large-market (i.e., S&P 500) fund in place of a large-growth fund. You will get enough exposure to large- and small-growth stocks via the S&P 500, total market, and small cap index funds, since they consist mainly of growth issues.

This is why I believe it is worthwhile to slice and dice the domestic component of our equity portfolios—we can pare down our exposure to overvalued growth stocks, particularly the smaller ones, which historically have had the lowest long-term returns.

There's a fifth domestic asset class to consider—real estate investment trusts (REITs), which we discussed in Chapter 2. Because they often behave very differently from the four corners of the market, most allocation experts consider them a separate asset class. Given the relatively high expected returns of REITs, they deserve serious consideration from every investor.

We've only scratched the surface of the many possible ways that the domestic market can be carved up. There are now ETFs and open-end funds that will allow you to invest in midcaps (companies midway in size between large and small caps) of the market, value, and growth variety. It is even possible to buy only value or growth stocks of all sizes in one portfolio (i.e., the Russell 3000 Value and Growth). And, of course, you can buy industry sectors in index form as well. But there comes a time when even the most devoted asset-class junkie says, "enough already." It is unlikely that there is any benefit to slicing the domestic equity market thinner than the five asset classes we've concentrated on above.

To summarize, the five major domestic asset classes you should use are:

- Large Market
- Small Market
- Large Value
- Small Value
- REITs

Timbers

The next material you will need to construct your portfolio is foreign equity. This is a much simpler task because you have relatively few choices. About the only indexed products you can buy are the foreign equivalents of "large-market" stocks. There are no indexed international small-market, large-value, or small-value vehicles available to individual investors.

What is available is the choice of region. You can invest in the whole shooting match—all foreign stocks in cap-weighted fashion, or you can divvy things up into the three main regions—Pacific (mainly Japan), Europe, and emerging markets (Mexico, Brazil, Turkey, Indonesia, Korea, Taiwan and the like). With some trepidation, you can invest in foreign value stocks reasonably efficiently using the Vanguard International Value Fund. This is not indexed, but does have low expenses and tracks an index of international value stocks reasonably well. In Table 13-3, I've listed this fund, plus the foreign index funds I'd recommend.

There are a few wrinkles to consider. Ideally, I would avoid owning the Vanguard Total International Fund in a taxable account, as it is a "fund of funds," consisting of the three regional funds. As such, it is not eligible for the foreign dividend tax exclusion, which allows you to deduct the taxes on dividends from foreign stocks on your U.S. tax return.

Pay attention to the fund size. If the fund is particularly small, say less than $100 million, I'd be wary—it is likely that the fund company may kill it due to lack of interest. The Emerging Markets Stock Index Fund levies 0.5% purchase and sales fees. Do not confuse these with a sales

Table 13-3. International Funds

Fund	Index	Type	Fees	Expense Ratio	Minimum Reg./IRA	Assets ($M)	Taxable/ Sheltered
Vanguard European Stock Index	MSCI-EAFE-Europe	Open-end	none	0.29%	$3,000/$1,000	4,813	Both
Vanguard Emerging Markets Stock Index	MSCI-EAFE-Emg. Mkt.	Open-end	**	0.58%	$3,000/$1,000	850	Both
Vanguard Pacific Stock Index	MSCI EAFE-Pacific	Open-end	none	0.37%	$3,000/$1,000	1,661	Both
Vanguard Total International	MSCI EAFE	Open-end	none	0.37%	$3,000/$1,000	3,003	Sheltered
Vanguard Tax-Managed International	MSCI EAFE	Open-end	*	0.35%	$10,000/NA	324	Taxable
Vanguard International Value	NA	Open-end	none	0.64%	$3,000/$1,000	910	Sheltered
Fidelity Spartan International Index	MSCI EAFE	Open-end	none	0.35%	$15,000/$15,000	349	Both
Schwab International Index	MSCI EAFE	Open-end	none	0.58%	$2,500/$1,000	613	Both

* 2% redemption fee for shares held less than one year, 1% for shares held 1–5 years.
* 0.5% purchase and sales fees, payable to fund.
(*Source:* Morningstar, Inc.)

load. These fees are paid to the existing shareholders in order to cover the transactional costs of shares just purchased. In other words, they directly benefit the existing shareholders, not a salesman or the fund company.

There are two other options to consider when looking at international vehicles. First, iShares does offer indexed ETFs for single nations. I'd recommend against them because of complexity and cost—these funds carry expense ratios of nearly 1%, far higher than those of the open-end funds. Second, there is Dimensional Fund Advisors (DFA). These folks are among the best and brightest in finance, with a strong connection to Eugene Fama and the University of Chicago.

DFA indexes just about any asset class you might want, including small, value, and even small value foreign markets. They also have individual funds for small stocks from the U.K., Continental Europe, Japan, Pacific Rim, and emerging markets. Better yet, their index funds for the U.S. market have much more focused exposure to value and small stocks than Vanguard or the other indexers. They even have tax-managed value index funds aimed at both U.S. and foreign value stocks.

But there's a hitch. DFA only sells their funds through approved financial advisors. Is it worthwhile to engage the services of a financial advisor just to gain access to DFA? Probably not. Their tax-managed, foreign-small and foreign-value funds carry expenses which are 0.2% to 0.6% higher than Vanguard's, and by the time you add in the advisor's expense, the advantage of these funds may be lost. But if you have decided that you need the services of a financial advisor, then you should certainly seek one with access to DFA.

Shingles

Like the shingles on a roof that shelter your house from the rain and snow, so do bonds provide comfort and succor (as well as dry powder) during troubled times in the market. Table 13-4 lists the recommended bond funds.

The overriding principle of bond investment is to *keep it short*. As we saw in Figure 1-10, long-maturity bonds can be quite risky. If you own a bond with a 30-year maturity and interest rates double, then your bond will lose almost half of its value. On the other hand, the excess return earned by extending bond maturities is minimal, as shown by the "yield curve" for the U.S. Treasury market I've plotted in Figure 13-2. Notice that you get about 4% of extra return by extending your maturity from 30 days out to 30 years. This is about as "steep" as the yield curve gets. Much of the time, the curve is much less steep—perhaps 1% to 1.5% difference between long and short yields—and

Table 13-4. Bond and Bond Index Funds

Fund	Index	Type	Fees	Expense Ratio	Minimum Reg./IRA	Assets ($M)	Duration (Years)
Vanguard Total Bond Market Index	Lehman Bros. Aggregate	Open-end	none	0.22%	$3,000/$1,000	12,437	4.6
Vanguard Short-Term Bond Index	Lehman Bros. 1–5 Y G/C	Open-end	none	0.21%	$3,000/$1,000	1,429	2.5
Vanguard Intermed.-Term Bond Index	Lehman Bros. Long G/C	Open-end	none	0.21%	$3,000/$1,000	1,806	5.8
Vanguard Inflation Protected Securities	NA	Open-end	none	0.25%	$3,000/$1,000	900	4.5
Schwab Total Bond Market Index	NA	Open-end	none	0.35%	$1,000/$500	887	4.9
Fidelity U.S. Bond Index	Lehman Bros. Aggregate	Open-end	none	0.31%	$100,000/$500	3,034	4.5
Vanguard Short-Term Corporate	NA	Open-end	none	0.24%	$3,000/$1,000	6,844	2.2
Vanguard GNMA	NA	Open-end	none	0.27%	$3,000/$1,000	15,839	3.6

(*Source:* Morningstar, Inc.)

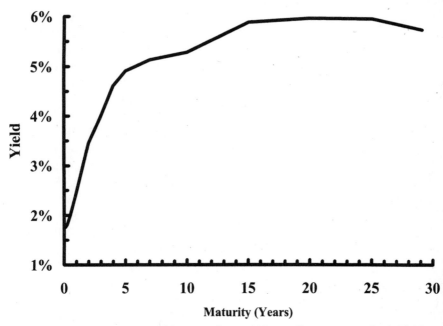

Figure 13-2. U.S. Treasury yield curve. *(Source: The Wall Street Journal, 3/14/02.)*

there are even times when the yield curve is "inverted," i.e., when long rates are lower than shorter rates.

In Figure 13-2, note that you get the most "bang for the buck" by about a five-year maturity. This is the steepest part of the yield curve—the part that rewards you the most. Beyond that, the extra return diminishes, with continually increasing risk. The stock portion of your portfolio is the place to take risk, not the bond portion, where the purpose is to shelter you from market downturns and provide ready liquidity. The curve is steepest in the first year or two. For the most part, then, you should keep the maturity of your bond portfolio between one and five years. There are a wide variety of bond funds that will accomplish this.

There are three main categories in the bond arena, and you will likely use all of them:

- Government securities. These are mainly Treasury bills (up to a one-year maturity), notes (one to ten years), and bonds (more than ten years). The others in this category are "agencies"—GNMA, FNMA, FHLB, FFCB, etc., which are backed by the U.S. government. Treasuries are subject to federal, but not state tax. Some of the agencies are exempt from state tax; some are not. Unless you are investing a small amount of money in Treasuries, there is no reason to buy a fund for this purpose. Since all Treasuries carry the same credit risk—zero—there is no need to diversify. Treasuries can be bought at auction directly from the government without a fee, allowing you to manufacture your own "Treasury Fund" at no expense. (You can reach Treasury Direct at 1-800-722-2678 and www.publicdebt.treas.gov/sec/sectrdir.htm.) Even if you are purchasing a Treasury at auction through a brokerage firm, the fee is nominal—typically about $25. For a five-year note worth $10,000, this equals an annual expense of 0.05%.

- High-quality corporate bonds and commercial paper. Corporates not only carry interest rate risk, but also credit risk. Even the highest-rated companies occasionally default. How often does this happen? Very rarely. According to bond-rating service Moody's, since 1920 the rate of default for the highest-rated AAA bonds was zero, 0.04% per year for AA-rated, 0.09% for A-rated, and 0.25% for BBB-rated. BBB is the lowest of the four "investment-grade" categories.

These categories are a tad deceptive, since, for example, it is highly unlikely that an AAA-rated bond would suddenly default—it would likely undergo successive downgradings first. For taking this risk, you have been rewarded historically with about 0.5% of extra return. Currently the "spread" between high-quality corporate bonds and Treasuries is over 1%. What does all this mean for investors? First, you will need wide diversification to invest in corporate bonds. You should only purchase these through a corporate bond mutual fund. You should not buy individual corporate bonds for the same reason you do not buy individual stocks, which is that you are bearing the unnecessary risk that your portfolio could be devastated by a single default—something you would not want to happen in the "riskless" part of your portfolio. The wise investor pays attention to the "spread" between high-grade corporate and Treasury yields that we plotted for junk bonds in Figure 2-6. When this gap is small, buy Treasuries. And when the gap is large, favor corporates. Another way of saying this is that when safety is cheap, you buy it (in the form of Treasury securities). At the present time, safety is *very* expensive.

- Municipal bonds. "Munis" are the debt issues of state and local governments, as well as other qualified quasi-governmental bodies, such as transit, housing, and water authorities. They are exempt from the taxes of the jurisdictions they are issued in. For example, New York City residents pay no federal, state, or city taxes on N.Y.C. munis. Munis issued by, say, Syracuse, are exempt from federal and state but not city tax to the N.Y.C. resident, and an Illinois muni would be exempt only from the federal tax to the N.Y.C. resident. Since they are tax-exempt, their yields tend to be lower than Treasury securities of comparable maturity and much lower than corporates. Like corporates, it is necessary to protect yourself from credit/default risk by buying a fund. Wealthy investors tend to assemble their own muni portfolios because they can buy enough issues to maintain adequate diversification. This is usually unwise because muni bonds are thinly traded and have very high bid/ask spreads—around 3% to 4%. Thus, even if you buy and hold these issues to maturity, you still will be paying a 1.5% to 2% "half-spread" on purchase, which amortizes out to about 0.2% to 0.3% per year, in addition to trading costs and management fees. This is the one field where Vanguard is all alone in the quality of its product—it offers many national and single-state muni funds, all with annual expenses of 0.20% or less. And since almost all are well in excess of $1 billion in size, the bid/ask spreads paid by these funds are estimated by Vanguard to be less than half that quoted above. So unless your name is Warren Buffett or Bill Gates, you're better off buying a Vanguard Fund. (Vanguard has recently brought out "Admiral" class shares, with muni bond fees in the 0.12% to 0.15% range. These carry $50,000–$250,000 minimums). In Table 13-5, I've listed Vanguard's national and single-state tax-exempt funds.

Obviously, it makes no sense to purchase municipal bonds in a tax-sheltered account. Here, the choice will be between government and corporate issues. In a taxable account, there are multiple possibilities, depending on the level of interest rates and taxes. Let's assume, for example, that you are subject to the 36% marginal federal rate and live in a state with a 5% marginal rate. In your taxable account, you can purchase the Vanguard Limited-Term Tax-Exempt Fund, which has a yield of 3.15%. Since you will pay state tax on most of this, the yield falls to 3.05% after tax. A Treasury note of the same maturity will yield 3.90%. But after paying federal, but not state, tax, its after-tax yield is only 2.50%. And finally, the Vanguard Short-Term Corporate Fund yields 5.18%, but after paying taxes at both levels, its after-tax yield falls to 3.15%. So, the nod here goes ever-so-slightly to the corporates. But there are times when either the Treasury or the muni fund will have a higher after-tax yield, and many times when it will be too close to call.

If you're confused, join the crowd. The choice of bond vehicles for your taxable accounts is a difficult decision, and the "right" answer may change from week to week. My advice is to split your taxable accounts among all three of the above bond classes (municipal,

Table 13-5. Municipal Bond Funds

Fund	Expense Ratio	Minimum	Duration (Years)	Assets ($M)
National Funds:				
Vanguard Short-Term Tax-Exempt	0.18%	$3,000	1.3	1,434
Vanguard Limited-Term Tax-Exempt	0.19%	$3,000	2.7	2,250
Vanguard Intermediate-Term Tax-Exempt	0.18%	$3,000	4.7	7,356
Vanguard Long-Term Tax-Exempt	0.19%	$3,000	7.5	1,389
Vanguard High-Yield Tax-Exempt	0.19%	$3,000	7.0	2,657
State Funds:				
Vanguard California Intermediate-Term Tax-Exempt	0.17%	$3,000	5.7	1,484
Vanguard California Long-Term Tax-Exempt	0.18%	$3,000	7.9	1,473
Vanguard Florida Long-Term Tax-Exempt	0.15%	$3,000	7.4	788
Vanguard Massachusetts Tax-Exempt	0.16%	$3,000	8.5	293
Vanguard New Jersey Long-Term Tax-Exempt	0.19%	$3,000	6.5	941
Vanguard New York Long-Term Tax-Exempt	0.20%	$3,000	6.7	1,313
Vanguard Ohio Long-Term Tax-Exempt	0.19%	$3,000	6.4	444
Vanguard Pennsylvania Long-Term Tax-Exempt	0.19%	$3,000	6.9	1,531

(*Source*: Morningstar, Inc.)

Treasury, and corporate), if you have enough assets to do so. The Treasuries will usually have a lower after-tax yield, but have the advantages of being perfectly safe and liquid, and free from state tax. Quite frankly, the yield differences aren't enough to be continually fretting over.

Surprisingly, unless you are investing a small amount (less than $5,000 to $10,000) in bonds, it makes no sense to buy a bond index fund. Why? Because about 50% of a such a fund is invested in Treasuries and other government securities, which you can own separately without paying ongoing fund fees. For that reason, I'd buy whatever Treasuries you want directly. (Remember, there is no need for diversification here.) I'd use the Vanguard Short-Term Corporate Fund (or the GNMA fund, which has a higher yield, but a longer maturity) for the non-Treasury part of your bond allocation—you'll get off cheaper, plus you'll have more control of your portfolio. And again, you'll need to be cognizant of the $10 Vanguard minimum account fee. If your total bond allocation is in the $10,000 to $30,000 range, it just may be advantageous to consolidate all of your bond holdings in one of their bond index funds to avoid the fee for fund accounts of less than $10,000.

What Kind of House Are You Building?

This is a trick question, for the most part. What I'm really asking is, what financial hand have you been dealt? There are the obvious questions of how much you will have and what your needs will be (and even more importantly, the ratio of the former to the latter), but in terms of portfolio design, the key question is, what is the tax structure of your portfolio? For example, many professionals have most of their portfolio assets in 401(k), IRA, Keogh, and pension accounts. This gives them the freedom to invest in almost any asset class they desire without regard to tax consequences. At the other end of the spectrum is the entrepreneur who has sold his business for a lump sum and has no tax-sheltered assets at all. This investor is severely limited as to the kind of assets he can own. The reason for this is the "tax efficiency" of the index mutual funds used for exposure to each asset class.

Tax-efficiency is an extremely important concept to understand. It is a measure of the percent of a fund's return you receive after the taxes on the distributions are paid. For example, a stock fund with no turnover will produce no capital-gains distributions; you will be taxed only on the relatively small amount of stock dividends the fund passes through to you. Such a fund is highly tax-efficient. On the other hand, a stock fund with high turnover will periodically distribute a large amount of capital gains to you, on which taxes must be paid. Such a fund is tax-inefficient. Worst of all are REIT and junk bond funds, which distribute almost all of their return in the form of dividends. Further, these dividends are taxed at the high ordinary income rate. Obviously, then, you will want to hold only tax-efficient funds in your taxable account, reserving the most tax-inefficient ones for your retirement accounts.

The problem, as we've already mentioned, is that certain asset classes are inherently tax-inefficient, such as junk bonds and REITs. Value funds are also relatively tax-inefficient, because if a value stock increases enough in price, it may no longer qualify for the value index and must be sold at a substantial capital gain. On the other hand, S&P 500, Wilshire 5000, and large-cap foreign index funds tend to be highly tax-efficient and are thus suitable for taxable accounts. Finally, some fund companies, including Vanguard, have brought out a class of super tax-efficient "tax-managed" funds for U.S. large and small and foreign large-cap stocks.

The taxable/sheltered question even dictates the overall stock/bond allocation to a certain extent. As we just saw above, after-tax bond yields are nothing to write home about. Since tax-efficient equity funds provide excellent deferral of taxation, the all-taxable investor will want a higher portion of stocks than the all-sheltered investor, all other things being equal.

Finally, there is the all-too-common situation of the investor with only a small amount of sheltered assets. In this case, he will want to prioritize which tax-inefficient asset classes to place in the sheltered portion of his portfolio.

A Duplex, Really

Actually, you're not building one house, but two. As we've touched on many times, you are really building two different allocations—one for risky assets (stocks) and one for riskless assets (generally, short-maturity bonds). In terms of how you allocate among different stock asset classes, it really doesn't matter what your overall stock/bond ratio is. The person who has an aggressive 80% stock/20% bond mix will have exactly the same kind of stock portfolio and bond portfolio as the person who has a conservative 20% stock/80% bond portfolio. What's different is the overall amount of assets in stocks versus bonds. We're not building houses so much as *warehouses*—one each for stocks and bonds. Once we've constructed them, we can then control our portfolio's risk and return by how much of our assets we load into each.

The most basic principle of portfolio design is that once you think you've designed an allocation for stock assets that is reasonable and efficient, then you keep that stock allocation across portfolios from the safest (all bond) to the riskiest (all stock). All you have to do to move up or down the risk/return scale is to vary the overall stock/bond ratio.

Recall from Chapter 2 that it is likely that long-term stock returns will not be much greater than bond returns. In such an environment, we find it hard to recommend an all-stock portfolio; 80% would seem to be a reasonable upper limit at the present time. Even wild-eyed optimists like Jim Glassman and Kevin Hassett, authors of *Dow 36,000*, admit that they could be wrong and recommend holding 20% bonds.

We'll illustrate these principles with four different investors: Taxable Ted, Sheltered Sam, In-Between Ida, and Young Yvonne.

Taxable Ted

Ted's life has not been a great deal of fun. Because of his straitened upbringing, he had to work his way through an electrical engineering degree by moonlighting as a bouncer. Then, after graduation, he rapidly grew tired of his first job in aircraft manufacturing and lit out on his own, starting a firm specializing in cellular phone transmission components. His professional life was a punishing succession of 80-hour weeks punctuated by labor troubles, parts shortages, incessant travel, payroll squeezes, and divorces. After 23 years of this, it did not take a lot of convincing for him to accept a seven-figure buy out offer from a larger competitor and leave the entrepreneurial life for good. Ted's now sitting on a large wad of cash to tide him over until he decides what to do when he grows up. He's never had the time or money to set up a pension plan or even an IRA. What should he do with it all?

From the point of view of his stock allocation, Ted is seriously constrained. He realizes that there are only three asset classes available to him: U.S. total market/large-cap, U.S. small-cap, and foreign large-cap. There is one other option available to him, and that's to open a variable annuity (VA) so that he can invest in REITs. I didn't have many nice things to say about these vehicles a few chapters ago, but here I'd make a rare exception. Vanguard does make available a relatively low-cost VA, and REITs are one of the few areas where this makes sense. This will enable him to hold REITs in his portfolio without being punished by the taxes on their hefty dividend distributions, since they would be sheltered inside the annuity account. Taxes are not paid until he withdraws the funds from the VA much later. The disadvantages are an extra 0.37% in insurance expense and not being able to withdraw funds before age 59½ without penalty. (Also, there is a $25 per-year fee for account sizes under $25,000, making investing under $10,000 in their VA uneconomical.) Here's what his stock allocation looks like:

- 40% Vanguard Total Stock Market
- 20% Vanguard Tax-Managed Small-Cap
- 25% Vanguard Tax-Managed International
- 15% Vanguard REIT (VA)

Ted's from California, so he decides to split his bond portfolio four ways. One quarter goes into a five-year "Treasury ladder." He does this with equal amounts of one-, two-, three-, four-, and five-year Treasuries.

As each matures, he rolls it into a new five-year note at auction. (Initially, the two- and five-year notes are bought at auction, the others in the "secondary market.") The other three-quarters of the bond allocation are split among the Vanguard Short-Term Corporate, Limited-Term Tax-Exempt, and California Intermediate-Term Tax-Exempt funds. The California fund appeals to him because of its higher yield and state tax exemption, but he also realizes that quite often, downgrades and defaults can concentrate in one state (as recently happened in California because of the electrical power squeeze), and he wants to keep his risk down. Also, the California fund has a longer average maturity, making it somewhat riskier. Here's what his bond portfolio looks like:

- 25% Treasury Ladder
- 25% Vanguard Short-Term Corporate Bond
- 25% Vanguard Limited-Term Tax-Exempt
- 25% Vanguard California Intermediate-Term Tax-Exempt

Note that Ted has no need of a separate "emergency fund," since in a pinch he can easily tap his bond money. Once Ted has arrived at efficient stock and bond allocations, they can be mixed to produce portfolios across the full range of risk. This is demonstrated in Table 13-6; note how all of the portfolios, from 100% stock down to 100% bond, maintain the same 8:4:5:3 ratio of large:small:foreign:REIT.

Now all Ted has to do is to determine his overall stock/bond mix. First he takes a look at Figures 4-1 through 4-5. Being an analytical type, he comes up with a table that relates his risk tolerance to his overall stock allocation. This is shown in Table 13-7. Take a good look at it. Realize that this is only a starting point.

Have you ever actually lost 25% of your assets? It is one thing to think about it, and quite another to actually have it happen to you. (Remember the aircraft-simulator crash versus real-aircraft crash analogy mentioned earlier.) The classic beginner's mistake is to overestimate his risk tolerance, then decamp forever from stocks when the inevitable loss hurts more than he had ever expected. When in doubt, tone down your portfolio's risks by shaving your exposure to stocks.

Finally, given that our estimates for future stock and bond returns are so close, it makes little sense to own more than 80% stocks, no matter how aggressive and risk-tolerant you are.

Sheltered Sam

Sam's a respected CPA in a small midwestern city. He lives with his wife of 25 years and their four children. Being a smart and disciplined tax professional, he's deferred as much income into his firm's pension

Table 13-6. "Taxable Ted's" Portfolios

Stock/Bond	100/0	90/10	80/20	70/30	60/40	50/50	40/60	30/70	20/80	10/90	0/100
Vanguard Total Stock Market Index	40%	36%	32%	28%	24%	20%	16%	12%	8%	4%	—
Vanguard Tax-Managed Small Cap	20%	18%	16%	14%	12%	10%	8%	6%	4%	2%	—
Vanguard Tax-Managed International	25%	22.5%	20%	17.5%	15%	12.5%	10%	7.5%	5%	2.5%	—
Vanguard REIT (VA)	15%	13.5%	12%	10.5%	9%	7.5%	6%	4.5%	3%	1.5%	—
Treasury Ladder	—	2.5%	5%	7.5%	10%	12.5%	15%	17.5%	20%	22.5%	25%
Vanguard Short-Term Corporate Bond	—	2.5%	5%	7.5%	10%	12.5%	15%	17.5%	20%	22.5%	25%
Vanguard Limited-Term Tax-Exempt	—	2.5%	5%	7.5%	10%	12.5%	15%	17.5%	20%	22.5%	25%
Vanguard California Intermediate-Term Tax-Exempt	—	2.5%	5%	7.5%	10%	12.5%	15%	17.5%	20%	22.5%	25%

Table 13-7. Allocating Stocks versus Bonds

I can tolerate losing _____ % of my portfolio in the course of earning higher returns:	Percent of my portfolio invested in stocks:
35%	80%
30%	70%
25%	60%
20%	50%
15%	40%
10%	30%
5%	20%
0%	10%

plan as possible. His oldest child is just beginning college, and he intends to retire when the youngest is done. He knows that by the time the last tuition bills are paid, his taxable savings, which he's placed mostly in Treasury notes, will be gone, and he will be left with only his retirement assets, which he intends to roll into an IRA when he closes up shop.

Sam has much more freedom in his choice of asset classes than Ted, because he can invest in any asset class he desires without tax consequences. In terms of stocks, he can embrace the forbidden fruit that Ted can't touch—value stocks and precious metals stocks. In addition, he can aggressively "rebalance" the foreign and domestic components of his portfolio. This process, which increases portfolio return and reduces portfolio risk, will be discussed in the next chapter. So instead of just owning the foreign market, he can break it down into regions. Finally, he can go flat out for yield in his bond portfolio and not have to worry about taxation until he withdraws his cash. Here's a reasonable stock allocation for Sam:

- 20% Vanguard 500 Index
- 25% Vanguard Value Index
- 5% Vanguard Small Cap Index
- 15% Vanguard Small Cap Value Index
- 10% Vanguard REIT Index
- 3% Vanguard Precious Metals
- 5% Vanguard European Stock Index
- 5% Vanguard Pacific Stock Index
- 5% Vanguard Emerging Stock Markets Index
- 7% Vanguard International Value

Note that he can hold the REIT fund in his IRA/pension. He does not need to resort to the expense and trouble of a VA, as Ted did.

For the bond portion of his portfolio, Sam can employ whatever kind of debt instrument he desires. He decides to put 60% in the Vangard Short-Term Corporate fund as his primary bond holding, because of its relatively high yield. And because he's a bit afraid of inflation, he will invest the remaining 40% of the bond portion in long-dated TIPS (Treasury Inflation Protected Security)—the $3\frac{3}{8}\%$ bond of 2032. Table 13-8 shows what Sam's portfolios, from all-stock to all-bond, look like.

Once again, Sam has no need for an emergency fund, since he is over $59\frac{1}{2}$ years of age and can tap the bond portion of his retirement accounts without penalty.

In-Between Ida

Our most difficult case study is In-Between Ida. Unfortunately, Ida, who is 57 years old, has just lost her husband after a long illness. But her late spouse planned well and left her with $1 million—$900,000 in personal savings and a life insurance policy, and $100,000 from his company pension plan, which she has now rolled over into an IRA.

Ida's situation is unlike Ted's and Sam's. Before we build her "two warehouses," we must first determine her stock/bond mix. The reason for this is that her stock/bond mix determines how much of her stock assets wind up in the taxable versus sheltered parts of her portfolio. For example, if she invests only 10% of her assets in stocks, she will have free rein to purchase whatever stock assets within the sheltered (retirement) part of the portfolio she chooses. On the other hand, if she invests all of the money in stocks, then she will be able to invest only the tax-sheltered 10% of it in the tax-inefficient asset classes—value stocks, gold stocks, and REITs.

So before Ida builds her two warehouses, she must first decide on her stock/bond mix. Assume that she picks a 50/50 mix. She will want to use the sheltered 10% of her portfolio to maximum advantage, so she will use it to purchase value stocks, which she would otherwise not be able to own on the taxable side. Since she wants to invest in REITs, she reluctantly agrees to open a VA to do so. Her bond portfolio, being taxable, will look very much like Ted's. For argument's sake, let's say she lives in Cleveland. Here's what she winds up with:

- 15% Vanguard Tax-Managed Growth and Income
- 5% Vanguard Value Index (IRA)
- 7.5% Vanguard Tax-Managed Small-Cap

Table 13-8. Sheltered Sam's Stock/Bond Mixes

Stock/Bond	100/0	90/10	80/20	70/30	60/40	50/50	40/60	30/70	20/80	10/90	0/100
Vanguard 500 Index	20%	18%	16%	14%	12%	10%	8%	6%	4%	2%	—
Vanguard Value Index	25%	22.5%	20%	17.5%	15%	12.5%	10%	7.5%	5%	2.5%	—
Vanguard Small-Cap Index	5%	4.5%	4%	3.5%	3%	2.5%	2%	1.5%	1%	0.5%	—
Vanguard Small-Cap Value Index	15%	13.5%	12%	10.5%	9%	7.5%	6%	4.5%	3%	1.5%	—
Vanguard REIT Index	10%	9%	8%	7%	6%	5%	4%	3%	2%	1%	—
Vanguard Precious Metals	3%	2.7%	2.4%	2.1%	1.8%	1.5%	1.2%	0.9%	0.6%	0.3%	—
Vanguard European Stock Index	5%	4.5%	4%	3.5%	3%	2.5%	2%	1.5%	1%	0.5%	—
Vanguard Pacific Stock Index	5%	4.5%	4%	3.5%	3%	2.5%	2%	1.5%	1%	0.5%	—
Vanguard Emerging Stock Markets Index	5%	4.5%	4%	3.5%	3%	2.5%	2%	1.5%	1%	0.5%	—
Vanguard International Value	7%	6.3%	5.6%	4.9%	4.2%	3.5%	2.8%	2.1%	1.4%	0.7%	—
Vanguard Short-Term Corporate	—	6%	12%	18%	24%	30%	36%	42%	48%	54%	60%
TIPS (3.375% of 2032)	—	4%	8%	12%	16%	20%	24%	28%	32%	36%	40%

- 5% Vanguard Small-Cap Value Index (IRA)
- 12.5% Vanguard Tax-Managed International
- 5% Vanguard REIT (VA)
- 12.5% Treasury Ladder
- 12.5% Vanguard Short-Term Corporate Bond
- 12.5% Vanguard Limited-Term Tax-Exempt
- 12.5% Vanguard Ohio Long-Term Tax-Exempt

Ida will admit that this portfolio is less than ideal. It does not contain as much of a value tilt as she would like, but there simply was not enough room in the sheltered part of her portfolio. And she's not wild about the Ohio muni fund's relatively long duration (6.4 years). Unfortunately, it was the only reasonably priced Ohio fund available.

Both Ida and Ted provide us with examples of the kinds of compromises that investors in the real world make because of their portfolio's tax structure. Ted is unable to own value stocks at all, and neither Ted nor Ida is able to take advantage of the excess return that comes from rebalancing with splitting their foreign stocks into regions.

Obviously, there are many intermediate cases between Ted's and Sam's; Ida's is just one. Take a look at Sam's portfolios in Table 13-8. At the risk/return level of 100% stocks, fully 60% of his asset classes are tax-inefficient (U.S. large and small value, international value, REITs, and precious metals). If an investor has decided on a 50% allocation to stocks, owning all these tax-inefficient asset classes mandates that at least 30% of his assets be tax-sheltered. And even in this case, it would actually be nice to have about 10% more sheltering for cash—in fact 40% of the total—to allow for rebalancing stock purchases in the case of a generalized market fall.

Young Yvonne

The highest hurdle of all in the investment game is the one faced by young people. Not only do they find it impossible to contemplate saving for retirement, but they face special problems relating to the small amounts involved. Young Yvonne will illustrate these issues.

At the moment, Yvonne doesn't have a penny to her name. Twenty-six years old and in between boyfriends, she's just begun work as an assistant district attorney. When she was barely into her teens, her father ran off, leaving her mother, twin brother, and her in desperate straits.

Through hard work, scholarship money, and frugality, she persevered and eventually earned her law degree through night school and passed the bar exam. And slowly but surely, the sun seems to be peeking through. She's got her own apartment, a health plan with her new job, and, according to her calculations, a bit of disposable income. After she pays for rent, food, gas and insurance on her 1985 Corolla, plus the odd night out with friends, she figures that she's left with about $4,000 per year to invest.

Yvonne has seen tough times. Unlike her friends, she doesn't need to be told that even at her tender age, job one is to save for her retirement and the inevitable rainy day. Sure, she'd like to spend a week in Maui or upgrade from her old junker, but her financial security comes first.

Yvonne's mom works in a bank trust department and has drilled into her that the first dollars set aside should go into retirement and emergency accounts. The one benefit not offered by her employer is a retirement plan, so Yvonne is going to have to set up her own IRA. How does she invest? Since her portfolio will be largely sheltered, she will aspire to one of Sam's allocations from Table 13-8. She picks the 60/40 version, modifying the bond portion to accommodate a taxable emergency fund:

- 12% Vanguard 500 Index
- 15% Vanguard Value Index
- 3% Vanguard Small-Cap Index
- 9% Vanguard Small-Cap Value Index
- 6% Vanguard REIT Index
- 1.8% Vanguard Precious Metals
- 3% Vanguard European Index
- 3% Vanguard Pacific Index
- 3% Vanguard Emerging Markets Index
- 4.2% Vanguard International Value
- 40% Cash, Bonds

Initially, however, Yvonne cannot own the sophisticated portfolio held by Sam, since all of the stock funds listed have $1,000 minimums for IRA accounts. Further, Vanguard's fee structure for IRAs has to be taken into account. Ten dollars per fund will be charged, but these fees are waived above aggregate assets of $50,000, or above $5,000 in each individual fund. Researching other fund families, she found that it is possible, in theory, to construct indexed retirement portfolios with Schwab, and was intrigued by the $500 minimums for its funds, but shocked by the quarterly fees of up to $40 for small accounts! And while Fidelity does not sport these onerous fees, she found its selection of index funds too limited.

Obviously, there's a tradeoff here between diversification and expense. Yvonne would like to own all of the asset classes shown above, but does not wish to pay up to 1% per year in extra fees for the benefit of owning a lot of small fund accounts. Even worse, it will be at least a few years before she can save enough to meet the $1,000 minimum for the 11 funds listed. For this reason, setting up a retirement account for a young person is a thorny problem. Yvonne can theoretically get around this by buying an "asset allocation fund" that invests in many different assets, but it is my opinion that these vehicles do not offer adequate diversification and often perform poorly. It is better to use a proper asset-class-based indexed approach from day one.

Here's how Yvonne should proceed. The first dollars of her savings should be placed in an emergency money market account. This should be a *taxable* account, so that penalties will not be incurred if she needs the money. Vanguard's Prime Money Market Reserves has about the lowest ongoing expense ratio of any money market, but it also has a $3,000 minimum. Not infrequently, fund families, in an effort to attract funds, will waive the expenses on their money market funds to boost yields and attract assets. Don't fall for this—eventually, the fees are reinstated and the yield falls. So most of her first year's savings will go into the emergency money fund. With the remaining $1,000 from her first year's savings she can purchase only one fund in her IRA. The logical choice is the Vanguard 500 Index Fund. So her initial target allocation will be split between just two asset classes—taxable cash and sheltered S&P 500.

Each year thereafter, she plans to contribute the maximum allowed in her IRA, placing the excess in her taxable money fund for emergencies. And thanks to the Tax Relief Reconciliation Act of 2001, the amounts that she can contribute to her IRA will increase from $3,000 in 2002 to $5,000 in 2008.

At what point does she start to diversify into other asset classes? I've already mentioned the tradeoff between diversification and fees; each asset class will provide her with additional diversification, but will also cost her the $10 per year fee for fund accounts of less than $5,000 (in addition to the $10 index fund fee for accounts under $10,000). There are many ways to approach this problem, but a reasonable compromise would be to add an additional fund for each $5,000 contributed. This will initially result in 0.2% extra expense—not a bad price to pay for the diversification obtained. I'd recommend adding in asset classes/funds in the following order:

1. $0–$5,000 added: Start with Vanguard 500 Index Fund.
2. $5,000–$10,000 total contributions: Add Vanguard Total International Fund.
3. $10,000–$15,000 total contributions: Add Vanguard REIT Index Fund.

4. $15,000–$20,000 total contributions: Add Vanguard Small-Cap Value Fund.

Note that we are not adding $5,000 to each fund in sequence. For example, Yvonne's asset allocation calls for a total of 13.2% foreign equity (the sum of the four international funds) and 6% REITs. So, of the second $5,000 added, only $1,500 will go into the Total International Fund. The other $3,500 is divided between the 500 Index Fund and the money market. And by the time $15,000 is added, only $1,000 will be put into the REIT Fund.

As the years pass, she will want to add in the Value, Small-Cap, and Precious Metals funds. Initially, however, her taxable emergency money market account will be considered to be the bond portion of her portfolio. But when she has convinced herself that she has enough emergency money saved up—say $10,000—she will want to add in the Short-Term Corporate Fund and TIPS fund and into her retirement account to maintain her targeted stock/bond ratio.

Finally, when the $50,000 level is reached, she'll split her Total International Fund into the Pacific, European, Emerging Markets, and International Value funds and arrive at a retirement fund composition looking like the allocation shown above. The above process is complex. For the sake of clarity, in Table 13-9 I've outlined what it looks like in actual practice, as the account grows in size. Funds are added from left to right, one at a time, for each $5,000 increment in portfolio growth.

Teach Your Children Well

The primary object of investing for the very young is not simply the management of cold, hard assets, but rather *financial education.* Instilling fiscal responsibility into the young is well beyond the scope of this book, but it is a fact that the way we handle financial risk and loss is probably determined at an early age. The sooner your children become acquainted with the risk/return nexus and the benefits of diversification, and the earlier they experience financial loss in a protective, supportive environment, the better.

I suggest that at approximately age ten you set up a small portfolio with two or three asset classes, as well as a money market fund in the child's name. Have him or her learn how to sort and file the statements properly as they arrive in the mail and teach the child how to track the value of each fund. Every quarter, sit down with all involved siblings and have an "investment conference" during which the performance of each account is discussed. Their reward for these chores will be the

Table 13-9. "Young Yvonne's" Investment Path: Vanguard Funds.
Note: Funds are added from left to right, in $5,000 increments. See text.

Total Amount	Money Market (Taxable)	500 Index	Total Int'l. Index	REIT Index	Small Value Index	Value Index	Small Cap Index	Short-Term Corporate	Prec. Met. Fund	European Index	Pacific Index	Emg. Mkt. Index	Int'l. Value Fund	Inflation Prot. Sec. (TIPS)
$5,000	$3,000	$2,000												
$10,000	$4,000	$4,500	$1,500											
$15,000	$6,000	$6,000	$2,000	$1,000										
$20,000	$8,000	$6,500	$2,500	$1,500	$1,500									
$25,000	$10,000	$3,500**	$3,000	$2,000	$2,000	$4,500								
$30,000	$10,000	$4,000	$3,500	$2,000	$2,500	$5,000	$1,000	$2,000						
$35,000	$10,000	$4,100	$4,600	$2,100	$3,100	$5,100	$1,000	$4,000	$1,000					
$40,000	$10,000	$4,800	$5,000	$2,400	$3,600	$6,000	$1,200	$6,000	$1,000					
$45,000	$10,000	$5,400	$5,800	$2,700	$4,000	$6,750	$1,350	$8,000	$1,000					
$50,000	$10,000	$6,000	***	$3,000	$4,400	$7,500	$1,500	$10,000	$1,000	$1,500	$1,500	$1,500	$2,100	
$55,000	$10,000	$6,600	***	$3,300	$4,950	$8,240	$1,650	$12,000	$1,000	$1,650	$1,650	$1,650	$2,310	
$60,000	$10,000	$7,200	***	$3,600	$5,400	$9,000	$1,800	$12,000	$1,080	$1,800	$1,800	$1,800	$2,520	$2,000
$65,000	$10,000	$7,800	***	$3,900	$5,850	$9,750	$1,950	$14,000	$1,170	$1,950	$1,950	$1,950	$2,730	$2,000
$70,000	$10,000	$8,400	***	$4,200	$6,300	$10,500	$2,100	$14,000	$1,260	$2,100	$2,100	$2,100	$2,940	$4,000
$75,000	$10,000	$9,000	***	$4,500	$6,750	$11,250	$2,250	$15,000	$1,350	$2,250	$2,250	$2,250	$3,150	$5,000
$80,000	$10,000	$9,600	***	$4,800	$7,200	$12,000	$2,400	$16,000	$1,440	$2,400	$2,400	$2,400	$3,360	$6,000
$85,000	$10,000	$10,200	***	$5,100	$7,650	$12,750	$2,550	$17,000	$1,530	$2,550	$2,550	$2,550	$3,570	$7,000
$90,000	$10,000	$10,800	***	$5,400	$8,100	$13,500	$2,700	$18,000	$1,620	$2,700	$2,700	$2,700	$3,780	$8,000
$95,000	$10,000	$11,400	***	$5,700	$8,550	$14,250	$2,850	$19,000	$1,710	$2,850	$2,850	$2,850	$3,990	$9,000
$100,000	$10,000	$12,000	***	$6,000	$9,000	$15,000	$3,000	$20,000	$1,800	$3,000	$3,000	$3,000	$4,200	$10,000

** When portfolio reaches $25,000 in size, approximately $3,000 is exchanged from the 500 Index Fund into the Value Index Fund.
*** When portfolio reaches $50,000 in size, the Total International Index Fund is exchanged into the International Value, European, Pacific, and Emerging Markets Index funds.

dividends from the stock and money market funds, as well as half of the remaining increase in investment value, if any, each December 31.

The most valuable part of the process comes during market declines, when they will suffer paper losses amounting to several months' or years' allowance in one fell swoop. The message during these periods should be as clear as it is gentle and kind:

> *It is all right to lose significant amounts of money in stocks as long as it is due to the vicissitudes of the overall stock market. Do not be afraid to do so and do not feel badly when it happens. This is the inevitable price you pay for the long-term superiority of stocks. In fact, a very famous investor once said that from time to time it was the duty of an investor to lose money.* (Don't tell your children it was Keynes.)

By imparting this invaluable lesson to your offspring at an early age, you will have gone most of the way towards making them competent investors. And in the process, you just might learn a few things yourself.

One Size Doesn't Fit All

Ted, Sam, Ida, and Yvonne are purely illustrative cases. It's a mistake to take a cookie-cutter approach to the allocation process—the above portfolios are only starting points. There are several factors that would cause you to modify the above recommendations. Among them:

- Your personal asset class preferences. The precious metals equity class is a good example of this. Some investors are deathly afraid of inflation and get a warm fuzzy feeling from having this ultimate hard asset in their portfolio. Others find it silly to hold a component with low expected return and high volatility. Still others find it emotionally difficult to perform the rebalancing operations necessary to extract its maximum return—buying low and selling high requires an iron discipline that not everyone possesses. Emerging markets investing is another frequent problem. Some investors are uncomfortable owning stocks in countries where the water is not safe to drink or where shareholder protection is not quite the priority it is in the developed world, despite knowing that such risk is often generously rewarded by the capital markets. Although you should not let your emotional responses dictate your allocation, you do need to sleep at night, and your personal preferences are an important part of your asset class structure.

- Your tolerance for "tracking error"—that is, the difference between the performance of your portfolio and that of the market. I'm reminded of Mencken's definition of a wealthy man as one who makes more money than his wife's brother-in-law. The same is true of portfolio performance. Whether you like it or not, you cannot help but compare the return of your equity portfolio to the market, by which most investors mean the S&P 500. The period from 1995 to 1999, when this index outperformed every other asset class, provided a powerful reality check in this regard. As already mentioned, diversification works whether we want it to or not. During those five years, the diversified investor felt pain as his stock portfolio lagged those of his family, friends, and neighbors by a large amount. If this tracking error doesn't irk you, then by all means, diversify away. But it's a fact that many investors find lagging the S&P 500 for a three or four years highly unpleasant, even if the long-term return of their stock assets is higher than that benchmark. As one of asset allocation guru Roger Gibson's clients put it, "I would rather follow an inferior strategy that wins when my friends are winning and loses when my friends are losing than follow a superior long-term strategy that at times results in my losing when my friends are winning." If such underperformance relative to the market, which can last up to a decade, bothers you, perhaps you should weight your portfolio more towards the S&P 500 and go lighter on the REITs, small, value, and international stocks than Sam, Ted, Ida, and Yvonne.
- Lastly, whether you know it or not, you are likely the proud owner of quite a lot of "human capital" that needs to be integrated into the rest of your portfolio. What this recently fashionable term refers to is the fact that you are probably the recipient of a steady salary, Social Security, or fixed pension payments that can be "capitalized" to their present value as we did in Chapter 2. Let's consider each of these in turn. Let's say you are an employee of General Motors. In this case, you are working for a "value company" and are vulnerable in rough economic times, just as are value stocks. In this case, it would not be a good idea to overweight your portfolio with value stocks, as in a severe economic slump you may lose both your job as well as a fair chunk of your portfolio. Similarly, if you work in high tech, it would be foolish to overweight growth stocks in your portfolio. This highlights the most common investment mistake made by corporate employees—owning company stock in their personal and retirement portfolios, as was recently demonstrated by the Enron

debacle. If the company gets into trouble, the risk of losing everything is high. There are also people who *should* own value stocks. These are employees of companies in "countercyclical" industries that do well even when times are bad, such as food and drug companies. The ultimate countercyclical jobs are in the pawn and repo business, which boom during economic slumps. If you work in either of these industries, you can knock yourself out and load up on value stocks if you so wish. Finally, if you are one of the vanishing number of individuals lucky enough to be getting a regular fixed pension, then you own, in essence, a bond issued by your former employer. If that employer was the government, you can capitalize (that is, discount) its payments by a low rate—say 6%. So, if you are relatively young, you essentially own a perpetual annuity, similar to prestiti and consols. If your payments are $30,000 per year, this is the same as owning a long bond with a value of $30,000/0.06 = $500,000. If you are older, its value will be commensurately less. Your Social Security payments should be capitalized in the same way. If your pension comes from Trump Casinos, I'd capitalize it at much higher rate— say 12%—making its present value only $250,000 ($30,000/0.12 = $250,000). In any case, it would not be a bad idea to increase your stock holdings to reflect the "bonds" you effectively own via your pension and Social Security.

Finally, never forget that stocks can have zero real return for periods as long as 20 years. We design our portfolios for the long term, not for emergencies, college, or even a home. This is not to say that a solid allocation does not have room in it for these expenses, but that is not its primary purpose. Obviously, if you have an adequate nest egg to which you've allocated 40% in bonds, there will be more than enough available for emergencies (as long as the "emergency money" is in a taxable account) or for a house down payment, as long as enough of the bonds are in a taxable account.

Although the central tenet of asset allocation is to consider the performance of your portfolio as a whole, it is psychologically comforting to occasionally backslide into what investment advisors call "two-bucket mode." This means envisioning your bonds as providing living expenses during the bad times and your stocks as providing support during the good times.

No matter what portfolio you choose, realize that looking back, you will always wish that you had allocated more to what turned out, retrospectively, to be the best assets. But since no one knows in advance what these will be, you should own as many as your circumstances allow. By indexing and diversifying, you are giving up bragging rights with the neighbors and the country club gang. But you are also minimizing the chances of impoverishing yourself and the ones you love.

CHAPTER 13 SUMMARY

1. The major stock asset classes you should own are domestic, foreign, and REITs. You may further break the domestic portion into the "four corners": large market, small market, large value, and small value.
2. Your overall stock/bond allocation is determined by your time horizon, risk tolerance, and tax structure. Since stock and bond returns may be quite similar in the future, you should hold at least 20% in bonds, no matter how risk tolerant you think you are.
3. The stock and bond asset classes you employ are primarily dictated by the percentage of your portfolio that is tax-sheltered.
4. The easiest asset structures to design are those where more than half of assets are tax-sheltered.
5. If you have less than 50% of your assets in sheltered vehicles, you should place value stocks and REITs in them. If you have room left over, you should break your foreign assets into regions (European, Pacific, and emerging markets) to benefit from rebalancing.
6. The present value of your Social Security and fixed pension payments should be factored into your asset allocation.

14

Getting Started, Keeping It Going

You are now, metaphorically speaking, a construction engineer. By this point, you should have a working set of blueprints (your allocation), and you should also have selected your building materials (mutual funds and Treasury securities). In what sequence do you begin to erect the structure?

Broadly speaking, your situation will fall into one of two categories:

- You are an investing novice with relatively little experience in the markets, with only a small amount of your assets in stocks.
- You are experienced with the ups and downs of the market. And since you are familiar with the markets and your own risk tolerance, your planned stock/bond allocation should thus be roughly the same as your current overall stock/bond mix. All you need to do is convert over to an indexed investment plan.

If you fall into the second category, then your task is relatively simple. If your stocks and funds do not carry a large amount of capital gains, all you will need to do is to sell them all and on the same day, if possible, purchase all of your new stock-index funds and bond funds/Treasuries. If you intend to use ETFs, then you can accomplish this from your existing brokerage account, assuming its fees will not be onerous.

If you decide to use Vanguard's, Fidelity's, or Schwab's index funds, then things get a little more complex. If you are selling individual stock positions, then I'd transfer the whole shooting match over to a brokerage account at Vanguard, Fido, or Schwab so that you can sell your individual stock and bond positions and establish your new fund positions at the same time. If at all possible, you should keep a cash buffer large enough so that you do not run into problems caused by settlement delays on your sales proceeds.

Things will be even more complicated if you have individual mutual fund accounts. Depending on your situation, you may be able to exchange your stock and bond fund shares to a money market account with check writing privileges that you can then deposit in your new fund accounts. Ideally, you should have already set up an account at Vanguard/Fido/Schwab so that your checks can be directly deposited. Conversely, it may be easier simply to transfer all of your old fund shares over to a brokerage account with Vanguard/Fido/Schwab, then sell them. In most cases, this will incur commissions.

If you hold a substantial amount of stocks and mutual funds that have appreciated significantly, then switching to the kind of asset-class-based indexed approach we've outlined may entail a large capital-gains jolt, and it may not be worth the cost, particularly if you already own a well-diversified portfolio of individual stocks. This represents a very difficult problem, and if you find yourself in this predicament, it would be well worth your while to engage the services of an accountant or tax attorney.

Getting Used to the Long Run

The beginning of this chapter is aimed at the first kind of investor—the novice whose current stock exposure is low. From a purely financial point of view, it is usually better to put your funds to work right away. However, if you are not used to owning risky assets, then getting started is a little like getting in shape to run a marathon. It is not a good idea to try to run 26 miles on the first day of training. Similarly, it takes a while to accommodate yourself to the ups and downs of the market. If your allocation to stocks has been low in the past and the allocation process we've described calls for a significant increase, then this is best done gradually, over a few years.

Once you've arrived at your target stock allocation, you are faced with a second problem—that of portfolio rebalancing. In the normal course of the capital markets, asset classes have different returns—sometimes radically different—and your portfolio composition will drift away from its planned percentages. It then becomes necessary to buy more of the losers and sell some of the winners—in other words, to rebalance it—to bring things back into line. It takes some time to convince yourself that rebalancing your portfolio is a good idea in the long run, particularly as you find yourself pouring cash into a prolonged bear market for one, several, or all of your assets.

Traditionally, investors working to accumulate stock shares use *dollar cost averaging,* or "DCA," to achieve their objectives. This involves investing the same amount of money regularly in a given fund or stock. The advantages of this approach are several-fold: Assume that a mutual fund fluctuates in value between $5 and $15 during the course of a year, and that $100 is invested monthly in the fund, allowing shares to be purchased at prices of $10, $5, and $15. The average price of the fund over the purchase period is $10, but through the magic of financial mathematics, using DCA in this manner gives you a lower average price. Here's how: we purchased 10 shares at $10, 20 shares at $5, and 6.67 shares at $15, for a total of 36.67 shares. The overall price per share was thus $8.18 ($300/36.67), even though the average of the three prices was $10. This is because we purchased more shares at the lower than at the higher price.

DCA is a wonderful technique, but it is not a free lunch. Purchasing those 20 shares at $5 took great fortitude because you were buying at John Templeton's "point of maximum pessimism." Security prices do not get to bargain levels without a great deal of negative sentiment and publicity. Imagine what it felt like to be buying stocks in October 1987, junk bonds in January 1991, or emerging markets stocks in October 1998, and you'll understand what I mean. Do not underestimate the discipline that is sometimes necessary to carry out a successful DCA program. DCA does entail risk; your entire buy-in period may occur during a powerful bull market and be immediately followed by a prolonged drop in prices.

Such are the uncertainties of equity investing. Always remember that you are compensated for bearing risk, and buying during a prolonged bull market is certainly a risk. If you've never invested in a bear market before, recall author Fred Schwed's warning that there are some things that cannot be explained to a virgin using words and pictures. For most investors, a prolonged down market is an experience unlike any other. Your first few forays into bear territory should be done with a relatively small portion of your capital.

There is an even better method than DCA, known as "value averaging," described by Michael Edleson in a book by the same title. A simplified version of his technique is as follows. Instead of blindly investing, say, $100 per month, you draw a "value averaging path," consisting of a target amount that increases by the same amount each month, $100 in this example. In other words, you aim at having $100 in the account in January, $200 in February, and so forth, on out to $1,200 by December of the first year and $2,400 by the end of the second year. In this case, you are not simply investing $100 per month. If the fund value declines, *more* than $100 will be required to reach the desired total each month. If the fund goes up, less will be required. It is even possible that if the fund value goes up a great deal, no money at all will have to be added in some months.

Further, assume that we plan an investment of $3,600 over three years. We will probably not complete our $3,600 investment in exactly 36 months. If, in general, the markets are up, it may require another three, six, or nine months to complete the program. If, on the other hand, there is a bear market, then we will run out of cash reserves long before 36 months are up. To show you how this works, let's start with Taxable Ted's allocation at the 50/50 stock/bond level (Table 13-6). I've assumed that Ted has a total portfolio size of $1 million and that he has finally decided that he wants a 50/50 portfolio, with $500,000 each in bonds and stocks. There is no reason why he should not invest all of his bond money immediately. Yes, there is a risk that he could be investing at a high point in the bond market and that he could lose some money, but bond bear markets are relatively painless affairs at the short maturities used in his portfolio.

That leaves $500,000 allocated to stocks. In Table 14-1, I've established a three-year "value averaging path" for his four stock assets at the Vanguard Group. The path consists of target amounts for each quarter that will be met with periodic investments. I've started at the fund minimum for each asset—$10,000 for all but the Total Stock Market Index Fund, which has a $3,000 minimum.

Table 14-1. "Taxable Ted's" Value Averaging Path (for $500,000 Stock Allocation)

	Total Stock Market Index	Tax-Managed Small Cap	Tax-Managed International	REIT (VA)
January 1, 2003	$3,000	$10,000	$10,000	$10,000
April 1, 2003	$19,417	$17,500	$19,583	$15,417
July 1, 2003	$35,833	$25,000	$29,167	$20,833
October 1, 2003	$52,250	$32,500	$38,750	$26,250
January 1, 2004	$68,667	$40,000	$48,333	$31,667
April 1, 2004	$85,083	$47,500	$57,917	$37,083
July 1, 2004	$101,500	$55,000	$67,500	$42,500
October 1, 2004	$117,917	$62,500	$77,083	$47,917
January 1, 2005	$134,333	$70,000	$86,667	$53,333
April 1, 2005	$150,750	$77,500	$96,250	$58,750
July 1, 2005	$167,167	$85,000	$105,833	$64,167
October 1, 2005	$183,583	$92,500	$115,417	$69,583
January 1, 2006	$200,000	$100,000	$125,000	$75,000

A few fine points should be mentioned. This is a somewhat simplified version of Edleson's method. In addition to increasing the target value for each quarter by a fixed amount, he also "builds in" further growth into the path. For ease of understanding, I have not done so. His book, by the way, is extremely hard to find. At the time of this writing, Fourstar Books, http://www.fourstarbooks.com, still has copies in stock.

It should be obvious that value averaging should *not* be done with exchange-traded funds, as doing so would incur a separate fee for each transaction. In the above example, it would cost Ted several hundred dollars each year.

There is nothing magic about quarterly investments or a three-year overall plan. Professor Edleson does recommend a quarterly investment program, but you can tailor the length of your plan to suit your tastes. I suggest a minimum of two to three years for funding; if market history is any guide, you should have an authentic bear market (or at least a correction) during this time. This will enable you to test your resolve with the relatively small mandated infusions and to ultimately convince yourself of the value of rebalancing.

Last, there will be some months when the market is doing very well, and you may actually be above the target for a given asset for that month on the path. Theoretically, you should sell some of the asset to get back down to the target amount. Don't do it, particularly in a taxable account, as this will incur unnecessary capital gains.

This method is about the best technique available, in my opinion, for establishing a balanced allocation. But it is not perfect. As already pointed out, if there is a global bear market, you will run out of cash long before three years is up. The opposite will happen if stock prices rise dramatically. If you are value averaging into both taxable and sheltered accounts, as In-Between Ida would have to do, it is likely that after a time the taxable and sheltered halves of the allocation will get out of kilter. Consider Ida's portfolio, which split the 10% of her portfolio that was sheltered between U.S. large-value and small-value stocks. What would happen if these assets did very poorly during the value averaging period? She would run out of sheltered money before she had reached her targets for those two assets.

In that case, she would have to compromise, either by stopping at that point, or perhaps putting more of her money into an asset with similar behavior—the "large market" and "small market" funds in her taxable accounts. If the opposite happens, the problem is less severe. If she is still in the value averaging phase and building up a position in these assets, then she will simply have to wait a few months before the "value path" eventually rises above her asset level, requiring additional purchases.

Value averaging has many strengths as an investment strategy. First and foremost, it forces the investor to invest more at market lows than at market highs, producing significantly higher returns. Second, it gives the investor the experience of investing regularly during times of market pessimism and fear—a very useful skill indeed. Value averaging is very similar to DCA, with one important difference; it mandates investing larger amounts of money at market bottoms than at market tops. You can think of value averaging as a combination of DCA and rebalancing. (Value averaging works just as well in reverse. If you are retired and in the distribution phase of your financial life cycle, you will be selling more of your assets at market tops than at bottoms, stretching your assets further.)

Playing the Long Game

Once you've established your allocation, you are left with the financial equivalent of gardening—maintaining the policy allocation you decided on in the last chapter. Mind you, this is very important work, from a number of perspectives. First, it keeps your portfolio's risk within tolerable limits. Second, it generates a bit of excess return. And third, and perhaps most important, it will instill the discipline and mental toughness essential to investment success.

In order to understand rebalancing, let's consider a model consisting of two risky assets; call them A and B. In a given year, each asset is capable of having only two returns: a gain of 30% or a loss of 10%, each with a probability of 50%. You can simulate the return for each simply by flipping a coin. Half the time you'll get a return of +30%, and half the time you'll get −10%.

The expected return of this "investment" is 8.17% per year. That's because, on average, you'll get one year of +30% for every year of −10%: 0.9 × 1.3 = 1.17, or a two-year return of 17%. If you annualize this out, you get 8.17% per year. (In other words, a return of +30% the first year and −10% the second is the same as a return of 8.17% in both.) Of course, you only get this 8.17% "expected return" if you flip the coin millions of times, so that the heads/tails ratio comes out very close to 50/50.

Now, imagine that you construct a portfolio of 50% A and 50% B. You thus have four possible situations:

| | | Year | | |
	1	2	3	4
Asset A	+30%	+30%	−10%	−10%
Asset B	+30%	−10%	+30%	−10%
50/50	**+30%**	**+10%**	**+10%**	**−10%**

One-quarter of the time, we flip two heads resulting in a +30% return. One-quarter of the time, we flip two tails, and the portfolio returns −10%. And one-half the time, we get one of each, and the return is the average of +30% and −10%, or +10%. The expected four-year return is thus $1.3 \times 1.1 \times 1.1 \times 0.9 = 1.4157$. This annualizes out to a return of 9.08%. (That is, had we gotten a return of 9.08% all four years, our final wealth would be the same 1.4157 we got from the above 30%/10%/10%/−10% sequence.)

The key point is this: *we got almost 1% more return (9.08%, versus 8.17%) simply by keeping our portfolio composition at 50/50.* Take a look at Year 2. If we started out that year with equal amounts of asset A and asset B, by the end, we would have had much more of A because of its higher return. In order to get back to 50/50, we sold some of asset A and with the proceeds bought some asset B. The next year, asset B did better than asset A, so we turned a profit with this maneuver. Had we not rebalanced, we simply would have gotten the 8.17% return of each asset.

But that's not all. Notice that instead of getting a return of −10% half of the time, as with a single asset, we now only get it one quarter of the time. *We have reduced risk by diversifying.*

This formulation, which I call the "two-coin toss" model of diversification and rebalancing, does overstate the benefits of diversification/rebalancing a bit. It is very unusual to find two assets with returns as independent as those of A and B and that have such a tendency to "mean revert"—that is, to have low returns followed by high returns, and vice versa. But to a certain extent, all diversified and rebalanced portfolios do benefit from this phenomenon. In real-life portfolios, the benefit of rebalancing stock portfolios is closer to 0.5%, and not the nearly 1% shown in this example.

Beyond risk control and extra return, there is yet a third benefit to rebalancing, and that is psychological conditioning. In order to make a profit on any investment, you must buy low and sell high. Both of these, particularly the former, are extraordinarily difficult to do. Buying low means doing so when the asset has been falling rapidly with poorer recent returns than other asset classes, generally accompanied by negative commentary from the experts. This is as it should be—you don't get low prices any other way. Selling high means just the opposite. The asset has had high recent returns and is outperforming other investments; it is the general consensus that it is the "wave of the future." This is also as it should be—you don't get very high prices in any other way.

Rebalancing forces you to buy low and sell high. It takes many years and many cycles of rebalancing before you realize that bucking conventional wisdom is a profitable activity. I like to refer to bucking the conventional wisdom as your "financial condition." By this, I don't mean how flush you are, but rather how strong your discipline and emotional balance are when it comes to investing. Like physical conditioning, "financial condition" requires constant exercise and activity to maintain. Periodically rebalancing your portfolio is a superb way of staying "in shape."

Another way of putting this is that rebalancing forces you to be a contrarian—someone who does the opposite of what everyone else is doing. Financial contrarians tend to be wealthier than folks who like to simply follow the crowd.

This concept also reveals the major benefit of a diversified portfolio: the advantage of "making small bets with dry hands." In poker, the player who is least concerned about the size of the pot has the advantage, because he is much less likely to lose his nerve than his opponents. If you have a properly diversified portfolio, you are in effect making many small bets, none of which should ruin you if they go bad. When the chips are down, it will not bother you too much to toss a few more coins into the pot when everyone around you is folding his hand. That's how you win at poker, and that's how you win the long game of investing.

It is often said that the small investor is at an unfair disadvantage to the professional, because of the latter's superior information and trading ability. This is certainly true of trading in individual stocks. It is even more true in the trading of futures and options, where more than 80% of small investors lose money, mainly to the brokerage firms and market makers. But when it comes to investing in entire asset classes, it is really the small investor who possesses an unfair advantage. Why? For two reasons.

First, because sudden market downturns affect smaller investors less, because they have a smaller portion of their portfolio invested in any one asset class. I came smack up against this at a recent conference of institutional bond investors. The junk-bond money managers at the meeting were easy to pick out—they were the ones with a vacant, deer-in-the-headlights stare. Not only were junk bonds falling rapidly in price, but in most cases, market conditions were so bad that they could not even find someone to trade with. In other words, *they did not even know what the bonds in their portfolios were worth.* Remember, the world of institutional investing is highly specialized—junk was most of what these poor folks traded, and my guess is that many of them had recently been on the phone to Momma inquiring about the availability of their old room. On the other hand, if only 2% of your portfolio was in junk, you didn't even notice the loss. And since prices were dirt cheap, why not rebalance or even increase your exposure a tad? Often, the small investor is the only player at the table with dry hands.

The second advantage of the small investor is more subtle—you have only your own gut reactions to worry about. The institutional manager, on the other hand, constantly has to worry about the emotions of clients, who likely will be annoyed with the purchase of poorly performing assets. In such a situation, rebalancing into a poorly performing asset may be an impossibility. An oft-quoted analogy likens successful investing to driving the wrong way up a one-way street. This is difficult enough with your own vehicle, but nearly impossible when you are a chauffeur piloting a Rolls Royce whose owner is in the back seat, squawking at every pothole and potential collision.

Let's take a look at how rebalancing works in the real world. Consider the four assets we examined from 1998 to 2000 in Chapter 4:

Asset Class	1998	1999	2000
U.S. Large Stocks (S&P 500)	28.58%	21.04%	−9.10%
U.S. Small Stocks (CRSP 9–10)	−7.30%	27.97%	−3.60%
Foreign Stocks (EAFE)	20.00%	29.96%	−14.17%
REITs (Wilshire REIT)	−17.00%	−2.57%	31.04%
Equal Mix Portfolio (25% Each)	**6.07%**	**19.10%**	**1.04%**

Assume for the sake of argument that we have decided on a portfolio holding 25% of each of these assets. In 1998, U.S. large stocks and foreign stocks did well, and U.S. small stocks and REITs did poorly. So at the end of that year, to get back to equal weighting, we'd have sold some U.S. large stocks and foreign stocks, and bought more small stocks and REITs. As you can see, this was a wash. In 1998 as in 1999, small stocks did better than the portfolio, but REITs did much worse. But at the end of 1999, we'd have sold some of the best performers—U.S. small stocks and foreign stocks—and tossed all of the proceeds into REITs, which were the runaway winner in 2000. The three-year return of the rebalanced portfolio was 8.48%. Had you not rebalanced back to equal weighting at the end of 1998 and 1999, your return would have been only 7.41%.[1]

This little exercise points out two things. First, rebalancing does not work all of the time—obviously, selling some foreign stocks at the end of 1998 was a bad move. But more often than not, it is beneficial. Second, although it doesn't always work, it always feels awful. Note that we had to endure two solid years of miserable REIT performance before we were finally paid off for our patience. It can be much worse than this—precious metals equity has had low returns for more than a decade, as have Japanese stocks.

How Often?

The question of how often to rebalance is one of the thorniest in investing. When you try to answer this question using historical data, the answer you get is "rebalance about every two to five years," depending on what assets and what time period you look at. But you have to be very careful in interpreting this data, because the optimal rebalancing interval is exquisitely sensitive to what assets you use and what years you study.

Personally, I think that about once every few years is the right answer for one good reason. If the markets were truly efficient, then you shouldn't be able to make any money rebalancing. After all, rebalancing is a bet that some assets (the worst performing ones) will have higher returns than others (the best performing ones). Research has shown that this tendency for the prior best-performers to do worse in the future and vice versa (which we saw in Chapter 7 in our survey of

---

[1]The rebalanced return is relatively easy to compute: just calculate the return for each year as the average of the four assets (or the weighted average if the compositions are uneven), and annualize over three years. i.e., $1.0607 \times 1.191 \times 1.0104 = 1.2765$. $1.2765^{(1/3)} = 1.0848$. Therefore, the rebalanced return is 8.48%. The unrebalanced return is a bit trickier. Here, you have to calculate the end-wealth after three years for each of the four assets in the same manner. For U.S. large, small, foreign, and REITs, these values are 1.4147, 1.1436, 1.3385, and 1.0598. The unrebalanced final wealth is the average of these numbers (or the weighted average if the compositions are uneven), which calculates out to 1.2391. $1.2391^{(1/3)} = 1.0741$. Therefore, the unrebalanced return is 7.41%. The calculation of the unrebalanced return is the source of not a little mischief. Many mistakenly calculate it as the weighted average of the annualized returns. This is incorrect and will always yield a value less than the rebalanced return. Rest assured that it is possible to lose money rebalancing, although it does not happen often.

five-year regional stock performance) seems to be strongest over about two to three years. In fact, over periods of one year or less, the reverse seems to be true—the best performers tend to persist, as do the worst.

Thus, you should not rebalance too often. The most extreme example of the advantage of waiting comes when you consider the behavior of the U.S. and Japanese markets in the 1990s. During this period, the U.S. market did almost nothing but go up, whereas the Japanese did almost nothing but go down. The longer you waited before selling U.S. stocks and buying Japanese ones, the better.

The above considerations apply only in the sheltered environment, where there are no tax consequences to rebalancing. In the example shown above—where we rebalanced a 25/25/25/25 mix of U.S. large and small, foreign and REITs—about 6.5% of the portfolio was traded each year. In a taxable account, rebalancing results in capital gains, which reduce your after-tax return. Although this does not trigger much in capital gains taxes in the early years, as time goes on most of the accumulated value in the funds would be subject to capital gains.

If, over the years, an average of 50% of the fund value consisted of unrealized capital gains, then this would cause about 3% of the portfolio value each year to be subject to capital gains taxes. At a combined federal/state rate of 25%, this would cost about 0.75% per year, wiping out the rebalancing benefit. Admittedly, you'd get some of this back in the form of a higher cost basis for the rebalanced shares, but it is still quite likely that rebalancing might put you behind the tax eight-ball. Thus, in taxable accounts, it makes sense to rebalance only with mandatory fund distributions (fund capital gains and dividends), inflows (that is, value averaging), and outflows.

Rebalancing in Retirement

Retirement is simply value averaging/rebalancing in reverse. Once again, sheltered accounts are easiest to deal with. Since the tax consequences of selling stocks and bonds are equivalent—everything gets taxed at the ordinary rate when you withdraw it from a retirement account—you sell enough of your best-performing assets to meet your living expenses so as to bring them back to their policy composition. If you are withdrawing only a small percent of your nest egg each year, you may not even notice the difference, and you will go on rebalancing every few years as if nothing has happened. On the other hand, if you are withdrawing a large percentage of your sheltered accounts each year, you may even have to sell some of your poorly performing assets to make ends meet.[2]

What this means, in general, is that during the good years, you will be selling stocks, and during the bad years you'll be living off your bonds—the two-warehouse psychology.

If you are going to be living on taxable assets, at least in part, then things can get extremely messy. For starters, let's think about Taxable Ted's 50/50 portfolio, with no sheltered assets at all. Assume he doesn't spend any money for a decade or two. (Ted just can't seem to slow down after all. He's taken up consulting and has yet to learn how to say no.) The stock portion of his portfolio has grown faster than the bond portion, and his portfolio is now 70/30 stocks/bonds. When he finally needs to tap his portfolio for cash, he's faced with an unpalatable choice. The "proper" way to do it would be to sell some of his stocks. But this will incur capital gains taxes—if there has been a doubling of his fund share price, then he'll pay about 10% on his total withdrawals. Spending down his bonds would be a real temptation, since this would avoid most capital gains, but would make the portfolio even more top-heavy with stocks.

There is no "right" answer to this dilemma. In most circumstances, a fully-taxable investor such as Ted should probably bite the bullet and spend down the stocks first, as slowly drifting towards a 100% stock allocation may put him at undue risk in the event of a serious and prolonged market decline. However, if Ted had so much money that he could comfortably get by on his bond holdings alone, then there would be nothing wrong with doing so and allowing his heirs to inherit his tax-efficient stock funds on a stepped-up basis. If you're Bill Gates, you don't need to own bonds.

Things get even more complex when investors have substantial amounts of both sheltered and taxable assets. The decision of how much to withdraw from each is one best left to an accountant and tax attorney. However, a few general statements are possible. If you have no other source of income, it is often advantageous to make at least some withdrawals from your retirement accounts if these can be made at a relatively low marginal rate. On the other hand, the compounding

---

[2]The easiest way to think about this is to imagine that you have $1 million in your retirement portfolio, split 50/50 between two assets, A and B. If asset A goes up 20% and asset B goes up only 10%, then you'll have $600,000/$550,000 of A/B. If you need $50,000, then taking it all from A gets you back to 50/50. If you need more than $50,000, then you will have to sell a bit of B as well. If you need less than $50,000, then you will still have to rebalance a bit from A to B to get back to 50/50.

and rebalancing advantages of a sheltered account are considerable, particularly over long time horizons, so you should also be trying to preserve these as much as possible.

For Those in Need of Help

Investment planning and execution are two completely different animals. It is one thing to plan periodic portfolio rebalancing and another to sell assets that have been doing extremely well so that you can purchase ones that have been falling for years. It is also one thing to calmly look at a graph, table, or spreadsheet and imagine losing 30% of your money. And it is most emphatically another to actually have it happen.

I thought long and hard before including these last few paragraphs, since I am an investment advisor and have no desire to appear self-serving.

I do believe that most investors are capable of investing competently on their own without any professional help whatsoever. But I have also learned from hard experience that a significant number of investors will never be able to do so. Most of the time, this is due to lack of knowledge of investment theory and practice. If you have gotten this far, however, you certainly should not be suffering any shortcomings in these departments!

But it is not uncommon to meet extremely intelligent and financially sophisticated people, oftentimes finance professionals, who are still emotionally incapable of executing a plan properly—they can talk the talk, but they cannot walk the walk, no matter how hard they try.

The most common reason for the "failure to execute" shortcoming is the emotional inability to go against the market and buy assets that are not doing well. Almost as common is an inability to get off the dime and commit hard cash to a perfectly good investment blueprint, also called "commitment paralysis."

But whatever the reason, a significant number of investors do require professional management. For those who do, I offer this advice:

- The biggest pitfall is the conflict of interest arising from fees and commissions, paid indirectly by you. But rest assured that you will pay these costs just as surely as if they had been lifted directly from your wallet. You will want to ensure that your advisor is choosing your investments purely on their investment merit and not on the basis of how the vehicles reward him. The warning signs here are recommendations of load funds, insurance products, limited partnerships, or separate accounts. The best, and only, way to make sure that you and your advisor are on the same team is to make sure that he is "fee-only," that is, that he receives no remuneration from any other source besides you. Otherwise, you will wind up paying, and paying, and paying, and paying. . .

- "Fee-only" is not without pitfalls, however. Your advisor's fees should be reasonable. It is simply not worth paying anybody more than 1% to manage your money. Above $1 million, you should be paying no more than 0.75%, and above $5 million, no more than 0.5%. Vanguard does offer personal advisory services, providing a useful benchmark for comparison: 0.65% from their $500,000 minimum to $1 million, 0.35% for the next $1 million, and 0.20% above $2 million. (Be aware, however, that Vanguard's advisory service will usually recommend some of their actively managed stock funds. If you do use them, insist on an indexed-only stock allocation.)
- Your advisor should use index/passive stock funds wherever possible. If he tells you that he is able to find managers who can beat the indexes, he is fooling both you and himself. I refer to a commitment to passive indexing as "asset-class religion." Don't hire anyone without it.

CHAPTER 14 SUMMARY

1. Only if you are an experienced investor who already has significant stock exposure should you switch rapidly from your current investment plan to one that is index/asset-class based.
2. If you are a relatively inexperienced investor or do not have significant stock exposure, you should build it up slowly using a value averaging approach.
3. Value averaging is a superb method of building up an equity position over time. This technique combines dollar cost averaging and rebalancing. Asset allocation in retirement is the mirror image of value averaging—you are rebalancing with withdrawals.
4. Rebalance your sheltered accounts once every few years.
5. Do not actively rebalance your taxable accounts except with mandatory withdrawals, distributions, and new savings.
6. Rebalancing provides many benefits, including higher return and lower risk. But its biggest reward is that it keeps you in "good financial shape" by helping maintain a healthy disdain for conventional financial wisdom.

15

A Final Word

We've surveyed a much wider swath of territory than is usually covered in the field of personal finance in one book, and I hope that you have found the journey rewarding. While each of the four overarching stories I've told (the theory, history, psychology, and business of investing), are worthwhile in their own right, they also form an essential part of an investor's repertoire. Let's recap what we've learned.

Pillar One: Investment Theory

- Risk and return are inextricably enmeshed. Do not expect high returns without frightening risks, and if you desire safety, you must accept low returns. The stocks of unattractive companies must, of necessity, offer higher returns than those of attractive ones; otherwise, no one would buy them. For the same reason, it is also likely that the stock returns of less developed and unstable nations are higher than those of developed nations. Anyone promising high returns with low risk is guilty of fraud.
- It is relatively easy to estimate the long-term return of a stock market simply by adding its long-term per-share earnings growth to its dividend yield. The long-term return of high-grade bonds is essentially the same as the dividend yield, since bond coupon payments do not grow.
- The market is brutally efficient and can be thought of as being smarter than even its wisest individual participants. Stock picking and market timing are expensive, risky, and ultimately futile exer-

cises. Harness the power of the market by owning all of it—that is, by indexing.

- It is not possible to predict what portfolio compositions will perform best in the future. A prudent course is to make the broad market (Wilshire 5000) and a lesser amount of small U.S. and large foreign stocks your core stock holdings. Depending on your tax and employment situation, as well as your tolerance to tracking error (performing differently from the broad market), you may also wish to add small and large value stocks and REITs to your portfolio as well.

Pillar Two: Investment History

- You simply cannot learn enough about this topic. The more you know, the better you will be prepared for the shocks regularly hurled at investors by the capital markets.
- Be aware that the markets make regular trips to the loony bin in both directions. There will be times when new technologies promise to remake our economy and culture and that by getting in on the ground floor, you will profit greatly. When this happens, hold on tight to your wallet. There will also be times when the sky seems to be falling. These are usually good times to buy.

Pillar Three: Investment Psychology

- You are your own worst enemy. It is likely that you are more confident of your ability to pick stocks and mutual fund managers than is realistic. Remember that the market is an 800-pound gorilla whose only pleasure is to make as many investors look as foolish as possible.
- If you are invested in the same assets as your neighbors and friends, it is likely that you will experience low returns. Your social instincts will corrode your wealth by persuading you to own what everyone else in the market owns. Successful investing is a profoundly solitary activity.
- Try to ignore the last five or ten years of investment returns and focus on the longer-term data as best you can. Yes, large growth stocks have had very high returns in recent years (and, until 2001, the very highest), but history shows that they still underperform both large and small value stocks. While there are no guarantees

that this will be true going forward, the odds always favor data gathered over the longest time periods.
- Resist the human temptation to imagine patterns where there are none. Asset class returns are essentially random, and patterns apparent in retrospect almost never repeat going forward.

Pillar Four: Investment Business

- The stockbroker services his clients in the same way that Bonnie and Clyde serviced banks. A broker's only hope of making a good living is to milk your account dry with commissions and spreads. He also occupies the lowest rung in the hierarchy of investment knowledge. The simple fact that you have finished this book means that you know far more about investing than he ever will.
- The primary business of most mutual-fund companies is collecting assets, not managing money. Pay close attention to the ownership structure of your fund company and of the fees it charges, but also realize that the expense ratio of a fund is just the tip of the iceberg.
- Ninety-nine percent of what you read about investing in magazines and newspapers, and 100% of what you hear on television is worse than worthless. Most financial journalists quickly learn that it is much easier to turn out a stream of articles about strategists- and fund managers-of-the-month rather than do serious analysis.

In the last section, we synthesized the knowledge in these four areas into a basic investment strategy that any investor should be able to employ. While it is possible to manage your finances with just the knowledge contained herein, you'd be foolish to do so. This book should be seen as a framework to which you'll be continuously adding knowledge, starting with the sources mentioned at the end of Chapter 11.

The overarching message of this book is at once powerful and simple: *With relatively little effort, you can design and assemble an investment portfolio that, because of its wide diversification and minimal expense, will prove superior to most professionally managed accounts.* Great intelligence and good luck are not required. The essential characteristics of the successful investor are the discipline and stamina to, in the words of John Bogle, "stay the course."

Investing is not a destination. It is an ongoing journey through its four continents—theory, history, psychology, and business. *Bon voyage*

Bibliography

Introduction

Lowenstein, Roger, *When Genius Failed.* Random House, 2000.

Chapter 1

Bernstein, Peter L., *The Power of Gold.* Wiley, 2000.

Erb, Claude B., Harvey, Campbell R., and Viskanta, Tadas E., "Political Risk, Economic Risk, and Financial Risk." *Financial Analysts Journal,* November/December 1996.

Fama, Eugene F., and French, Kenneth R., "The Cross-Section of Expected Stock Returns." *Journal of Finance,* June 1992.

Fama, Eugene F., and Kenneth R. French, "Value versus Growth: The International Evidence." *Journal of Finance,* December 1998.

Homer, Sidney, and Sylla, Richard, *A History of Interest Rates.* Rutgers University, 1996.

Ibbotson, Roger G., and Brinson, Gary P., *Global Investing.* McGraw-Hill, 1993.

Jorion, Philippe, and Goetzmann, W., "Global Stock Returns in the Twentieth Century." *Journal of Finance,* June 1999.

Keynes, John M., *The Economic Consequences of the Peace.* Harcourt Brace, 1920.

Modigliani, Franco, and Miller, Merton H., "The Cost of Capital, Corporation Finance, and the Theory of Investment." *American Economic Review,* Vol. 48, No. 3 (June) 1958.

Nocera, Joseph, *A Piece of the Action.* Simon and Schuster, 1994.

Norwich, John J., *A History of Venice.* Alfred A. Knopf, 1982.

Siegel, Jeremy J., *Stocks for the Long Run*. McGraw-Hill, 1998.

Strouse, Jean, *Morgan: American Financier*. Random House, 1999.

Chapter 2

Bogle, John C., *Common Sense on Mutual Funds*. Wiley, 1999.

Chancellor, Edward, *Devil Take the Hindmost*. Penguin, 1999.

Clayman, Michelle, "In Search of Excellence: The Investor's Viewpoint." *Financial Analysts Journal*. May/June 1987.

Crowther, Samuel, and Raskob, John J., interview, *Ladies' Home Journal*. August 1929.

Ellis, Charles, *Investment Policy: How to Win the Loser's Game*. Irwin, 1992.

Fisher, Irving, *The Theory of Interest*. Macmillan, 1930.

Graham, Benjamin, and Dodd, David, *Security Analysis: Principles and Techniques*. McGraw-Hill, 1934. Reprinted 1996.

Peters, Thomas J., and Waterman, Robert W. Jr., *In Search of Excellence: Lessons from America's Best Companies*. Harper Collins, 1982.

Templeton, John, interview, *Forbes*. 1995.

Wanger, Ralph, *Acorn Funds Annual Report*. 1996.

Williams, John B., *The Theory of Investment Value*. Harvard University Press, 1938.

Chapter 3

Berkshire Hathaway Annual Report, 2000.

Bernstein, Peter L., *Against the Gods*. Wiley, 1996.

Bernstein, Peter L., *Capital Ideas*. Macmillan, 1992.

Bogle, John C., *John Bogle on Investing*. McGraw-Hill, 2001.

Brooks, John, *The Go-Go Years*. Wiley, 1973.

Clements, Jonathan, "Can Peter Lynch Live up to his Reputation?" *Forbes,* April 3, 1989.

Clements, Jonathan, "Getting Going." *The Wall Street Journal*. April 10, 2001.

Dreman, David N., *Contrarian Investment Strategy: The Psychology of Stock Market Success*. Random House, 1979.

Fama, Eugene, "The Behavior of Stock Prices." *The Journal of Business*. January 1965.

Graham, John R., and Harvey, Campbell R., "Grading the Performance of Market Timing Newsletters." *Financial Analysts Journal,* November/December 1997.

Jensen, Michael C., "The Performance of Mutual Funds in the Period 1945–64." *Journal of Finance,* 1965.

Leinweber, David, "Stupid Data Miner Tricks." Annotated slide excerpts, First Quadrant Corporation.

Morningstar Principia Pro Plus, April 2001.

Nocera, Joseph, *A Piece of the Action.* Simon and Schuster, 1994.

Surz, Ronald, Unpublished data, 2001.

Chapter 4

Brinson, Gary P., Hood, L. Randolph, and Beebower, Gilbert L., "Determinants of Portfolio Performance." *Financial Analysts Journal,* July/August 1986.

Brinson, Gary P., Singer, Brian D., and Beebower, Gilbert L., "Determinants of Portfolio Performance II: An Update." *Financial Analysts Journal,* May/June 1991.

French, Kenneth R, online data library. http://web.mit.edu/~kfrench/www

Morningstar Principia Pro Plus, April 2001.

Chapters 5 and 6

Ambrose, Stephen E., *Undaunted Courage.* Simon and Schuster, 1996.

Bary, Andrew, "Vertigo: The New Math Behind Internet Capital's Stock Price is Fearsome." *Barrons,* January 10, 2000.

Brooks, John, *Once in Golconda.* Wiley, 1999.

Chamberlain, Lawrence, and Hay, William W., *Investment and Speculation.* New York, 1931.

Chancellor, Edward, *Devil Take the Hindmost.* Penguin, 1999.

Galbraith, John K., *The Great Crash.* Houghton Mifflin, 1988.

Johnson, Paul M., *The Birth of the Modern: World Society 1815–1830.* Harper Collins, 1991.

Kindleberger, Charles P., *Manias, Panics, and Crashes.* Wiley, 2000.

Mackay, Charles, *Extraordinary Popular Delusions and the Madness of Crowds.* Harmony Books, 1980.

Maddison, Angus, *Monitoring the World Economy 1820-1992.* OECD, 1995.

Malkiel, Burton G., *A Random Walk Down Wall Street.* W. W. Norton, 1996.

Nocera, Joseph, *A Piece of the Action.* Simon and Schuster, 1994.

Ritter, Jay R., "The Long Run Performance of Initial Public Offerings." *Journal of Finance,* March, 1991.

Santayana, George, *The Life of Reason*. Scribner's, 1953.

Siegel, Jeremy J., *Stocks for the Long Run*. McGraw-Hill, 1998.

Smith, Edgar L., *Stocks as Long Term Investments*. Macmillan, 1924.

Sobel, Dava, *Longitude*. Walker & Co., 1995.

Strouse, Jean, *Morgan: American Financier*. Random House, 1999.

White, Eugene N., ed., *Crashes and Panics*. Dow Jones Irwin, 1990.

Chapter 7

Benzarti, S., and Thaler, Richard H., "Myopic Risk Aversion and the Equity Premium Puzzle." *Quarterly Journal of Economics,* January 1993.

Brealy, Richard A., *An Introduction to Risk and Return from Common Stocks*. M. I. T. Press, 1969.

DeBondt, Werner F.M., and Thaler, Richard H., "Further Evidence On Investor Overreaction and Stock Market Seasonality." *Journal of Finance,* July 1987.

Fuller, R.J., Huberts, L.C., and Levinson, M.J., "Returns to E/P Strategies; Higgledy Piggledy Growth; Analysts Forecast Errors; and Omitted Risk Factors." *The Journal of Portfolio Management,* Winter 1993.

Kahneman, D., and Tversky, A., "Judgment under Uncertainty: Heuristics and Biases." *Science,* September 1974.

Lowenstein, Roger, "Exuberance is Rational." *The New York Times,* February 11, 2001.

Chapter 9

Anonymous and Harper, Timothy, *License to Steal*. Harper Business, 1999.

Barber, Brad M., and Odean, Terrence, "Trading is Hazardous to Your Wealth: The Common Stock Performance of Individual Investors." *Journal of Finance,* April 2000.

Ellis, Charles D., *Winning the Loser's Game*. McGraw-Hill, 1998.

Lewis, Michael, "Jonathan Lebed's Extracurricular Activities." *The New York Times,* February 24, 2001.

Nocera, Joseph, *A Piece of the Action*. Simon and Schuster, 1994.

Rothchild, John, *A Fool and His Money,* Wiley, 1997.

Schlarbaum, Gary G., Lewellen, Wilbur G., and Lease, Ronald C., "The Common-Stock Portfolio Performance Record of Individual Investors: 1964–70." *The Journal of Finance,* May 1978.

Chapter 10

Bogle, John C., *John Bogle on Investing*. McGraw-Hill, 2001.

Morningstar Principia Pro Plus, April 2001.

Nocera, Joseph, *A Piece of the Action*. Simon and Schuster, 1994.

Pressler, Gabriel, "Buying Unloved Funds Could Yield Lovable Returns." *Morningstar Fund Investor,* January 2001.

Zweig, Jason, Unpublished speech.

Chapter 11

Anonymous, "Confessions of a Former Mutual Funds Reporter." *Fortune*, April 26, 1999.

Bogle, John C., *Common Sense on Mutual Funds*. Wiley, 1999.

Quinn, Jane B., "When Business Writing Becomes Soft Porn." *Columbia Journalism Review,* March/April 1998.

Nocera, Joseph, *A Piece of the Action*. Simon and Schuster, 1994.

Chapter 12

Cooley, Phillip L., Hubbard, Carl M., and Walz, Daniel T., "Retirement Savings: Choosing a Withdrawal Rate That Is Sustainable." *American Association of Individual Investors Journal,* February 1998.

Chapter 13

Gibson, Roger C., *Asset Allocation*. McGraw-Hill, 2000.

Chapter 14

Edleson, Michael E., *Value Averaging*. International Publishing, 1993.

Schwed, Fred Jr., *Where Are the Customer's Yachts?* Wiley, 1940.

Index

Note: locators in **bold** indicate additional display material.

2010 Postscript

What Have We Learned from the Meltdown?

In the two years between the publications of my first finance book, *The Intelligent Asset Allocator*, in 2000, and this volume in 2002, the investment world turned upside down as the bubble in tech stocks burst, taking much of the rest of the market with it.

In the subsequent eight years, another full market cycle took place. A massive rise in liquidity and credit inflated the value of nearly all assets—not only of stocks and bonds of all descriptions, but also of houses, commercial real estate, and commodities. This bubble then led to the second-worst collapse in U.S. market history.

As the dust settles, current market valuations for stocks are not radically different from what they were in 2002, and thus the expected returns listed on page 72 are not, with two exceptions, in serious need of modification. Those two asset classes, REITs and precious metals stocks—particularly the latter—have seen their valuations climb to the point where they are unlikely to deliver the salutary results that they have in the past.

What, then, have we learned since 2002? For the most part, the recent turmoil has reinforced the themes emphasized in this book:

- Costs still matter.
- Diversification still works.
- Risk tolerance should still not be overestimated.
- The current investment conventional wisdom should still be avoided.

Nevertheless, a few things really are different this time:

- Short-term interest rates are very low; money market funds and Treasury bills now offer near-zero yields.
- Exchange-traded funds (ETFs) have begun to eclipse traditional open-end mutual funds.
- The most frequently traded and highest-quality corporate and municipal bonds proved to be remarkably illiquid in the teeth of the crisis, probably even more so than during the Great Depression. (In plain English, just when you most needed to sell them to raise cash for living expenses or to scoop up stocks on the cheap, you could not do so without taking a significant haircut.)

We'll discuss each of these in turn.

Eternal Truths

Costs still matter, and the performance of active managers does not persist. Duh. The laws of arithmetic continue to apply: since professional investors *are* the market, in the aggregate they must receive the market return *minus expenses*. I'm not going to bore you with the mass of mutual fund statistics and academic studies on the inadequacies of active management that has accumulated since 2002. I cannot, alas, resist relating the sad story of Bill Miller.

As skipper of the Legg Mason Capital Management Value Trust, Mr. Miller beat the S&P 500 *each and every year* between 1991 and 2005, yet in the subsequent three years, his fund did so poorly that it almost completely wiped out the previous fifteen years' worth of stellar performance. From the beginning of his tenure as manager in 1991 to the end of 2008, he beat the S&P 500 by only a small margin: an 8.50% annualized return versus 7.93% for this index. Only his lucky few early investors ever got those returns.[1] The vast majority of his fundholders, suckered in by his blistering previous results, arrived too late to the party, got taken over a cliff, and lagged even the badly battered S&P 500 by over 15% per year between 2006 and 2008. And, oh yes, I almost forgot: for the privilege of accompanying Mr. Miller on this doomed runaway train, Mr. Miller's fund charged the passengers a 1.7% management fee. Worse, this 1.7% fee did *not* include the considerable transactional costs incurred by the trading in his ever-more-bloated fund.

The trajectory of the Legg Mason Value Trust—a small number of early investors earning initially high returns, inevitably triggering a stampede of gullible performance-chasers into the fund, who then got nailed when its performance returned not so gently to earth—gets repeated with a depressing regularity. (If this story sounds vaguely familiar, then you might reread the sad tale of Robert Sanborn on pages 84–85.) The moral remains the same: performance comes and goes, but expenses are forever.

• • •

Diversification still works *in the long run.* That, of course, is not what you're hearing these days, and for good rea-

---

[1] Tom Lauricella, "The Stock Picker's Defeat," *Wall Street Journal,* December 10, 2008, p. C1.

son. Consider the returns of the following asset classes during the great bear market of 2007–2009:

Asset Class	Nov. 2007–Feb. 2009
S&P 500	−50.95%
U.S. large-cap value stocks (Russell 1000 Val.)	−54.39%
U.S. small-cap stocks (Russell 2000)	−52.05%
U.S. small-cap value stocks (Russell 2000 Val.)	−51.88%
Real estate investment trusts (DFA REIT)	−65.58%
Int'l. large-cap stocks (EAFE)	−56.40%
Int'l. large-cap value stocks (EAFE Value)	−58.59%
Int'l. small-cap stocks (EAFE Small Cap)	−59.49%
Emerging markets (MSCI EM)	−61.44%

During the most recent market turmoil, there was simply no place to hide; all stocks got hammered, and the further investors strayed from the good old S&P 500, the more they lost.

Next, let's look at the bear market of 2000–2002. Here, diversification seemed to work a bit better. The madness of the preceding 1990s was confined largely to tech stocks and to the largest growth companies, which investors saw as the new wired world's primary beneficiaries. During the 1990s bubble, everything else languished. Real estate? Obsolete in the New Economy. Small banking, manufacturing, and retail concerns? Doomed as well. Consequently, only tech and large-cap growth stocks, which were most heavily represented in the S&P 500 and the EAFE, and which had run up ridiculously in the previous five years, collapsed. REITs and U.S. small-cap value stocks, which had languished in the 1990s, actually made money between the broad market top of 2000 and the bottom in 2002.

Asset Class	Sept. 2000–Sept. 2002
S&P 500	–44.73%
U.S. large-cap value stocks (Russell 1000 Val.)	–23.66%
U.S. small-cap stocks (Russell 2000)	–30.64%
U.S. small-cap value stocks (Russell 2000 Val.)	+3.46%
Real estate investment trusts (DFA REIT)	+26.28%
Int'l. large-cap stocks (EAFE)	–42.17%
Int'l. large-cap value stocks (EAFE Value)	–35.92%
Int'l. small-cap stocks (EAFE Small Cap)	–27.92%
Emerging markets (MSCI EM)	–34.02%

Now, the punch line: consider how these asset classes fared over the full decade of the 2000s:

Asset Class	Jan. 2000–Dec. 2009
S&P 500	–9.10%
U.S. large-cap value stocks (Russell 1000 Val.)	+27.62%
U.S. small-cap stocks (Russell 2000)	+41.23%
U.S. small-cap value stocks (Russell 2000 Val.)	+121.31%
Real estate investment trusts (DFA REIT)	+170.86%
Int'l. large-cap stocks (EAFE)	+16.97%
Int'l. large-cap value stocks (EAFE Value)	+48.47%
Int'l. small-cap stocks (EAFE Small Cap)	+94.29%
Emerging markets (MSCI EM)	+161.96%

During the past decade, the further you diversified away from a traditional portfolio of large-cap stocks, the better you did. And mark this well: the period covered by this last table is probably within shouting distance of the worst decade any person is likely to encounter during his or her investing career, encompassing not one, but two of the biggest market collapses in U.S. history.

Investment wisdom begins with the realization that long-term returns are the only ones that matter, and that over the long term, diversification protects your portfolio. Logically, you should care little that many days, or even years, along the way your portfolio suffers significant losses. Logic, unfortunately, is the hardest-won investment discipline.

In other words, it is how well diversification works over the decades, and not over the days, months, or even years, that matters most. If you still doubt the value of diversification, just ask Japanese investors, who have lost 1.9% per year *for the past two decades*, while everyone else earned decent, and in many cases more than decent, returns.

I doubt that U.S. stock returns over the next two decades will look anything like Japan's over the last two. But why take the risk? Because we cannot predict the future, we diversify. This is the only free lunch there is in investing; sample as many plates from the all-you-can-eat table of the world's capital markets as you can.

●   ●   ●

If the 2007–2009 market collapse served any useful purpose, it was to reinforce the notion that high returns come attached to ferocious risk. Put more simply, if you expect high returns, you should also expect to suffer serious losses from time to time. As I explained in Chapter 4, it is one thing to train for a crash landing in a flight simulator; the real thing is something else entirely. In the same way, no matter how good your math skills and no matter how complete your knowledge of market history, nothing comes close to helplessly watching a large chunk of your net worth disappear into thin air.

Most investors' allocations have become a good deal more conservative since 2008, and a significant minority has sworn off equities for good (or at least until the next bubble). For those who are nearing retirement, this is not necessarily a bad thing. But for young investors, who I hope are still aggressively saving for retirement, the opposite conclusion should be drawn. In Chapter 2, I noted that bear markets were the friends of the young, allowing them to accumulate stocks cheaply, and indeed, those who followed the dollar cost averaging technique, or, even better, the value averaging method, described in Chapter 14 wound up with near triple-digit returns on the stock purchases made in late 2008 and early 2009.

• • •

The conventional financial wisdom is almost always wrong. The Internet didn't change everything—at least not in the world of investments—and along with it, bricks, mortar, and real estate didn't become obsolete either. After the collapse of the tech bubble, real estate did indeed turn around, but it didn't, as its new enthusiasts predicted, climb forever. The business cycle wasn't abolished, and the newfangled derivatives didn't quite eliminate risk.

The word these days? The economies of the old, developed Western nations are entering a "new normal" of slower economic growth, and stocks and bonds in the United States, Europe, and Japan will languish along with them. The place to be? Emerging markets, of course, with their blistering economies.

This line of reasoning has more than a few flaws. First of all, it turns out that, on average, the stocks of nations with rapidly growing economies have *lower* returns than those of more mature, developed nations. For example, since 1993, China has had one of the world's highest economic growth rates—at times exceeding 10% per year—yet between 1993 and 2008, its stock market *lost* 3.31% per year. The same is true, to a lesser extent, for markets in the Asian "tigers" (Korea, Singapore, Malaysia, Indonesia, Taiwan, and Thailand), which since 1988 have all had lower returns than those in the low-growth United States.[2] By contrast, stodgy old England, which during the twentieth century tumbled from world hegemon to open-air theme park, actually had high returns between 1900 and 2000.[3] More systematic data confirm this pattern: good economies tend to be bad stock markets, and vice versa.

What's going on here? In my opinion, three factors contribute to the "good economy/bad market" phenomenon. First, just as the prices of the stocks of poorly performing companies must fall to the point where they will entice investors with higher future returns, the same happens at the country level. Like unglamorous stocks, unglamorous stock *markets* must offer higher returns to attract buyers.

Second, both new and existing companies are constantly raising capital by issuing new shares, which dilutes the pool of existing shares. In many foreign countries, particularly in Asia, the rate of new share issuance is particularly high. This reduces per-share earnings and dividends, which in turn erodes overall stock returns.[4]

---

[2] Source: Morgan Stanley Capital Indexes, www.mscibarra.com.

[3] Philippe Jorion and William N. Goetzmann, "Global Stock Markets in the Twentieth Century," *Journal of Finance* 54, no. 3 (June 1999), pp. 953–980.

[4] Jeremy Siegel, Stocks for the Long Run (New York: McGraw-Hill, 2007), pp. 124–125; William J. Bernstein and Robert D. Arnott, "The Two-Percent Dilution," *Financial Analysts Journal* (September–October 2003), pp. 47–55; Larry Speidell et al., "Dilution Is a Drag . . . The Impact of Financings in Foreign Markets," *Journal of Investing* 14, no. 4 (Winter 2005), pp. 17–22; Jay R. Ritter, "Economic Growth and Equity Returns," November 1, 2004, working paper; and Elroy Dimson et al., *Triumph of the Optimists* (Princeton, N.J.: Princeton University Press, 2002), p. 156.

Third, in many developing markets, governments do not protect shareholders from the rapacity of management as well as they do in nations with more established legal systems. In other words, in these countries, management and controlling shareholders find it disturbingly easy to loot a company.

And even if I'm wrong about developing-market equities, their return will no doubt come at the cost of very high risk: twice in the past fifteen years, emerging-markets indexes have lost about two-thirds of their value, something that you don't often hear emerging-markets enthusiasts discuss.

New Truths

As this postscript is being written, cash-like assets—Treasury bills, money market funds, and bank certificates of deposit—are yielding a near-zero return. Somewhat higher yields can be had by buying notes and bonds of longer maturity, but at the cost of higher risk. What's an investor to do?

As the old Wall Street saw goes, "More money has been lost reaching for yield than at the point of a gun." In such situations, I find Pascal's Wager to be a particularly useful paradigm.

Blaise Pascal, a seventeenth-century French mathematician and philosopher, famously chose to believe in God because of what we would today call "asymmetric consequences." If the devout person is wrong, then all he has lost is a single lifetime of fornication, imbibing, and the pleasure of skipping a lot of boring church services. But if God does exist, then the atheist roasts eternally in Hell. The rational person thus chooses to believe in Him.

The financial markets work the same way, and the canyons of Wall Street are littered with the bones of those who forgot this simple principle. Here's how it works with today's bond market: it is entirely possible that the Fed's unprecedented "kitchen sink" approach to both monetary and quantitative easing will savage long-term bond investors through hyperinflation. Or not. I know a lot of very smart folks on both sides of this question and am myself an agnostic on the issue. I do, nonetheless, know one thing for sure: if you fear inflation, consequently keep your bond maturities short, and then turn out to be wrong, you've lost only a few percent of yield. But if you make the opposite bet, that is, ignore the inflationary possibility and reach for yield, and you turn out to be wrong, you may well find yourself greeting people at a Wal-Mart front door. Were Blaise Pascal around today, I suspect he'd be shortening his bond maturities.

• • •

The criticism most frequently leveled at this book's original printing was the short shrift given ETFs. Indeed, since the book was first published in 2002, the popularity of these vehicles has grown to the point where they are seriously challenging more traditional "open-end" mutual funds. Nonetheless, I remain dubious; there is nothing really wrong with ETFs, but I continue to believe that most investors are better off with the older open-end fund format. I do so for four reasons. First, the commissions and spread costs incurred by trading ETFs quickly eat up their minuscule expense advantage. Many ETFs are in fact more expensive to own than the corresponding Vanguard or Fidelity index funds. Second, the convenience of being able to trade ETFs throughout the day is in reality a disadvantage; unless you are able to predict intraday market moves—a fool's errand if ever there was one—you are faced with the often paralyzing choice of exactly when to buy or sell. Third, ETFs carry with them considerable institutional risks. Many ETFs have already been liquidated, and I do not trust most of the ETF providers to support these products over the very long term. Last, avoid bond ETFs at all costs. The so-called authorized participant process by which arbitrageurs minimize the discounts and premiums of these funds to their true net asset value does not work well with thinly traded corporate and municipal bonds. In late 2008, the discounts and premiums on many bond ETFs reached several percent for many of these funds, a problem that is not encountered with open-end funds.

That said, there are some areas in which an equity ETF does make sense. The first is the iShares MSCI EAFE Value Index, for which Vanguard offers no corresponding index/passive open-end mutual fund. The second is the Vanguard FTSE All-World ex-US Small-Cap ETF, which does not charge the 0.75% purchase fee levied on investor class shares and also carries a much lower expense ratio (0.38% vs. 0.60%). A third would be the iShares EPRA/NAREIT Developed Real-Estate ex-US ETF, for which there is no equivalent open-end fund available to most small investors.

• • •

Finally, the extreme market turbulence of late 2008 and early 2009 starkly illuminated the role of Treasury securities, money market funds, and certificates of deposit (CDs) in a well-managed portfolio. Consider the graph on the next page, which plots the return of one dollar invested in short-term (one- to five-year maturity) Treasury and corporate notes.

Observe that Treasury notes had salutary returns in the teeth of the crisis, while the corporate notes took about a

Source data: Barclays Capital Indices

7% hit. Over the full two-year period, however, corporates had a higher return.

One could conclude from this graph that all was right
in the world, and that the markets were efficient; yes, the
corporates had higher risk, but investors were ultimately
rewarded with higher return for bearing it.

But suppose you needed liquidity in late 2008 or early
2009. Say you lost your job, a not unlikely event in a
downturn. Or, more important for our purposes, say you
needed cash to rebalance your portfolio by purchasing
stocks at fire-sale prices. Selling short-term corporate
bonds to do so would have incurred a considerable haircut. (Selling longer corporate bonds or even TIPS would
have been worse; municipal bonds also incurred losses,
although less than corporates.)

Conclusion: hold enough Treasuries, money markets,
and CDs to see you through a prolonged period of down-
turn-related unemployment and to execute rebalancing
purchases. These highly liquid assets will probably yield

lower long-term returns than riskier bonds, but when the going gets tough, you'll be glad you have them.

• • •

Consider yourself privileged, then, to have lived through one of history's most dramatic periods of financial distress. Carry its brutal lesson about the connection of risk and return with you forever. Remember, the capital markets are fundamentally a mechanism that distributes wealth to those who have a strategy and can adhere to it from those who either do not or cannot. Know what to expect, develop your own strategy, and stick to it.

About the Author

William Bernstein, Ph.D., M.D., has become a grassroots hero to independent investors everywhere. He has made a name for himself by questioning the value of Wall Street wisdom, skewering the recommendations of self-serving stockbrokers, and showing legions of investors how to successfully manage their own investments with intelligence and long-term vision.

Bernstein's first book, *The Intelligent Asset Allocator*, remains one of the most honored investment books of recent times. Hailed by national publications, including *BusinessWeek*, and by independent investment icons, including Vanguard founder John Bogle, it has become an instant classic for its well-researched analyses and rules for successful investing. He has more recently published *The Investor's Manifesto*. He has also authored two works of economic history: *The Birth of Plenty* and *A Splendid Exchange*, the latter short-listed for the Financial Times/Goldman Sach's Business Book Award in 2008.

Bernstein is the editor of the asset allocation journal *Efficient Frontier*, founder of the popular Web site EfficientFrontier.com, and a co-principal in Efficient Frontier Advisors. He is often quoted in national publications, including *The Wall Street Journal*, has written for *Barron's* and *Money*, and has also contributed to academic finance journals. He lives in Portland, Oregon.